# Brazilian Society

# Brazilian Society

T. Lynn Smith

UNIVERSITY OF NEW MEXICO PRESS
Albuquerque

©The University of New Mexico Press. All rights reserved.
Manufactured in the United States of America
Library of Congress Catalog Card Number 74-27445
International Standard Book Number 0-8263-0365-X
First Edition

*Dedicated To*
*Six Brazilian Friends*
*José Vicente and Lili de Freitas Marcondes*
*José Arthur and Regina Rios*
*Hilgard O'Reilly and Carolina Sternberg*

# Contents

# Tables

# Illustrations

# PART I

# Introduction

Only two chapters are used in this introductory section. The first contains a brief exposition of the basic purpose of the book, its scope, and the general approach or point of view. used in this study of Brazilian society. Chapter 2, also introductory, focuses on the development of sociology in Brazil and the United States, and upon the relationships between sociologists in the two countries. This study was prepared as one in a series of three lectures in Portuguese given at the União Cultural Brasil-Estados Unidos in São Paulo in November 1969, when my wife and I were the guests of the União for two weeks to participate in the inauguration of its ultramodern linguistic laboratory named in my honor.

# 1

---

## Introduction

---

This volume contains the results of endeavors to analyze and interpret changes in Brazilian society during the last quarter of a century and especially during the last decade. It is the fruition of sustained efforts, particularly from 1963 on, to understand and pass on to others verified and systematized knowledge about the momentous changes that are metamorphizing Brazilian society. In no way is it intended to replace my earlier work entitled *Brazil: People and Institutions,*[1] but rather to complement and to carry to a more advanced stage the fundamentals contained in that volume. Indeed, since perforce the various matters treated in this book do not constitute a complete analysis of modern Brazilian society, even though much attention has been given to the integration of the materials presented here, it is hoped that readers who wish to have comparable data and analysis about other important aspects of the social structure and processes in Brazil will seek to find it in the fourth edition of my earlier book. This applies especially to information about the situation and trends in such basic societal features as the domestic and educational institutions and the class system.

It should be stressed that the studies contained in this book all are part and parcel of my lifelong endeavors to play a significant part in building a genuine science of society, a scientific discipline that would deserve a place among the natural sciences as a group made up of such specific sciences as geology, botany, and zoology. From the time when, as an undergraduate student, I made the decision to do graduate work in sociology and to devote my life to a professional career in that then slightly esteemed field, I have held steadfastly to the belief that the only difference between sociology and any one of the others named should be found in the subject

3

matter studied. And that there should be no differences in the intellectual objectives and the logical methods, i.e., the types of observation and inference, used by sociologists, on the one hand, and geologists, botanists, and zoologists, on the other. I have always realized, of course, that social facts frequently are more elusive and complicated than those in the other natural sciences. It has been perfectly obvious, too, that it is more difficult, perhaps impossible, to obtain objectivity that is as complete and a scientific attitude to the same degree, by the person who studies such phenomena as the family, the church, and the class system as may be attained by the one who deals with the scientific study of plants, animals, and stones. But such considerations have never led me to the idea that therefore one need make no attempt to be fully scientific in the study of societal structures, processes, and changes.

All of the chapters in this volume reflect, at least implicitly and frequently explicitly as well, my efforts to apply a genuinely comparative method in the study of societies. By such a method is meant the procedures by which one and the same observer and analyst, using exactly the same general frame of reference (in this case the "sociological spectacles" through which he views societies), and essentially at the same time, compares and contrasts various aspects of the social organization and processes of two or more societies. In my own case, the frame of reference used contains components, such as the set of concepts that figure in the treatment of "Ways of Farming," that never would have been included in this volume, or in any of my other writings for that matter, had I not been confronted for lengthy periods with the problem of trying to understand and interpret differences in the levels and standards of living in various parts of Latin America. In any case, to the best of my ability, the continuous effort to compare and contrast the essentials of life and labor of people in Brazil with those of their fellows in the eighteen Spanish-American countries, on the one hand, and with those of the inhabitants of the United States and Canada, on the other, is portrayed in this book.

As stated above, this volume is the fruition of sustained efforts during the last decade to ascertain and pass on to others verified and systematized knowledge of the momentous changes that are producing a complete metamorphosis of Brazilian society. It focuses upon the haste with which that society literally has "cut across lots" in the change from a societal entity that for centuries had been almost exclusively rural, agricultural, and pastoral to one in which most of its people would live in cities and towns and derive their livelihoods from manufacturing and processing, trade and commerce, transportation and communication, construction and maintenance, and other nonagricultural activities. In fact, the changes have been so numerous and so great that time and energy have not sufficed for all the study and analysis that would have been needed in order to do justice to the transformations in all aspects of Brazilian society. Therefore, the subjects treated in this book are highly selected. Some of the chapters are devoted to crucially important matters such as the growth of population and the race or *desafio* between population and the food supply, and to the vitally significant process of urbanization. Together these things are providing the "thrust" that is completely redoing the organization, structures, and processes of Brazilian society. Others focus upon selected features of the social structure, some of the basic social institutions, and a few of the processes of change and development.

Neither this volume nor most of my other writings about Brazil and the Brazilians would have been possible had not a major part of my time during the last quarter of a century, and what well might be considered an imprudent expenditure of a sizable portion of the family budget, gone into the acquisition of a voluminous collection of Braziliana. This collection includes hundreds of census reports and other compendia of statistical data, long runs of many of the more important journals, books about various features of Brazilian society written by persons in many countries and in many languages, and well over one thousand monographs, pamphlets, separates, reprints, etc. In connection with the writing of my *Brazil: People and Institutions* in the years 1943-45 I had learned the vital importance of having such materials readily at hand where any one of the items could be consulted and or rechecked at a moment's notice. Indeed the nucleus of the collection assembled at that time continues to save thousands of hours every year over what would be the case if it were necessary to try to get access to the materials in various libraries. Therefore, in more than a dozen revisits I have made to Brazil since 1945, I have expended considerable amounts of time and money in the effort to secure the materials I needed for my research, and thereby to be able to avoid to a considerable extent the debilitating feelings of frustration one suffers when a known source, and especially one which needs to be cited, cannot be used at crucially important moments in the exacting intellectual work of analysis, interpretation, and verification. Specifically, the studies on which the various chapters in this book are based could not have been made had not the source materials and other references been around me in my office and in my study where I could use them at the times that best suited my own convenience.

A few of the periods alluded to above, that I spent in Brazil, were so important in connection with the building of my reference collection that it seems worthwhile to offer a few more details about them. Most important of all, probably, was the journey of four months in 1951 undertaken for the specific purpose of making the contacts and arrangements needed in order to get the demographic materials that would result from the 1950 Census of the Americas. Every one of the Latin American countries was visited on that occasion, and the month I spent in Brazil, at places from São Paulo to Belém, was the one in which I was able to make the arrangements and initiate the exchanges that have brought me a continuous flow of the documents most significant for my work from that day to the present. In 1952 a couple of months spent in Brazil as advisor on agrarian reform provided the opportunity to make other firm friendships, and to initiate other exchanges, some of which are still being continued. And the same may be said of the four weeks spent in Brazil in 1953 as observer for the International Labour Office at the Seminar on Rural Welfare in Latin America; the six weeks I was in Brazil, again from Belém to São Paulo, in 1956 on a lecture tour under the auspices of the U.S. Department of State; the two weeks in Brazil in 1961, as a participant in a seminar on agrarian reform; the six weeks in 1963 that I served as technical director and leader of the sessions on ''social aspects'' of the International Course Agrarian Reform, when my ''students'' included officials from most of the states in Brazil; and the two weeks in Brazil in 1969, when my wife and I were guests of the União Cultural Brazil-Estados Unidos in São Paulo, to see and visit the modern linguistic laboratory to which my name has been given. On all of these occasions contacts were made and exchanges begun, many of which are still continuing. Naturally hundreds of books and monographs also were purchased in the course of these visits, large portions of which I would never have been able to secure had I not been on the spot and in position to take advantage of the information about publications that was passed on to me by friends and associates. In any case, the collection has been built up in these ways; by purchases from the works listed in the catalogues of dealers in all parts of the United States, Canada, England, Spain, Portugal, Italy, Germany, and Austria; by exchanges with scholars in Japan, Italy, France, Spain, Portugal, the Netherlands, and other countries; and through other miscellaneous procedures. And it has served me well in my teaching as well as my research, has been indispensable in the programs of many of my graduate students, and its use shared rather generously with professors and students at other universities, who appealed for assistance.[2]

Finally a word may be in order about the sequence in which the materials are presented. This and one other chapter of an introductory nature are given in this section, Part I of the book. Part II consists of three chapters dealing with the population and related matters. In Part III there are four chapters in which selected aspects of the social structure and the social institutions are treated. Finally, Part IV is made up of five chapters on subjects directly related to sociocultural change and development, including the two concluding chapters on urbanization.

# 2

## Sociology and Sociologists in Brazil and the United States: Some Aspects of Their Interrelationships

The sociologists of Brazil and the United States jointly are employed in three highly important tasks. These are: building a genuine science of society; disseminating the systematized body of theoretical knowledge of which it is made up; and helping to bring sociological facts and principles to bear upon the problems with which mankind is confronted at all levels, from those pertaining to family life to those involving the relationships between nations. This means that many dedicated sociologists in both countries are fully convinced of the value of the scientific attitude and appreciate the discipline it places upon men's thoughts and actions. For better or worse they are determined to have a part in bringing their scientific attitude to bear upon social and cultural phenomena. It also means that they seek opportunities to improve their perceptiveness and objectivity as observers, their skill as analysts, their insight based upon a knowledge of previous work on the subject or related subjects, their facility in organizing and synthesizing the results of their scientific activities, and their effectiveness in transmitting to others the knowledge they have acquired. It is true, of course, that considerable self-restraint and even resignation is required on the part of those genuinely entitled to be called sociologists. With great frequency they see others, men and women, apparently unrestrained by the rules of the scientific attitude and method, receiving great

First published in *America Latina* 14, Nos. 1-2 (January-June 1971); 83-100 and republished with the permission of Manuel Diégues, Jr., editor.

acclaim for the pronouncements they make upon the very same subjects that the sociologists are studying. This, though, is matter common to genuine social scientists in Brazil, the United States, and other parts of the world.

I will discuss briefly a few of the ways in which the work of sociologists in Brazil and in the United States has been intertwined. In so doing I use a simple chronological scheme for organizing my thoughts, and I comment in turn briefly upon each of the four following matters: (1) the influence of August Comte, brilliant French philosopher who coined the word "sociology," upon the early work in sociology and upon the development of this science in Brazil and the United States; (2) the early work in sociology in the two countries; (3) some of the first relationships between sociology and sociologists in Brazil and the United States; and (4) a few aspects of the present interrelationships.

## The Influence of August Comte

It would hardly be possible to commence a discussion of our subject without some reference to the work of August Comte, although in reality the man who gave the name to our science actually seems to have had very little direct influence upon the development of sociology either in Brazil or in the United States. This is not to say, however, that the ideas of this great philosopher played only minor roles in the intellectual circles of the two countries. Quite the contrary, Comte was a major influence in both, and especially in Brazil.

It seems well to recall for the moment that Comte's work falls into two sharply different periods and categories. As a young man he produced his monumental *Cours de Philosophie Positive.* This probably is best characterized as a brilliant polemic of a new positive philosophy, eventually designated in the work as sociology, against the traditional metaphysical philosophy.[1] During the later years of his life he organized and set forth his *Systeme de Politique Positive,* which was quite the antithesis of the early work and indeed constituted a "religion of humanity." Naturally such a complete reversal of thought created sharp division among his followers or disciples, of whom there were many. Perhaps no one has better summarized the nature and profundity of the split than was done by Fernando Azevedo in his monumental *A Cultura Brasileira,* from which I wish to quote a highly meaningful extract:

> After the death of August Comte, which occurred about this time (1857), Positivism was divided into two schools, one of which, under the direction of Pierre Lafitte, was the one which gained most territory in foreign countries and especially in Brazil, where it succeeded in bringing together a team of workers. For those who were bound up with this faction of Positivism, the theories which E. Littré, the chief of the other branch, regarded as the product of the mental illness of Auguste Comte, were perhaps the most precious things that the French thinker had left behind him. It was this current, that of orthodox Comtism, as Euclides da Cunha called it, which in the south of the country acquired the larger number of adherents among us, precisely for those theories of Comte which were rejected by Littré and which were concerned with the political and religious organization of society.[2]

With these thoughts in mind let us consider briefly the influence of August Comte and his ideas upon intellectual life, in general, and sociology, in particular, in the two most populous nations in the western hemisphere. In this respect there was a tremendous difference between the two. In the United States it seems fair to say that Comte's contributions were restricted largely to the use of the name[3] he had coined as the designation for the new science, the propagation of his theory of the "three stages," and study in general of his early work as contained in Harriet Martineau's free translation and condensation of his *Cours de Philosophie Positive.* This was published in London in 1853 under the title *The Positive Philosophy of August Comte.* The following year (1854) appeared the first two books published in the United States that made use of the neologism "Sociology" in their titles; and it was many years later before any others specifically identified as sociological works were to be printed. One of the first two was by an intellectual, Henry Hughes, who belonged to the planter aristocracy in the great cotton-producing section of Mississippi. It was entitled *Treatise on Sociology, Theoretical and Practical,* and was published in Philadelphia.[4] The second, which appeared almost simultaneously, was by George Fitzhugh, who seems to have clung rather tenuously to a position among Virginia's proud, traditional, slave-owning elite. It bore the title, *Sociology for the South, or the Failure of Free Society,* and was published in Richmond, Virginia.[5] Other than the name, and a favorable attitude towards Comte's partiality for highly and rigidly stratified or caste-dominated societies, these apologics for slavery seem to owe very little to the positivist philosophy. Even the extent to which they are pragmatic and empirical probably is more validly attributed to the influence of the thinking of Francis Bacon in the intellectual circles of Britain and the United States than to the brilliant exposition of such positivism eventually elaborated by Comte.

When it did appear, Comte's later work embodying the religion of humanity, which his disciples sought to establish, enjoyed very little popularity in the United States. In part this was probably due to the far-reaching effects of our deep-cutting and protracted Civil War; but the prominent roles played in the intellectual circles of the United States by Protestant clergymen, who saw little of merit in Comte's ideas for remaking religious life and organization, also probably was a factor. In any case the failure of positivism as a basis for religious activities in the United States was almost total.[6]

In Brazil, as I scarcely need remind my readers, the impact of Comte's ideas and doctrines were profoundly different from what they were upon intellectual life in the United States. In the first place I have been unable to discover any early books, i.e., those published before 1860, that made use of the word sociology in the title or made use of Comte's strong preferences for a castelike social structure as the basis for a defense of slavery. On the other hand, there was no parallel in the United States for the profound effects of Comte's mathematics upon the officers of Brazil's Escola Militar.[7] Nor was there in my country any Benjamin Constant. Finally, there was no successful establishment of an Igreja Positiva. In brief, were I to analyze society in the United States in a way comparable to what I have done for society in Brazil, there would be no place for a paragraph such as the following which appears in *Brasil: People and Institutions:*

> Positivists. More significant in their influence than in their number are the members of the Igreja Positiva Brasileira. Each week the Rio de Janeiro papers carry announcements of the meetings of this society and résumés of the sessions. This offshoot of Comtian philosophy counted in 1912 only 153

members, of whom 90 were men. Probably it does not have many more now, but the group has always included persons who were influential in public and intellectual affairs.

As early as the year 1850, a thesis on statistics introduced Comte's ideas into Brazil. In 1876 the first Positivist society was formed, its principal objectives being the creation of a library and the establishment of courses in science. Prominent among the original members were Dr. Antonio Carlos de Oliveira Guimarães, who took the initiative in the establishment of the society, and Dr. Benjamin Constant. In 1878 the society became the Igreja Positiva do Brazil. The census of 1890 reported a total of 1,327 persons who were affiliated with this church. Of these, 377 were in the Federal District, 321 in São Paulo, 146 in Santa Catarina (mostly in Brusque), 144 in Rio Grande do Sul, and 105 in Minas Gerais. Prior to the end of the year 1912 the group had presented and pushed vigorously 437 projects in connection with state and federal legislation. They fostered such measures as the improvement of relations between Brazil and Argentina, the freeing of the slaves, and the secularization of cemeteries. On the other hand, they opposed compulsory education, obligatory vaccination, anonymity in the press, and Chinese immigration. The 1940 census enumerated only 1,299 Positivists in Brazil, and the 1950 census did not classify them separately.[8]

### The Beginnings of Sociology in the United States and Brazil

We need not linger long in the consideration of the real beginnings of sociology in the two most populous countries in the Western Hemisphere. In both there were numerous important studies in what today certainly is entitled to be designated as sociology, long before social scientists began using Comte's neologism as a designation for their work. In Brazil, for example, I personally evaluate very highly the work of A.P. Figueiredo, who lived and worked in Recife during the middle of the nineteenth century,[9] and João Cardoso de Meneses e Souza,[10] who was active in Rio de Janeiro in the years around 1875. Comparable names might be mentioned of those who lived and worked in the United States, but for present purposes that probably is not necessary. Moreover, we can be very brief in our mention of the founding fathers of sociology as such in both countries. In discussing this I begin with the United States, because the use of the word sociology in the designation of university courses, in the names of books and articles, and as the discipline being professed came somewhat earlier there than it did in Brazil.

Perhaps the beginnings of sociology in the United States, other than the very early endeavors of Hughes and Fitzhugh already mentioned, may be treated adequately for present purposes by a few brief comments about five pioneer sociologists. First, of course, in the list is Lester F. Ward, whose name frequently is given along with those of Comte and Spencer in the group of the three men most responsible for the development of sociology, the science of society. Originally trained in law, Ward spent much of his life working in the fields of geology and botany. His two-volume work entitled *Dynamic Sociology* was published in 1883. I believe it was the third book published in the United States, and the first after the somewhat abortive efforts of Hughes and Fitzhugh, to employ the word sociology in the title. In any case it was circulated shortly after the publication of the first volume of Spencer's *Principles of Sociology* and before the last volume of that great classic appeared. Ward was strongly influenced by Darwin and also by Comte, Hegel, and William Wundt.

Albion W. Small was trained in theology and ordained as a Protestant minister. Subsequently he went to Germany for advanced study, and there he fell strongly under the influence of that country's social economists. Upon his return to the United States he taught social science (then embracing what eventually became the separate disciplines of history, economics, and political science) at Colby College in Maine. About 1890 he began offering a course in sociology, apparently the second such course to be given in the United States. (Sumner seems to have introduced the first course only a few years before at Yale.) From Colby College, Small moved to the University of Chicago where he established the first department of sociology ever to come into existence. There in collaboration with one of his students, the first man ever to take a Ph.D. degree in sociology in the United States, George E. Vincent, he published in 1894 the first textbook in sociology. It is entitled *An Introduction to the Study of Society*. (Vincent rose rapidly to the deanship of the College at Chicago, and to the presidency of the University of Minnesota; later he was to become the first president of the Rockefeller Foundation. At the Foundation, he conceived, organized, and put into effect the great world health program of that Foundation, which, in the last analysis, is the cause of our present world population crisis to be discussed in Chapter 5.) In 1895, Small founded the *American Journal of Sociology,* our first professional review.

Franklin H. Giddings was trained in engineering, but much of his life was spent in the profession of journalism. In this capacity he became deeply involved in the problems of organized labor. He succeeded Woodrow Wilson as professor of politics, or political science, at Bryn Mawr College in 1888. In 1894, he accepted a newly established chair of social science at Columbia University, where he devoted himself to establishing sociological studies. As a sociologist he was strongly influenced by Darwin, Spencer, Gumplowicz, Tarde, and Durkheim. In 1896 he published his *Principles of Sociology.* I early came to appreciate his work for two reasons: (1) my first teacher in the field of sociology, John C. Swenson, had done graduate work at Columbia under Gidding's direction; and (2) the first really sociological studies of rural communities, by James M. Williams, Warren H. Wilson, and Newell L. Sims, respectively, all were done under Gidding's encouragement and direction as doctoral dissertations at Columbia University.[11]

Charles H. Cooley, perhaps the first genuine social psychologist, and noted among other things for his formulation of the concept of the "primary group," was trained in engineering and economics. He was profoundly influenced through reading by the work of William James, the psychologist. In 1892 he began teaching sociology at the University of Michigan where he remained until his retirement, which did not come until I was professionally occupied as a sociologist. In 1899 and 1902, though, shortly before I was born, he published his first two books in the field of sociology.

William Graham Sumner's early training was in theology at Yale University. From there he went to Europe for advanced study at Geneva, Gottingen, and Oxford. Upon his return to the United States, he taught mathematics and Greek at Yale. Then he went to New York where he served as assistant pastor of a Protestant church. In 1872 he became professor of political and social science at Yale, where he worked mainly as a classical economist. Here he offered, apparently, the first course in sociology to be given at any university in the United States. In 1906 he published his great classic entitled *Folkways*.

Such are a few of the important facts about the origins and development of sociology in the United States. Obviously, at that time, owing to the difficulty of communication between the United States and Brazil, if for no other reason, there was little if any Brazilian influence on the early development of sociology in North America. Nor do I need to dwell upon the fact that the development of those who specialized professionally in the science of sociology and the production of books that carried the word sociology in their titles were still a thing of the future in Brazil. However, there were six men most entitled to be called the founders of sociology in Brazil. These are Fernando de Azevedo, Delgado de Carvalho, F.J. Oliveira Vianna, Francisco Cavalcanti Ponte de Miranda, Gilberto Freyre, and Antonio Carneiro Leão. Fortunately, I have numbered all of them except Ponte de Miranda, whom I never met, as personal friends.

Fernando Azevedo worked under the influence of French scholars, and indeed may be thought of as Durkheim's influence at its best. Ponte de Miranda, whose *Introdução a Sociologia Geral* was published in 1926, got his principal stimulations from Germany. Oliveira Vianna also was influenced mainly by European thinkers, including the racial theorists such as Gobineau, Ammon, Lapouge, and Chamberlain. Except for the ideas on racial or zoological determinism expressed in one part of his *Evolução do Povo Brasileiro,* however, I personally have found his works to be fully equal to any of those published anywhere in the world at the time he wrote. I hope that eventually they will be much more widely known in the United States than presently is the case.

The other three, Delgado de Carvalho, Gilberto Freyre, and Carneiro Leão, all were strongly influenced by sociological activities as they were developed in the United States. On my first visit to Brazil in 1939 I met Delgado, obtained copies of his sociology textbooks, and learned of the complete suppression of sociological activities at the Universidade do Distrito Federal in Rio de Janeiro.

Delgado de Carvalho's work was of a general nature, with emphasis on theoretical matters and educational sociology. Gilberto Freyre, from my point of view, should be remembered as the one who introduced a genuine cultural sociology in Brazil. At the time he was doing the master's thesis at Columbia University, which eventually was published as *Casa Grande e Senzala,* I was deeply involved in emphasizing the importance of the cultural factor among my associates, largely graduate students in sociology and anthropology in the United States. May I say that in those days, the 1920s and the 1930s, the reliance upon zoological or racial factors, along the lines followed by Oliveira Vianna, was somewhat the rule rather than the exception in both the United States and Brazil, as well as throughout Europe. For this reason I consider the work of Freyre, and also that of our friend and associate, Arthur Ramos, especially significant. Carneiro Leão was also influenced greatly by sociology and sociologists in the United States, both in his *Fundamentos de Sociologia* and in his *A Sociedade Rural,* the first systematic work in rural sociology to be published anywhere in Latin America.[12]

Some may object that I have not named Euclydes da Cunha in this short list of the founding fathers of sociology in Brazil. This is not because I do not esteem his work. On the contrary, I consider *Os Sertões* to be among the most important studies ever made of rural society, and in my publications devoted to the development of rural sociology in Latin America I single out his great classic, along with those of Oliveira Vianna, Gilberto Freyre, and Carneiro Leão, as being of the highest importance. However, I am sure that Euclydes never considered himself to be a sociologist, and in his work I find no mention of Comte, Spencer, or any other noted sociologist.

## U.S. Sociologists in Brazil

The presence in Brazil of sociologists from the United States as teachers in the universities, as researchers, or in any other capacity is comparatively recent. The first of these to do anything of consequence that I know of was Samuel H. Lowrie who spent much of the decade of the 1930s at the Universidade de São Paulo. Undoubtedly, the numerous articles he published here as a result of his studies and those of his students had a considerable impact. I am not familiar with the circumstances that brought him to Brazil nor with the details of his activities while he was there.

At about the time Lowrie returned to the United States, Donald Pierson arrived at the Escola de Sociologia e Política to begin a rather long career at that institution. In 1934 Dr. Robert E. Park, who would have been included in my list of the founding fathers of sociology in the United States had that list been a little longer, was then relinquishing the headship of the department of sociology where Pierson was doing graduate work, and proceeded to spend a year on a leisurely trip around the world. Park's career had included a lengthy period as a journalist from which he moved into the field of public relations and specifically into service as private secretary to the great Negro leader Booker T. Washington. From that, with an intense interest in everything having to do with race and race relations, he went to the University of Chicago where he established studies in urban sociology and especially in urban ecology. With this background, one of his major interests on his trip around the world was the development of an encyclopedia of the Negro, and with this in mind, he spent some time in Brazil discussing his project with many of the intellectuals he thought might be most interested in collaborating in the venture. He soon discovered that Brazilian concepts and patterns of race and race relations were vastly different from those he knew in the United States and had encountered elsewhere on his trip. This led him to the conclusion that the Brazilian patterns should be studied.[13] Accordingly, after his return to Chicago he looked around for a promising graduate student who might be sent to Brazil to make such a study for his doctoral dissertation. Pierson was chosen and he spent two years (1935-37) in Bahia gathering the materials for his study. Eventually, this was submitted as a dissertation at Chicago, and subsequently it was published as *Negroes in Brazil* (Chicago: University of Chicago Press, 1940). The preface for this work was written in 1939 when Pierson was at the Escola de Sociologia e Política. Through his classes there, his association with Brazilian sociologists, his translations into Portuguese of many sociological works, and through the students (including Flavio Nobre de Campos) he encouraged to study at the University of Chicago, and through his own books and articles, Pierson had a tremendous influence upon sociology in Brazil.[14]

The reference to the work of Pierson brings us to the point at which some of my own efforts might be mentioned. People in Brazil, the United States, and elsewhere often have asked me how I came to devote such a large part of my life to studying, teaching, lecturing, and writing about Brazil. Indeed, I have had standing invitations from the editors of some of the sociological journals in the United States for accounts of my pioneering activities in the study of Brazilian society (and also of my own part in the development of sociological studies of Spanish-American societies; the establishment of the journal *Rural Sociology;* the organization of the Rural Sociological Society; the transition from deductive to pragmatic work in the field of Population Study; my experiences as a graduate student and assistant to P.A. Sorokin and Carle C. Zimmerman; and a number of other items in the building of a science of society).

After receiving excellent undergraduate training in the liberal arts at Brigham Young University, where I majored in history and sociology, I entered the University of Minnesota in the fall of 1928 to begin graduate work in sociology. There it was my good fortune to have as my major professors, Dr. Pitirim A. Sorokin, whom many of us consider to have been the greatest sociologist of all time, and his brilliant associate, Carle C. Zimmerman.[15] Following two years of graduate study at the University of Minnesota, I went along in 1930 when Sorokin moved to Harvard University to establish and head a new department of sociology at that renowned institution. A year later, in the summer of 1931, I began my own professional career as assistant professor of sociology at the Louisiana State University, a position in which I divided my time between teaching courses in the College of Arts and Sciences and carrying on research at the Louisiana Agricultural Experiment Station. As soon as I could get my teaching and research in Louisiana fairly well established, I began extending my area of professional observation to Latin America. The first venture along these lines was in Mexico where, accompanied by Carle C. Zimmerman, I spent part of the summer of 1935 on a general reconnaissance survey. By 1939, my endeavors to apply a genuinely comparative method in the study of Latin American societies were far enough along that, aided by a small grant from the Julius Rosenwald Fund, I spent four months visiting almost all of the Latin American countries. On this occasion I was privileged to be in Brazil for a period of three weeks.

Among the memorable events connected with my first experiences on the great Brazilian half continent were long conversations with Paul Vanorden Shaw, then teaching at the University of São Paulo, and many hours of professional exchanges with Arthur Ramos,

Delgado de Carvalho, and others at the University of Brazil in Rio de Janeiro. This was the occasion when I began to perceive the disastrous effects of governmental repression of sociological work at Brazilian universities, a phenomenon which, unfortunately, has recurred from 1939 to the present. Inasmuch as many of the younger sociologists, even Brazilian sociologists, seem to be unacquainted with the happenings in 1939 it seems well to note here a few of the things that had taken place under the Vargas regime immediately prior to my visit. I learned many of these details during my first visit and others in subsequent trips to Brazil. Apparently either unwilling or unable to make a distinction between "sociology" and "socialism," Getúlio Vargas and some of his henchmen had completely suppressed the excellent work in sociology that had been started at the University of the Distrito Federal (later the University of Brazil) in Rio de Janeiro. (In São Paulo, fortunately, the position of Fernando de Azevedo was so firmly established that even Vargas lacked the will or the way to abolish his chair or transfer his activities to another department.) Be that as it may, in Rio de Janeiro, Gilberto Freyre's position in sociology was eliminated entirely; Delgado de Carvalho's work in sociology was discontinued, and he was transferred to a professorship of geography; and Arthur Ramos's work was all labeled as anthropology. Undoubtedly, these and other changes at the time set back by decades the development of sociological teaching and research at Brazilian institutions of higher learning.

Perhaps the most important result of my first visit to the Portuguese-speaking half of South America was my meeting with Arthur Ramos. The fame of this noted Brazilian physician and social scientist had already spread to the United States prior to 1939; and, indeed, it was Kimball Young who, upon learning that I planned to visit Brazil and other parts of South America, emphasized that by all means I should seek to meet and become acquainted with Ramos.[16] Even in the course of two short weeks in Rio de Janeiro, the conversations with Ramos convinced me that Young's high esteem of Ramos's work in social psychology and on the African sociocultural heritage in Brazil was fully justified. As a result, following my return to Louisiana, I set about securing funds from the General Education Board and making arrangements to bring Ramos to the Louisiana State University as visiting professor of sociology for the first semester of the 1940-41 academic year.

There he taught our regular seminar on race relations and a special course on "Races and Cultures of Brazil," which we introduced to take advantage of his field of specialization. In these courses he exercised a strong formative influence upon a considerable number of brilliant young graduate students who subsequently played substantial roles in the development of a pragmatic type of sociology in the United States. Moreover, from this beginning in 1940 (which may have been the first sociology course devoted to Latin America to be taught in the United States), the study of Latin American institutions has become a well-established feature of the work in the department of sociology at the Louisiana State University. Furthermore, from the modest beginning there in 1940, sociology courses devoted to the study of Latin American societies have multiplied until presently several hundred colleges and universities throughout the United States now include such work as parts of their regular offerings.

In February 1942, along with my wife and children, I returned to Brazil to spend a full year seeking to learn about the structure and functions of Brazilian society. This time I was serving as a member of the Auxiliary Foreign Service of the U.S. Department of State and I was on assignment to the Embassy in Rio de Janeiro and specifically commissioned to make sociological studies of the vast rural portions of Brazil. In this capacity I traveled extensively on visits to all sections of the country, making the observations and gathering the data for various aspects of life and labor in Brazil, much of which subsequently was used as integral portions of my book-length study entitled *Brazil: People and Institutions*.[17] During this year also, at the request of Cyro Berlinck and Donald Pierson, I taught a seminar on research methods in sociology at the Escola Livre de Sociología e Política in São Paulo. This seminar was convened each time it was possible for me, in the course of my travels, to pass through São Paulo; and the perceptive, industrious group of young professionals whom at that time, by means of my extremely poor Portuguese, I sought to instruct, included such now well-known Brazilian sociologists as J.V. Freitas Marcondes, Lucilla Herman, Olavo Baptista Filho, and Carlos Borges Schmidt. Those visits to São Paulo also were the occasions of lengthy professional conversations with Donald Pierson and Emílio Willems, both of whom were then teaching at the Escola.

During my stay in Brazil in 1942-43, I also was enabled to begin

my efforts to get promising young Brazilians to the United States
for graduate training in sociology and related disciplines. Actually,
the first students I was able to assist in this way were two young
geographers, Hilgard O'Reilly Sternberg and his wife, Carolina.
They were awarded assistantships by the Louisiana State University
that enabled them to go there for advanced study, where they
worked under the able direction of Richard J. Russell. Through the
Sternbergs, subsequently, we were able to bring the first of my
Brazilian graduate students in sociology to work for the M.A.
degree at that university. This was José Arthur Rios. Eventually it
was my good fortune to have as graduate students in universities in
the United States such excellent Brazilian sociologists as João
Gonçalves de Souza and his wife, Norma, J.V. Freitas Marcondes,
John V.D. Saunders, Fernando de Oliveira, and Fabio Barbosa da
Silva.

In 1945 I was privileged to return to Brazil for additional field
study in Goiás and the São Francisco Valley; and in 1946 I spent
two months as visiting professor, teaching demography, in the
department of geography at the University of Brazil. While in Rio
de Janeiro at this time I also offered a course in rural sociology at
the Universidade do Povo at the Casa do Estudante do Brasil, where
my wife and I occupied an apartment. Among my students in this
class was the now internationally known Brazilian sociologist,
Manuel Diégues Junior. At this time, I also presented a lengthy
series of lectures on the relations of man to the land in Brazil to the
officials of the Ministry of Agriculture.

The important work of securing the services of Brazilian
sociologists for positions as visiting professors in the United States,
which I helped initiate by inviting Arthur Ramos to the Louisiana
State University in 1940, has remained a major interest of mine
from that time to the present. Among the Brazilian scholars my
associates and I have succeeded in getting to instruct undergraduate
and graduate students at the universities with which I have been
connected are José Arthur Rios (first at Vanderbilt University and
later at the University of Florida), Emílio Willems (Vanderbilt),
J.V. Freitas Marcondes (Florida), Hiroshi Saito (Florida), and
Sugiyama Iutaka (Florida). All of these have assumed full
responsibility for regular courses and proved to be exceptionally
competent. Many others have taken part for shorter periods in the
intellectual activities in our universities as lecturers and in other

special capacities. This list includes such eminent Brazilian scholars as Antonio Carneiro Leão, Teiti Suzuki, Manuel Diégues Junior, René Ribeiro, Padre Avila, and Thales de Azevedo. All of this, I hope and I believe, has facilitated considerably the meaningful relationships between sociology and sociologists in Brazil and the United States.

Another of the more significant aspects of the extended efforts to further genuine understanding and interchange between sociologists and other scholars in the United States and those in Brazil has been the encouragement and direction given to candidates for advanced degrees in sociology to select Brazilian subjects for the research that must be done in connection with the preparation of their theses and dissertations. Those who have worked in Brazil and on Brazilian topics under my direction for these purposes include José Arthur Rios (at Louisiana State), Paul H. Price and Marion T. Loftin (at Vanderbilt), and John V.D. Saunders, J.V. Freitas Marcondes, Fabio Barbosa da Silva, Lowell C. Wikoff, F. Herbert Minnich, Harold M. Clements, J. Parke Renshaw, and John Mayer (at Florida).

From the beginning a major part of my own professional activities has been devoted to the work of increasing and disseminating a body of comprehensive, systematized, and empirically tested knowledge about Brazilian society. In doing this, I have been led on by the hope that my own studies and the courses and seminars dealing with Brazilian peoples, social institutions, social structures, social processes, and sociocultural systems would contribute significantly to the development of a genuine science of society. In any case, from 1946 on, I have returned frequently to Brazil, for periods ranging in length from ten days to three months, for a variety of purposes. These include my own research assignments as advisor to Brazilian governmental agencies, representative and observer for various international bodies at seminars and symposia held in Brazil, participation as a specialist in various national and international conferences, teaching in specialized courses organized by international organizations, lecture tours, and so on. The auspices under which these visits were made include Brazil's Ministry of Agriculture, the U.S. Department of Agriculture, the International Labour Office, the U.S. Department of State, the Inter-American Institute of Agricultural Sciences, the John Simon Guggenheim Memorial Foundation, and Brazil's Ministry of Education.

As a result of this, as must be apparent to anyone who reads my books in general and those dealing with Brazil in particular, my own sociological work has been strongly influenced by many Brazilian scholars. Not a few of these have been among my closest personal friends over a considerable period of time. Through me I trust that parts of their own scientific accomplishments have had a significant impact upon many of my own students and upon the students of my students. Obviously, for present purposes, any list of the Brazilians who have had the greatest influence upon my own scientific activities necessarily must be greatly abbreviated, but I can hardly do other than to include the names of a few of them. Alphabetized in the distinctive Brazilian way according to the first letter in the first given name, this greatly shortened list is as follows: Antonio Carneiro Leão, Arthur Cezar Ferreira Reis, Arthur Ramos, Augusta de Carvalho, Carlos Borges Schmidt, Delgado de Carvalho, Emílio Willems, Fernando de Azevedo, Fernando de Oliveira, Florestan Fernandes, F.J. Oliveira Vianna, Gilberto Freyre, Hilgard O'Reilly Sternberg, Hiroshi Saito, José Arthur Rios, J.V. Freitas Marcondes, Manuel Diégues Junior, M.A. Teixeira de Freitas, M.B. Lourenço Filho, Olavo Baptista Filho, René Ribeiro, Sugiyama Iutaka, Teiti Suzuki and Thales de Azevedo.

In recent years the contacts between sociologists in Brazil and the United States have multiplied enormously. Especially since about 1955, Pierson's sustained efforts and my own attempts to promote genuine interchange between sociology and sociologists in the two countries have come to be just small parts of the whole. Dozens of well qualified sociologists from each of these countries have participated, almost as "interchangeable parts," in the scientific and educational institutions and processes of the other. Even the shortest of lists of Brazilians who have done the most to enrich the content and broaden the scope of sociological activities in the United States must include the names of the following: Thales de Azevedo, Olavo Baptista Filho, Manoel Berlinck, J.V. Freitas Marcondes, Gilberto Freyre, Florestan Fernandes, Sugiyama Iutaka, José Pastore, José Arthur Rios, Hiroshi Saito, and Emílio Willems. And among sociologists from the United States who have contributed most to the development of sociological activities in Brazil are Herbert Blumer, Rex Crawford, Bert L. Ellenbogen, Archibald O. Haller, Donald E. Johnson, John H. Kolb, Olen E. Leonard, Lowry Nelson, John V.D. Saunders, Ray E. Wakeley and E.A. Wilkening.

In conclusion, it seems fair to state that during the second half of the twentieth century neither the unity of purpose nor the volume of exchange between sociology and sociologists in Brazil and the United States is exceeded by the activity between any other two countries in the entire world with the possible exception of Canada and the United States.

# PART II

# The Brazilian Population

With a population that already has passed the 100-million mark, with fully one-third of the people in all twenty Latin American countries, and with a rate of increase that is among the highest in the world, reliable information about Brazil's population is among the most important aspects of the general study of Brazilian society. Three chapters are included in this section. The first of these, Chapter 3, contains a general profile of the population of the Brazilian half continent. Heretofore there has been a tremendous lag between the time Brazil's census was taken and the time the published data from the same were available for study by social scientists. Fortunately this problem was largely overcome in the 1970 census, and as a result the materials collected in 1970 have figured strongly in the preparation of the profile presented here. So much is said throughout the world about the racial composition of Brazil's population that a consideration should be given to a presentation of the most reliable information about the racial make-up of the Brazilian population and trends in the same. Chapter 4, the second in this part, is devoted to this subject. Finally, Chapter 5 is an attempt to present the most salient facts about the all-important race between population and the food supply, as this great *desafio* occupies the spotlight during the 1970s.

# 3

## Demographic Profile

Thanks to the censuses taken in 1940, 1950, and 1960, and 1970 and the increase in the knowledge of demography, the verified facts and tested hypotheses about Brazil's people are increasing rapidly. In this chapter an attempt is made to present some of the more important facts about the number, distribution, characteristics, vital processes, and growth of the population in Brazil.[1]

### Number and Distribution

The latest official census taken as of September 1, 1970, showed the total population of Brazil to be about 94,500,000. Lest some may be of the opinion that little or no credence may be given to this figure, it should be indicated that Brazil's recent censuses were either done under the competent guidance of Professor Giorgio Mortara, or taken by those strongly influenced by him. This authority has calculated that the percentage of omissions in 1940 was only 1.7, which compares not too favorably with an index of 1.4 percent for the corresponding census of the United States.

In evaluating these figures it may be helpful to consider that Brazil contains approximately 2.4 percent of the population of the world, 50 percent of the people of South America, and about 35 percent of all the inhabitants of the extensive area known as Latin America. It is also of interest to know that Brazil's population in 1970 was about 46 percent as large as that of the United States, up from about 39 percent in 1960. About 18 percent of all the inhabitants of the Americas are Brazilians.

Even though it contains more than one-third of the population of Latin America, Brazil's boundaries encircle more than 41 percent of the total land area south of the Rio Grande; so the average density of population is considerably less than that in some other parts of Latin America. Thus the number of persons per square mile was only 28.7 in 1970, which is practically the same as the 27.8 average for the South American continent, but somewhat greater than the specific figures for some other countries, such as 21.5 in Argentina and 25.7 in Peru. It was much less than the 64 persons per square mile of national territory in Mexico, 192 in Cuba, and 434 in El Salvador.

The striking thing about the distribution of population in Brazil is the degree to which it is concentrated within a few hundred miles of the seacoast (see Figure 1). Over the immense stretch of the coastal plain, from the mouth of the Amazon to the Uruguayan border, there are only a few areas that are not rather densely populated. Most of the large cities are directly upon the seashore or only a short distance inland, and the narrow coastal band is also the home of the bulk of the rural population. On the other hand, except in the southern portions of the country where the twentieth century has seen the population surging to the interior in a tremendous burst of colonizing activity, there are only a few scattered localities in which the fingers of dense settlement have pushed inland to any great extent. Exceptions to this rule are penetrations along the Paranagua River, which forms the boundary between the states of Maranhão and Piauí, the band of densely settled territory extending into southern Ceará from Paraíba, the fairly well-populated stretch of territory along the railway that runs from Salvador to Joazeiro in the state of Bahia, and another in the southern part of that state. By far the greatest penetration of settlement into the interior is the one which has pushed up into central Goiás along the highway to Brasília and the railway that extends from São Paulo through the Triangulo of Minas Gerais to the thriving little city of Anapolis; and, although it does not show on the map, since the building of the Belém-Brasília highway in the 1960s several million people have flocked into the zone adjacent to it.

Throughout a large portion of all Brazilian territory the population density is very low. However, only a small part of it is entirely unoccupied; for even in the vast interior, one occasionally will find a small village, a cattle *fazenda,* a post for dispensing supplies to and assembling the products of those who gather rubber and other things the forest has to offer, and, at widely separated intervals, a

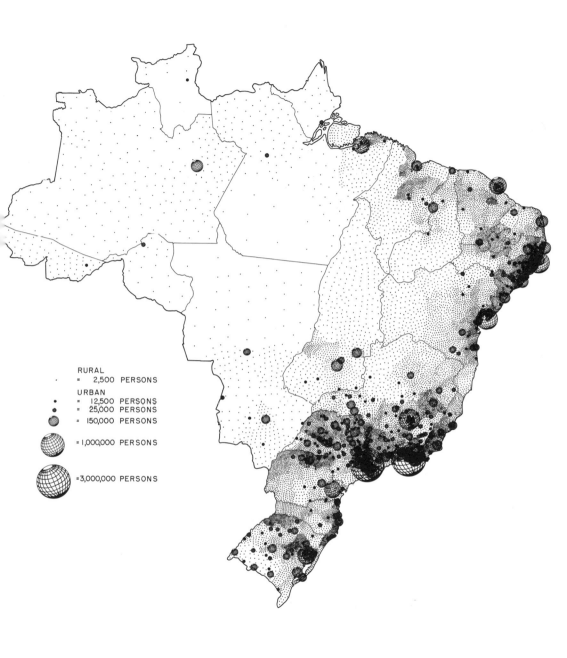

RURAL
· = 2,500 PERSONS
URBAN
· = 12,500 PERSONS
• = 25,000 PERSONS
⬤ = 150,000 PERSONS
◯ = 1,000,000 PERSONS
◯ = 3,000,000 PERSONS

FIGURE 1. Distribution of the Population of Brazil, 1960

town or city of considerable importance. But the distances between each of these are enormous, and most of the interior can hardly be thought of as settled territory. The great expanses of central Brazil are practically devoid of inhabitants.

The center of population in 1970 fell far to the south, being located in the east south-central portion of the state of Minas Gerais not far from its capital, Belo Horizonte, and almost due north of Rio de Janeiro. Furthermore, between 1920 and 1970 the center of population moved a short distance to the south in a slightly easterly direction. This reflects the tremendous growth of the two immense Brazilian conurbations, São Paulo and Rio de Janeiro.

## Characteristics of the Population

*Racial Elements*

There are few places in the world in which the racial make-up of the population is more involved and complex than it is in Brazil. All the principal varieties of mankind, all the basic stocks into which the human race may be divided, have entered into the composition of the population of this great half continent.

During the twentieth century the addition of several hundred thousand Japanese immigrants to São Paulo and the adjacent states, where they are multiplying at a very rapid rate, added the last of the great types of mankind to the Brazilian population.

In the 1950 census, the latest one in which such a classification was used, the population of Brazil was classified according to color into the following groups:

| Color | Number | Percent |
|---|---|---|
| White | 32,027,661 | 61.7 |
| Black | 5,692,657 | 11.0 |
| Yellow | 329,082 | 0.6 |
| Brown | 13,786,742 | 26.5 |
| Undeclared | 108,255 | 0.2 |

Although there is little doubt that the Caucasian races have contributed most to the biological make-up of the Brazilian population, these figures should be viewed with a degree of caution. In the first place, the category of whites must be thought of as designating those who are white or "whitish," and a considerable number of those who were placed in this category have a substantial strain of Indian heritage. Furthermore, the admixtures of genes from Negroid sources, although probably of less importance than the Indian, are by no means lacking entirely in a substantial part of those who are classified as whites. The number of persons classed as blacks, or Negroes, certainly is the absolute minimum, and any change whatsoever in the criteria used probably would have increased this number. It is unfortunate that the single category of *pardo,* or brown, was used to designate the mixtures of two fundamentally different types, the crosses of whites and Negroes and also those of whites and Indians as well as the Indians themselves. As it stands, the two mixed groups are probably represented in about the same proportions, although, as indicated above, many who might be placed in this mixed category are included with the whites. *Cafusos,* representing the Negro-Indian cross, although not entirely lacking, are too few to make any substantial difference in the total figures.

The census data also offer an opportunity of observing how the proportions of the different races vary from one part of the country to another. These have been mapped in Figure 2. This illustration has the advantage of showing the relative importance of the total population of each state at the same time that it reveals how the inhabitants of each are distributed among the several color categories. It deserves careful study by anyone who has an interest in the fundamental types of mankind as they are represented in the population of Brazil.

Lest some may think that the importance of the white element in Brazil is overstressed, attention should be directed to the southern part of the country. Note especially that São Paulo, the most populous state in Brazil, Rio Grande do Sul (which ranks fourth in population), Santa Catarina, and Paraná contain very small proportions of Negroes and racially mixed persons. In all of these, the descendants of recent immigrants from Europe constitute the bulk of the inhabitants. The high proportions of whites in Minas Gerais, the Distrito Federal (now the state of Guanabara), the state of Rio de Janeiro, and in Espírito Santo also should be taken into account.

The concentrations of the Negroid elements deserve comment. The data in Figure 2 bear out the general impression that, from the racial standpoint, Bahia is the darkest spot on the map of Brazil.

Not only are the absolute number and relative importance of Negroes large in the state, but the mixed category in Bahia undoubtedly consists principally of mulattoes. Other states in which the majority of those in the mixed category are white-Negro crosses are Rio de Janeiro, Sergipe, Alagoas, Pernambuco, Paraíba, and Maranhão; as well as Guanabara, which also belongs in this group.

Indians and their crosses with whites make up the principal non-Caucasian strain in the populations of such states as Amazonas

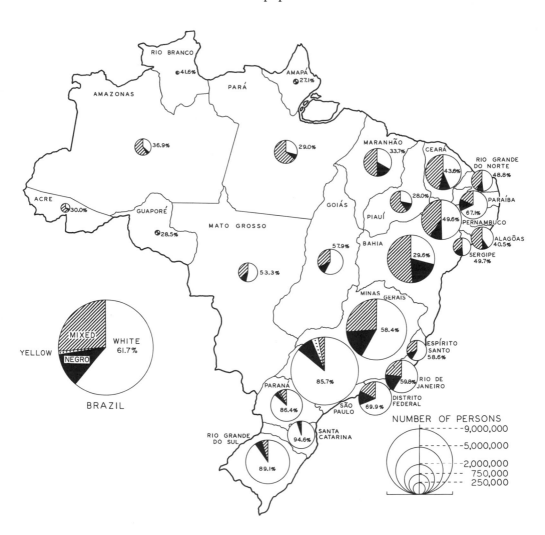

FIGURE 2.  Racial Composition of the Population, by States

and Pará, and they also are of considerable importance in Mato Grosso, Goiás, Piauí, Ceará, and Rio Grande do Norte. As a matter of fact, throughout the inland, or *sertão,* portions of the entire northeast, the Indian strain is prominent; but of course the more densely populated, sugar-cane-growing, coastal districts, in which the Negroes and mulattoes constitute the lion's share of the population, tip the balance greatly in favor of the black element in all of the states from Bahia to Paraíba.

## National Origins

Among the nations of the world, and even among those of the Western Hemisphere, Brazil is outstanding in the extent to which large numbers of immigrants from various countries have been incorporated into the population.

In 1920, 1,565,961 persons, or about one out of every 20 persons living in Brazil (5.2 percent), had come from another country. Of these the largest contingent, 558,405, or 35.7 percent, was from Italy, with Portugal (27.7 percent), Spain (14.0 percent), Germany (3.4 percent), and Turkey (3.2 percent) following in the order named. Uruguay, Poland, Russia, Japan, Austria, Argentina, Paraguay, and France, also in the order of their importance, were the other countries which had contributed 10,000 or more persons to help swell the population of South America's largest country. Most of these immigrants were located in a few of the southern states, 52.4 percent of them being in São Paulo, 15.1 percent in the Distrito Federal, 9.7 percent in Rio Grande do Sul, 5.5 percent in Minas Gerais, 4.0 percent in Paraná, 3.4 percent in Rio de Janeiro, and 2.0 percent in Santa Catarina. On a relative basis the foreign-born were most important in the Distrito Federal, where they constituted 20.8 percent of the inhabitants; then followed São Paulo (18.2 percent), Mato Grosso (10.4 percent), Paraná (9.2 percent), and Rio Grande do Sul (7.1 percent).

Immigration to Brazil, which was very large from 1887 to 1897 and from 1912 to 1914, never regained its former importance after the close of World War I, although it was substantial between 1920 and 1930. From 1965 to 1969 it averaged only 9.700 per year.[2] As a result the total number of foreign-born in the population has been falling steadily from 1920 on. By 1950 it was only 1,224,184, 2.3

percent of the national population; and in 1970 just 1,214,184, or 1.3 percent of the inhabitants.

The 1950 data indicate that of these the largest number, 336,826, or 27.5 percent, were natives of Portugal; and the second largest contingent, 242,337, or 19.8 percent, was from Italy. The other six countries which had contributed most heavily to the foreign-born population of Brazil and the number of persons from each are as follows: Spain, 131,608, or 10.8 percent; Japan, 129,192, or 10.6 percent; Germany, 65,184, or 5.4 percent; Poland, 48,806, or 4.0 percent; and Syria and Lebanon, 44,718, or 3.7 percent. Persons originating in these eight countries made up 82 percent of all the foreign-born in Brazil.

By 1950 the immigrant population of Brazil was much more highly concentrated in a few sections of the country than was the case in 1920. At mid-century São Paulo alone contained 693,321 foreign-born persons, or 56.6 percent of all those in Brazil. The Distrito Federal was the home of an additional 210,454 (17.2 percent). Therefore the two together had almost three-fourths of the foreign-born population of Brazil. The four other states containing the largest contingents of the foreign-born in 1950, with the corresponding numbers and percentages, are as follows: Rio Grande do Sul, 78,134, or 6.4 percent; Paraná, 76,502, or 6.3 percent; Rio de Janeiro, 38,395, or 3.1 percent; and Minas Gerais, 32,896, or 2.7 percent.

*Rural-Urban Residence*

For several centuries, both quantatively and qualitatively, Brazil's population was among the most rural in the world. No other fact is of greater importance than this for one who would understand Brazil and the Brazilians. In the words of Dr. F.J. Oliveira Vianna, noted sociologist and culture historian:

> From the first days of our history we have been an agricultural and pastoral people. . . . Urbanism is a modern element in our social evolution. All of our history is that of an agricultural people . . . the history of a society of farmers and herdsmen. In the country our race was formed and in it were molded the intimate forces of our civilization. The dynamism of our history in the colonial period came from the

countryside. The admirable stability of our society in the Imperial period was based in the country.[3]

The quantitative aspects of the subject are made abundantly clear from the data gathered in the 1940 census. According to the criteria employed, 69 percent of the population was classified as rural and the remainder as urban. However, these criteria provided that the inhabitants of every seat of a countylike *municipio* and those of many district seats, regardless of the number of inhabitants, were to be placed in the urban category, so that this group actually embraced the residents of several thousand very small villages and hamlets, including one in the faraway part of Mato Grosso having only 61 inhabitants. Brazil's towns and cities of 5,000 or more inhabitants numbered only 319, and of these only 27 of them had as many as 40,000 residents. Had criteria similar to those used in the United States Census been employed, the percentage of the population in the urban category probably would have been between 20 and 25.

From the qualitative standpoint, also, the population of Brazil in 1940 was extremely rural. With its people spread throughout an enormous territory, with relatively few important focal points of urban and industrial cultural influences, with a high proportion of the population engaged directly in agricultural and collecting activities, and with the systems of communication and transportation still in a rudimentary form, it should be evident that the degree of rurality in Brazil was very high. And even in the 1970s, the inhabitant of the average little town or village in Brazil is conditioned to a far greater extent by cultural influences arising from the surrounding rural environment, and less by those emanating from large urban centers, than is the resident of a center of equal size in the United States or Western Europe. It will still be many decades before good roads, automobiles, electricity, telephones, radios, television sets, newspapers, and the many other traits which have come to be considered as necessities in the average rural community in the United States are found to any considerable extent in many of Brazil's rural districts. Meanwhile the footpath, trail, or stream; the canoe, pack animal, riding horse, and oxcart; the homemade candle and lamp; and communication by word of mouth remain as the basic elements in the rural scheme of living in much of Brazil. There is no reason for doubting that while

Brazilian cities have moved ahead in the stream of modern progress, many of her rural districts have continued decade after decade with little or no visible change. Cultural lag has been tremendous. Whereas in the United States social changes since 1920 have tended to eliminate the differences between the ways of living in rural and urban districts, in Brazil the same forces have tended to accentuate even more the differences between the two.

Since 1950, however, drastic changes have taken place in the rural-urban distribution of Brazil's inhabitants. An exodus of tremendous proportions has transplanted millions of persons, primarily those of humble origins and low socioeconomic status. It has uprooted them from the rural districts in which they were born and put them down in teeming cities and towns, or in the miserable "suburbs" which encircle each of them. My own estimates indicate that the overwhelming rush of population from the open country to cities and towns between 1950 and 1960 involved about 7,000,000 persons; that is, about one out of every ten persons enumerated in the 1960 census had migrated from a rural area to an urban center during the preceding ten years. As large as are this number and proportion, they must be strictly in accord with the expectations on the part of anyone who has been in a position to observe the mushrooming of existing cities and towns, the sudden appearance of great sprawling slums in the zones surrounding all the principal metropolitan centers, and the emergence and growth of hundreds of additional urban areas. In 1950, on the eve of the mass movement of Brazilians from country to city, Brazil contained only eleven cities with as many as 100,000 inhabitants apiece. By 1960 the corresponding figure had risen to thirty-one; and in 1970, the latest census showed a total of sixty cities that had passed the 100,000 mark. About 1965 Brazil's population became more urban than rural, and in 1970 over 52 million persons, 55.9 percent of all Brazilians, were classified in the urban category.[4] Between 1960 and 1970 a net movement of about 10,300,000 persons from rural to urban districts took place; or, in other words, of the 94,500,000 persons enumerated in 1970 more than one in ten was a recent migrant from rural to urban areas.

## The Age Distribution

Few aspects of a population are of greater significance than the manner in which it is distributed according to age. As is true in any country in which the birth rate is very high, the population of Brazil is highly concentrated in the younger age brackets. (See Figures 3 and 4.) In fact, except for some differences due almost exclusively to the much larger numbers of immigrants in the United States, in 1970 the age distribution of Brazil's population corresponded closely to the one for the United States a century earlier. (See Figure 5.) Thus, according to the 1970 census, 42.2 percent of the population was less than fifteen years of age, whereas the same year in the United States the corresponding percentage was only 28.5. On the other hand elderly people in Brazil are much less important, relatively, than they are in countries such as the United States,

FIGURE 3. Comparison of the Age Distribution of the Populations of Brazil and the United States, 1970

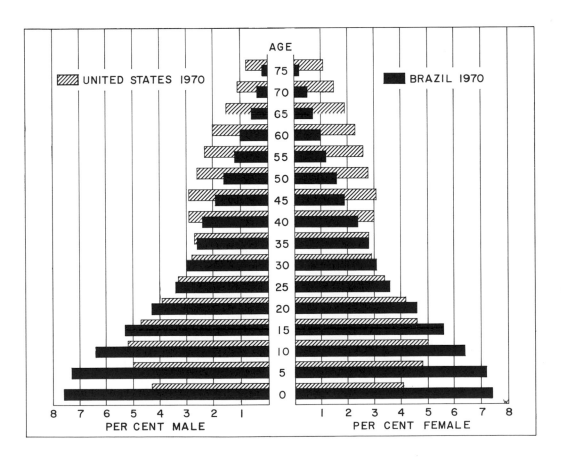

France, Great Britain, Germany, and Australia, where the birth rate
is lower and life expectancy greater. The specific type of age profile
that is characteristic of Brazil and other Latin American countries
affects every aspect of institutional life, but is particularly
significant in the economic and educational spheres. As compared
with his fellows in North America or Western Europe, the average
Brazilian in the productive years of life has more mouths to feed.
Therefore, he must either produce more goods and services, or he,
his children, and his parents who have passed the productive ages

FIGURE 4. Variations in the Relative Importance of Children of
Less Than Five Years of Age in the Populations of Brazil, Canada,
England, France, Japan, and the United States, 1900 to 1970

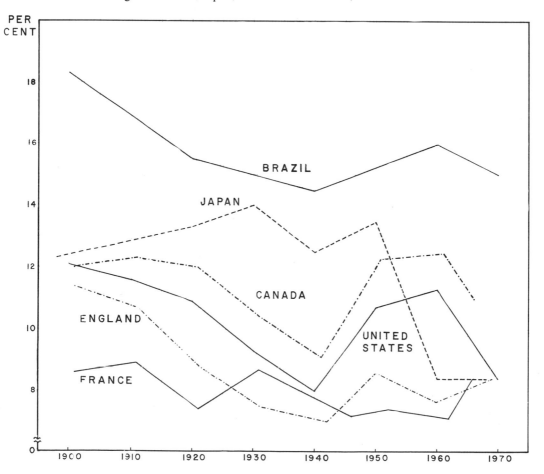

must get along on a much lower per capita consumption. Such an age distribution also favors a situation in which thousands of youngsters, many of them hardly more than babes in arms, are thrust out into the world to make their own ways.

The nature of the age distribution of the Brazilian population means that the proportions of those who should be attending primary and secondary schools are inordinately high. This greatly magnifies Brazil's task of keeping the solemn pledge she made when her representatives signed the Charter of Punta del Este, popularly known as the Alliance for Progress, thereby making a commitment

FIGURE 5. Comparison of the Age Distribution of Brazil's Population in 1970 with That of the Population of the United States in 1870

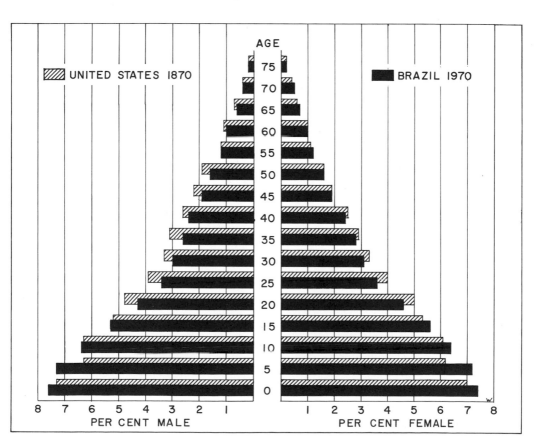

to provide before 1970 access to a minimum of six years of elementary schooling for every child of appropriate age throughout her immense territory.

It also is important to indicate that the chances are slight that any substantial modification in the basic features of Brazil's age distribution will take place in the immediate future. Immigration and emigration could swell to many times their present levels without producing any readily observable effects upon the proportions of the very young, those in the productive ages, and those who have lived for more than sixty-five years; and the effects of the now rapidly falling death rate are spread over all of the age groups. Therefore, any marked changes in the proportions of the population in the various age groups must result primarily from a sudden, drastic fall in the birth rate. Such a significant trend may develop within the next quarter of a century, as the population becomes more and more concentrated in large urban centers, and as a knowledge of modern birth control techniques are made available to the masses. Indeed we may witness in Brazil a sudden drop in fertility rivaling that which took place in the United States between 1900 and 1930 and that in Japan since 1947.

If such a large and rapid fall in the birth rate materializes, there will come a time when in Brazil there will be more persons aged fifteen to twenty than those under five, for example; and a considerable number of other closely related shifts in the relative importance of the age groups in the lower part of the age-sex pyramid. A pronounced change of this nature could produce, as it did in the United States of 1930, a situation in which the population was highly concentrated in the economically and biologically productive ages. But, we must hasten to add, no abrupt decline in the birth rate is yet observable although it appears to have begun. Moreover, even after it gets well under way a quarter of a century may be required for its effects upon the age distribution to become pronounced. Finally, a fall sharp enough to bring about drastic changes in the relative importance of the very young, those between fifteen and sixty-five, and the aged, may not take place at all.

As generally is the case, there is a marked contrast between the age distributions of the urban and rural segments of Brazil's population. This may be illustrated with data which show the percentage classified as urban for each of the age groups used in the official tabulations. (See Figure 6.) One should note especially the high degree to which the very young are concentrated in the rural population, and the large proportions of those in the biologically and economically productive ages in the cities and towns. Moreover, even though persons who have passed their sixty-fifth birthdays are relatively scarce in Brazil, the small segment of the population that is made up of such persons is concentrated to a considerable degree in the nation's cities.

FIGURE 6. Proportion of Brazil's Population in Each Age Group Classified as Urban, by Sex, 1970

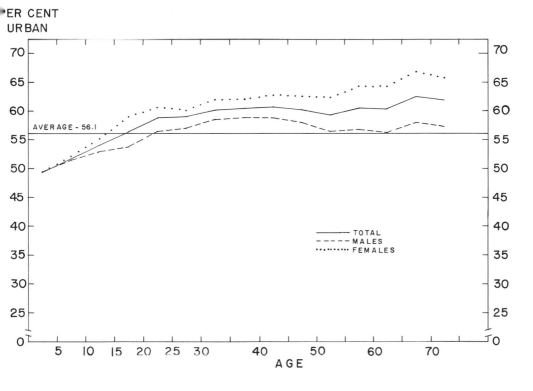

## Marital Status

Even though Brazilians seem less prone to shun formal marital ties than Colombians, Venezuelans, and some other Spanish Americans, legal mating is far less prevalent among them than it is in most European countries, the United States, Canada, and Japan.[5] At all ages the percentages of Brazilians, male and female, who are living in the marital state are comparatively low by the standards prevailing in the United States and Western Europe, although they are high in comparison with those in many Spanish-American countries. (See Figures 7 and 8.) The fact that the curves

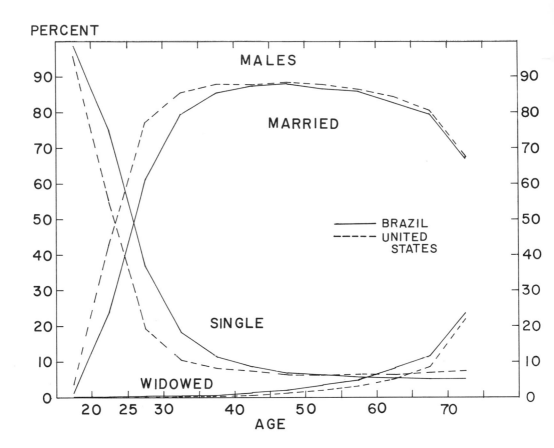

FIGURE 7. Marital Status of Brazilian Males, by Age, 1970

representing the percentages of single persons in the population drop less precipitously in Brazil than in the United States indicates that the marriage age in the former is somewhat higher than it is in the latter. The differences between the same curves at the more advanced ages indicate that the Brazilian woman is more likely to live out her entire life without contracting matrimony than her sister in the United States. No comparable differential prevails between the male populations of the two countries. These sex differences may be due in part to the fact that the higher rates in Brazil give the old bachelors greater opportunities for marrying widows than are present in the United States. Such a hypothesis receives some

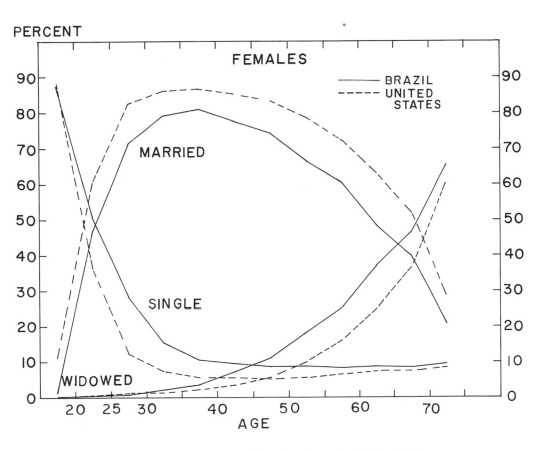

FIGURE 8.  Marital Status of Brazilian Females, by Age, 1970

support from the nature of the differences in the curves representing the percentages of widows in the populations. But the greater relative importance of immigrants, among whom the men greatly outnumber the women, in the United States could also have an important bearing on the difference.

Higher death rates among all age groups in Brazil than death rates in the United States are responsible for the fact that the curves representing the widowed rise more rapidly in that country than in our own. This in turn creates more opportunities for widowers to remarry; so the differences between the male populations of the two countries are far less than those between the female populations.

In Brazil before the women have completed their sixty-sixth year the number of widows in the population has increased to the point where it exactly equals the number of married women. This situation does not prevail in the United States until the sixty-ninth year of age. The chances are equal that the Brazilian woman who lives to be sixty-eight years of age will be a widow, while in the United States the corresponding age is seventy-one. The basic facts which deserve emphasis are that the population of Brazil contains high portions of single and widowed persons and relatively low proportions of those living in the married state.

## The Vital Processes

The rate of reproduction and the mortality rate, or expectation of life, are the two most important items in national accounting. Unfortunately it will be some time before either of them can be accurately gauged in Brazil, but even so it is essential that the present state of affairs be known as fully as possible.

### The Rate of Reproduction

Until recently it has been impossible to learn much about the birth rate in Brazil except that it had to be very high. Even in the 1970s the registration of births is inadequately organized, so that the number of births recorded in the civil registers is much lower than the number of baptisms reported annually by the Catholic Church. By working with the data on baptisms and other materials, it was possible to reach the conclusion that the birth rate in Brazil in 1940 must have been 40 per 1,000 inhabitants or above.[6] Subsequently Professor Giorgia Mortara, after a most careful study of the thoroughgoing materials pertaining to human fertility which were collected in the 1940 census, concluded that the birth rate in Brazil was at least 42, being highest in the state of Santa Catarina at 45.5 per 1,000 inhabitants and lowest in the state of São Paulo at 37.8.

Presently it seems certain that the true rate is between 40 and 45 per 1,000 population.

Another simple index of the rapidity with which a given population is reproducing is obtained by determining the number of children under five per 100 women aged fifteen to forty-four, inclusive. Computations based on the 1960 census data support the conclusion that the birth rate in Brazil is very high. Thus in 1960 there were 72.4 children under five for each 100 women in the childbearing ages as specified above. Comparable indexes for a few other countries at about the same time are as follows: Italy, 40; Mexico, 82; Sweden, 37; France, 40; Australia, 46; and the United States, 46.[7]

Since Brazil's high rate of reproduction is considerably above that in most parts of the world, it means that most of the factors which have reduced the fertility of western populations during the last century are still inoperative in the great South American country. However, even with crude devices it is possible to demonstrate that there is a tremendous rural-urban differential, which leads to the belief that, as Brazil speedily urbanizes and industrializes, the birth rates there may soon fall precipitiously just as they did in Europe and North America.

## The Death Rate

The collection of vital statistics in Brazil must be greatly improved before it will be possible to determine with any degree of accuracy the death rate or life expectancy for the country as a whole. That the mortality rate is high is evident from a few soundings that have been made here and there and from the nature of the age-sex pyramid, but just how high is not known. It is probably about 12 to 15 per 1,000 inhabitants, and it surely is being reduced substantially. If the birth rate remains high, however, the death rate may get as low as 7 or 8 per 1,000 inhabitants, without life expectancy at birth rising much above sixty years.

Figures on infant mortality in Brazil can be little more than considered guesses. Since this particular index, one of the most sensitive measures of the well-being of a people or a society, is secured by relating the number of infants who die in the course of a given year to the number of live births occurring during that year, the present deficiencies in the registries of births makes it impossible for anyone to make the necessary calculations. However, among the rates that are reported for the period 1967-69 are the following ones for the municipios containing some of the nation's principal cities: Recife, 157; Fortaleza, 139; São Luis, 133; Salvador (Bahia), 107; Belo Horizonte, 103; Belém, 80; Curitiba, 80; São Paulo, 78; Brasília, 77; Porto Alegre, 66; and Rio de Janeiro, 56. Most of these figures are highly suspect; and the deficiencies of the data are such that some of them no doubt are much too high.

## Growth of Population

As has been indicated above, the latest census enumeration placed the population of Brazil at 94,500,000 as of September 1, 1970. This figure represented an increase of about 23.5 millions (31 percent) over the population in 1960, a truly phenomenal rise; and it played a major role in bringing about the now rather widely known fact that in the second half of the twentieth century the population of the twenty Latin American countries is in the forefront of the huge upsurge of world population that is taking place. Over the sixty-year period 1890 to 1950 the annual rate of Brazil's population increase was high, and between 1950 and 1970 it was the amazing figure of 3.1. In this connection it is well to have in mind the fact that prior to 1950 an annual rate of growth of more than 3 percent had never been experienced by the population of any large segment of the earth's surface, with the single exception of the United States between 1800 and 1860.

Prior to the 1940 census, counts of Brazil's inhabitants left a great deal to be desired. Even so, however, the censuses from 1890 on were much better than the crude enumerations which took place during the Empire. It is probably impossible to get data on the long-time growth of population in the half continent under consideration that are any more reliable than those assembled in Table 1.

The rapidity with which the population is increasing varies greatly from one part of Brazil to another. For the period 1950-70, for which the definitive results of the necessary censuses are available, these regional variations are shown clearly in Figure 10 (Chapter 13). And for the period 1960-70, the results of the 1970 census indicate that the largest increases were in the states of São Paulo, Paraná, Minas Gerais, and Bahia. In these four states between 1960 and 1970, the increases were 4,700,000; 2,460,000; 1,480,000; and 1,430,000, respectively, so that in 1970 their enumerated populations were as follows: São Paulo, 17,716,000; Paraná, 6,741,000; Minas Gerais, 11,280,000; and Bahia, 7,421,000. The most rapid rate of increase during the latest intercensal period was in the new Distrito Federal, where the mushrooming of Brasília and its satellites brought about a growth of 403,000 during the decade under consideration, an increase of 284 percent, for a total of 545,000 in 1970. In the other states the most rapid increases were registered in Mato Grosso, 62 percent, with the 1970 data still incomplete; Paraná, 58 percent; Goiás, 52 percent; and Rio Grande do Norte, 39 percent.

**TABLE 1**

**GROWTH OF POPULATION IN BRAZIL, 1808-1970***

| Year | Population | Year | Population |
|------|-----------|------|-----------|
| 1808 | 2,419,406 | 1900 | 17,318,556 |
| 1823 | 3,960,866 | 1920 | 30,635,605 |
| 1830 | 5,340,000 | 1940 | 41,565,083 |
| 1854 | 7,677,800 | 1950 | 51,944,397 |
| 1872 | 9,930,478 | 1960 | 70,967,185 |
| 1890 | 14,333,915 | 1970 | 94,500,000 |

*Sources: *Recenseamento do Brazil,* 1920, Vol. I, Rio de Janeiro: Typ. de Estatística, 1922, pp. 403-21; *VII Recenseamento Geral do Brasil–1960,* "Sinopse Preliminar do Censo Demográfico," Rio de Janeiro: Serviço Nacional de Recenseamento, 1962, pp. 2-3; and Inter-American Statistical Institute, *Statistical Compendium of the Americas, 1971,* Washington, D.C.: Organization of American States, 1971, p. 2.

Finally, it is important to stress that the great bulk of Brazil's recent population growth has taken place in its cities and towns and relatively little of it either in the established rural settlements or on the frontier. For the period 1950-70 this is demonstrated clearly by a study of Figure 10. Northern Paraná and north-central Maranhão are, of course, important exceptions to this generalization. But in Brazil as a whole between 1960 and 1970 the urban population experienced an increase of 19,600,000 or 60 percent, whereas the rural population mounted by only 3,460,000 or by a little over 9 percent.

# 4

## Racial Composition

A thorough study of the racial make-up of the Brazilian population and of the manner in which the various elements are distributed among the regions and classes of the country would in itself be a life's work. If the United States is described as a "melting pot," Brazil must be considered a caldron. No other country has had for four hundred years such large numbers of white, red, and black people thrown into so close physical and social contact with one another. To the already extremely heterogeneous population, composed of these three original strains and of which the white Portuguese component was already a composite of many elements, the nineteenth and twentieth centuries brought millions of Europeans, mainly Italians, Germans, Poles, Portuguese, and Spaniards, and the twentieth century has added large contingents of Lebanese and Japanese.

### Racial Elements

Nearly all known ethnic stocks have contributed to the present-day racial elements of which Brazil's population is composed. However, until well along in the nineteenth century Portugal's colonial policy was one of severe restriction of immigration, with the result that the bulk of the people in Brazil are descended from the three more important strains: (1) the Portuguese colonists; (2) the native Indians whom the colonists enslaved and by

Reprinted from T. Lynn Smith, *Brazil: People and Institutions,* fourth edition (Baton Rouge: Louisiana State University Press, 1972), pp. 51-74, and republished with the permission of the Louisiana State University Press.

whose women they produced a mixed-blood offspring, the *mamelucos,* whose exploits as Indian hunters probably have never been equaled; and (3) millions of Negro slaves who were imported from Africa. To these only need be added the elements introduced by immigration of Europeans (especially Italians, Germans, and Poles) during the late nineteenth and early twentieth centuries, and the importation of Japanese since 1908.

If one would know the reasons underlying Brazil's population history, he should first remember that the central theme of the nation's social and economic history is *falta de braços,* which can best be translated as "lack of hands." To secure a cheap supply of agricultural labor has been the dominating motive in Brazil's population policy from the earliest colonial days to the present time. If during early centuries the need for workers on sugar plantations in Bahia, Pernambuco, the lower Paraíba, and other coastal areas dominated the national immigration policy and determined the elements that were added to the population, in later years São Paulo's coffee and cotton fazendas have played a similar role. Therefore, a brief consideration of Brazil's struggle to secure an abundant labor supply for its agriculture is a logical beginning in the analysis of the elements that have entered into its population make-up.

## The Long-Continued Labor Shortage

That the shortage of workers, *falta de braços,* is the central theme of Brazil's social and economic history is well known by all who are acquainted with that nation. Thousands of books, pamphlets, and articles have been written about this or that aspect of Brazil's social, economic, agricultural, and industrial problems. They are written in all degrees of quality and in many languages. However, in this immense literature it would be difficult to find a single treatise which does not make reference to the nation's need for more workers. If one travels through Brazil he will hear the same refrain, *falta de braços,* from Amazonas to Rio Grande do Sul, from Rio Grande do Norte to Mato Grosso. This is not surprising if three important items are kept in mind: (1) that most of Brazil's vast territorial expanse is underpopulated; (2) that much of Brazil is more "occupied" than "settled"; (3) that the dominant position of the huge landed estate in Brazil has determined that the nation's immigration policy should be designed to secure laborers to work on the fazendas rather than independent proprietors to carve new farms out of the wilderness.

That most of Brazil is underpopulated is indicated by the huge distances which, except near the coast, separate the nuclei of population from one another. One sees little to distinguish the *vila* or *povoação* in Minas Gerais or Rio de Janeiro from the "town" or "village" in Mato Grosso or Amazonas. But in the former states these small population centers will be encountered every few miles, while in the latter frequently they are separated by hundreds of miles. The underpopulation of the country is also indicated by the fact that its territory, more extensive than the United States minus Alaska, contains only about one-third as many inhabitants as our own country. Furthermore, although northeastern Brazil suffers severely from periodic droughts, the proportion of the country where low annual rainfall dictates a sparse population is extremely small in comparison with the huge expanses of our western plains and intermountain regions. Millions of additional Brazilians could grow prosperous in areas which at present seldom or never feel the impress of a human foot, if they were properly equipped with those portions of the man-made environment that would enable them to safeguard health and to magnify the strength of the human arm in its struggle with the jungle.

The emphasis on the need for more workers also grows in part out of the fact that much of Brazil is still more occupied than settled. With minor exceptions, particularly in parts of São Paulo and Rio Grande do Sul, only a narrow stretch of the littoral is really settled. The remainder of the country is more correctly described as merely occupied. This is to say that the greater part of Brazil is cut up into huge estates on which a few cattle are grazed, or a scattered population is engaged in the collection of mate, rubber, rosewood, babassú, carnaúba, Brazil nuts, and hundreds of other forest products, searching for diamonds or other precious stones, washing for gold, or merely in hunting and fishing. The landowner and the handful of people whom he employs to work on his vast acreages, or who are permitted to live there, have occupied the territory, but they have not settled it. When, as is now the situation in western São Paulo, northern Paraná, and northeastern Rio Grande do Sul, hundreds of new farms and thousands of new families are established on acreages that formerly merely provided a meager livelihood for a *fazendeiro* and a few of his *agregados,* the significance of this distinction between settlement and mere occupation becomes evident. But even in the 1960s in all the vast expanse of territory between the Colombian frontier and the Uruguayan border there were few sections in which thousands of settlers could not find land and natural resources awaiting exploitation by man. As one studies Brazil's land system, it becomes clear why in Brazilian terminology latifundium means not merely a large landed estate but has the additional significant connotation of large acreages purposely withheld from productive uses.

Finally, it is important to note that in Brazil underpopulation and the demand for more people take the form of a cry for more workers and not, as a rule, for more families to carve homes for themselves out of the wilderness. Very early most of the land passed into the private possession of a limited number of people.[1] From the very first, Brazil has been a country of large landed estates in which the overwhelming proportion of the population was engaged in working the land of others, first as slaves and later as laborers. Therefore, most of the nation's recent efforts to stimulate immigration, and particularly the vigorous policy of São Paulo, have been especially designed and administered to attract a supply of agricultural laborers. It cannot be overemphasized that Brazilian immigration policy has been dominated by the shortage of workers on its fazendas and not by the immensity of the sparsely populated portions of the national territory. It is largely because of this dominance of the large landed estate that *falta de braços* has been the dominant note in Brazil's social and economic history.

Highlights in the four-hundred-year-old struggle to supply enough hands for Brazilian fazendas are (1) the hunting, capture, and enslavement of the native Indian populations, (2) the importation of millions of Negro slaves from Africa to work the sugar plantations of the littoral, and (3) São Paulo's long-continued and vigorous efforts to supply its coffee and cotton fazendas with cheap agricultural labor. Probably the most significant aspects of the latter have been the importation of more than a million Italians, an immigration which has contributed to a radical change in the ethnic composition of São Paulo's population, and the admission of a recorded immigration of some 200,000 Japanese between 1925 and

1940. Together with their descendants these members of the yellow race now number almost 500,000 persons, or more than 4 percent of the state's population.


## Enslavement of Indians

Brazilian Indians were not pushed westward, or killed, like those of the United States, or gathered together into missions and taught the elements of Christianity like those in some parts of Spain's colonies.[2] They were hunted down and enslaved to provide a supply of laborers for the rapidly expanding sugar plantations. These and other large-scale agricultural undertakings set the pattern and guided the policies in the peopling of Brazil from colonial times until the present time.

During the entire colonial period Brazil was dominated by the large sugar plantation—the *engenho*. According to Oliveira Vianna, Brazil did not know the small farm until the last century. From the first Brazil was a land of latifundia. "All the long colonial period was a time of the splendor and glory of the large landed property."[3] To clear and cultivate the land for these large sugar estates, to wait upon and serve the members of the landowning aristocracy, and to perform the other multifarious tasks of the little world which was the engenho required a large number of workers. Oliveira Vianna cites authorities who place at two hundred the average number of slaves per Brazilian sugar plantation.[4] In the formative years these slaves were Indians.

Although the Portuguese possessed African slaves before they began the settlement of Brazil, comparatively few Negroes were introduced into the colony during the first two centuries of its existence. The wars with Holland were largely responsible for this and for forcing the Portuguese in Brazil to look elsewhere for a labor supply. The native Indian population was a logical source. The hunting down and the enslavement of the Indians, again to use the words of Oliveira Vianna, became "a true profession of warlike character, practiced by intrepid *sertanistas* [frontiersmen], who, in the north, as well as in the south, entered the interior at the front of their formidable bands of mamelucos, assaulted the villages of the poorly armed savages, and carried to the latifundia of the coastal areas thousands of Indian slaves."[5]

Of all these early man hunters those of São Paulo gained the greatest notoriety. Paulista *bandeirantes* ranged far and wide throughout the entire length and breadth of what is present-day Brazil, from the *sertões* of Ceará on the north to the upper reaches of the Amazon on the west and the plains of Rio Grande do Sul on the south, in search of their human quarry.[6] Not content to confine their enslaving activities to the Indians who remained in their native state, they fell upon and carried into captivity the thousands of red men whom the Jesuit fathers had collected into compact villages and educated far along in the religious and agricultural practices of the whites.[7] The exploits of these bandeirantes from São Paulo constitute as significant a chapter in the history of Brazil as those of the Indian fighters and frontiersmen in the annals of the United States.

But the supply of Indians was not sufficient for all purposes; the red men were not tractable workers and were constantly fleeing the plantations; and the wars with Holland finally came to an end. African slaves replaced Indians in agricultural work, and as Indian slavery was gradually abandoned, the red man was used mainly in pastoral areas to look after the corrals and the herds, and as a fighter.[8]

## The Magnitude of the "Traffic"

Just how many Negroes were imported into Brazil as slaves is a moot question that probably can never be adequately answered. The same applies to the kindred query as to how prolific were the members of the Negro race during the colonial epoch. Certain it is that there was no exceedingly large emigration of Negroes from Brazil,[9] but unless it is granted that they failed almost entirely to reproduce[10] or that they died like flies in the new country, one can hardly accept even the more conservative estimates as to the number of slaves that were transported from Africa to Brazil. The necessity of extreme caution in the evaluation of all estimates of the numbers involved in the "traffic" is indicated by the wide discrepancies that appear in the early estimates, those made by people "familiar with the scene," "on the ground," and "in a position to know." Thus the famous Padre José de Anchieta set the population of the Portuguese colony in Brazil as 57,000 in the year 1585. Of this number he said that some 14,000 were African slaves, of whom 10,000 were in Pernambuco, 3,000 in Bahia, and about 100 in Rio de Janeiro. But for the period 1584 to 1590, approximately the same date, Fernão Cardim placed the African slave population of Pernambuco at only 2,000 and that of Bahia at 4,000.[11]

The Negroes brought to Brazil included not only representatives of all the various Bantu groups, which also supplied a large share of the slaves for the United States, but also many from the Sudanese groups, including the Minas, Yorbes, Gêges, Haussás, and others from the northern parts of Africa. These peoples in race and culture were considerably different from the Bantus. Many of them through contact with Arabs knew the Arabic language and were of the Islamic faith. Negroes of this type were especially important in Bahia,[12] although they could also be found in Rio de Janeiro.[13]

*Portuguese Colonists*

From the mother country, Portugal, came of course the original white colonists, mostly men. This movement of Portuguese to the New World colony, empire, and republic went on incessantly and continues today. This is the migration which furnished the basic white stock for Brazil's upper strata, and it continues to supplement the white blood which in smaller or greater proportion courses through the veins of large percentages of people in the middle and lower classes. It should not be forgotten, however, that in number the colonists were comparatively few and that the present-day importance of their descendants is out of all proportion to the numerical size of the original white population. This point will be developed further in the sections having to do with race mixture and the "bleaching of the population."

Small as was the contingent of Portuguese colonists who came to the New World to establish themselves, a significant percentage of them were of Semitic stock—the "new Christians" *(cristãos novos)*. These former Jews came in relatively large numbers, settled in the small ports along the seacoast where they engaged in trade, skilled labor, and the professions, and became the moneylenders who supplied the capital on loan to the *senhores de engenho*.[14] From the accounts extant it would seem to be a rare case in which the sugar planter was not heavily indebted to one of these traders and moneylenders—persons engaged in professions the Portuguese disdained.[15]

## Other Early White Colonists

In addition to the various elements of white racial stock, including Semites and Moors, who are included among the Portuguese colonists, small groups of French, Dutch, and English early made contributions to the makeup of the Brazilian population. Of most importance among these extraneous elements were the Dutch, whose seventeenth-century occupation of northeastern Brazil has left important racial traces. This is particularly true in Pernambuco. The French, too, attempted to seize various coastal points, notably the bay of Rio de Janeiro; but probably more important still was their long-continued trade in brazilwood. The touch-and-go contacts growing out of this forbidden traffic probably resulted in a considerable infusion of French blood among the Indian peoples inhabiting the coastal areas. Finally, at least a few Englishmen, Italians, and Germans were present among the colonists and contributing their share to the future population of Brazil.[16]

## Nineteenth- and Twentieth-Century Immigration

As has been indicated, for the first three centuries of Brazil's existence, the peopling of its vast territory consisted of (1) a small trickle of Portuguese colonists, mostly adventurers seeking a fortune in sugar growing and, later, mining; (2) the numbers added by the hunting down and enslaving of the Indians and through crossbreeding the production of a large mixed white-Indian progeny; (3) the importation of millions of African slaves, by whose women another large mixed-blood contingent was brought into existence. It is true that French and Dutch also established themselves on the coast and contributed to the racial elements of present-day Brazil. However, in comparison with the Portuguese, the Indian, and the African racial elements, they have been of very minor importance.

In the nineteenth century, following the establishment of the empire's capital at Rio de Janeiro and especially after independence, steps were taken to break down the barriers insulating Brazil from the non-Portuguese world. Some of the ports were opened to trade, printing was legalized, scientists and other explorers were admitted, and an attempt was made to induce immigrants other than Portuguese to come to Brazil. The emperor's Teutonic wife probably was largely responsible for the concessions made to German and Swiss immigrants and their introduction and planting in such colonies as Petrópolis, nestled in the high valleys of the Serra do Mar, where the emperor's summer palace was located.

Following the abolition of slavery late in the nineteenth century the population was swelled and greatly changed in composition by the immigration of over a million Italians, mostly to São Paulo and Rio Grande do Sul; thousands of Polish who settled largely in Paraná; and more thousands of Germans, who concentrated in Santa Catarina, Rio Grande do Sul, São Paulo, and Espírito Santo. Large contingents of Portuguese, Spaniards, and Lebanese also entered Brazil in the late years of the nineteenth century. The Portuguese continued to settle in the cities, especially Rio and São Paulo. The Spaniards went mostly to São Paulo, and many of them located in the newly opened agricultural areas. The Lebanese settled in the city of São Paulo for the most part, although they also spread throughout the small interior trading centers from southern Mato Grosso to the Amazon.

During the twentieth century the immigration of these European elements has continued, although that of the Italians greatly diminished in volume. Otherwise, the introduction of some 200,000 Japanese immigrants, who have already multiplied to about 500,000 persons, is the most significant new factor in the racial composition of Brazil's population. The Europeans and Lebanese who immigrated after 1900 have settled for the most part in the areas previously occupied by their compatriots. The Japanese have located for the most part in São Paulo and the neighboring areas of Paraná, Mato Grosso, and Minas Gerais, although two sizable groups settled on the Amazon. The immigration of these peoples will be treated in detail elsewhere. Here it is sufficient to point out that the introduction of these Europeans and Asiatics, especially in the years since Brazil gained her independence, has done much to change the racial stock of southern Brazil. Today Rio Grande do Sul is largely German and Italian; Santa Catarina, German; and Paraná, Polish, German, and Italian. São Paulo, although it contains Brazil's greatest agglomeration of races, runs heavily to Italian. However, the German, Japanese, Lebanese, and Spanish elements are of very considerable size and importance. Portuguese, of course, also are important in Brazil's leading state.


## Race Mixture

Not only have the various ethnic strains been present in Brazil, but conditions have been conducive to their mixing and blending. From the very first the relative absence of white women,[17] the inferior status of the woman in the family, and the superior status of the white master class gave men of the white race almost unhampered access to Indian female slaves. During the first century of Brazilian history there was much more intermixture between the white and the red races than there would have been had more European women been introduced into the colonies, had those who did come wielded a stronger influence over their husbands, had more of the native-born white women married, and had the social positions of the white and the Indian races been more nearly equal. As a result the genes of upper-class white men have not only been passed on to legitimate offspring who have remained at the top of the social pyramid, but they have contributed greatly to the "bleaching" of the darker populations of the lower social strata.

The rapidity with which this bleaching of the Brazilian population has progressed is startling. This applies equally to the lightening of color derived both from Indian and Negroid strains. For example, when the Portuguese first established settlements at Bahia they found living there as patriarch of his own village one Corrêa (Indian name Caramurú or "man who makes lightning"), a sailor or possibly a noble, who may have been marooned there by Cabral. For the most part the entire village population consisted of the children and grandchildren of this white chief. Thus, before the Portuguese had a real foothold on the coast, there were already half-breeds and quarter-breeds who were descendants of this prolific progenitor. Even the first priests are said to have followed Corrêa's example,[18] and the flock that of their pastor's, so that by 1550 the already marriageable half-breeds and quarter-breeds were being supplemented by numerous additional offspring of mixed racial stock. As was to be expected, many of the Portuguese colonists chose as wives the half-blood women and produced offspring who were three-quarters white; at the same time the newcomers also contributed through extramarital relations to the rapidly increasing population of half bloods. The process of supplying representatives for all the possible gradations in the color scale went on very rapidly. By 1570 selective mating for color had already produced a native-born elite who were almost entirely white; whereas the matings between persons of various degrees of mixed blood, plus the numerous illegitimate progency of the upper-class men, were rapidly diffusing white blood throughout all classes in the population.[19] Later, with the importation of Negroes from Africa, an exactly comparable pattern of miscegenation took place between upper-class (white or near-white) men and Negro women. Throughout the centuries that have elapsed selective mating of upper-class men with the whitest women has produced a Brazilian elite in whom Indian or Negro traces are infinitesimal, while their extramarital relations with lower-class women constantly are adding to the proportion of white blood in middle-class and lower-class Brazilians.[20]

This indicates that a comparatively few white men contributed far out of all proportion to the present-day ethnic composition of Brazil.[21] In addition to their numerous progeny of legitimate descendants of the white race, through the keeping of concubines (mulheres da cama) and other extramarital relations, their genes have been distributed far and wide throughout the masses of the population who have a darker hue. It should not be overlooked that the name caboclo, originally applied to the domesticated Indians and later to the white-Indian cross, has now with much reason become a generalized term to denote the Brazilian peasant or rural laborer. As indicated above, from the very first the mixture of the white and red races went on rapidly; but family pride, an endogamous marriage system, and the inheritance of private property preserved a small elite of whites at the very top of the social pyramid. Later, and especially throughout the seventeenth, eighteenth, and nineteenth centuries, the same complex of factors operated in a similar way to make the racial heritage contributed by the comparatively few white people who came during the colonial period almost as important in the make-up of the present-day population as the contribution of great masses of Negro slaves imported from Africa.

It was not long before the numbers of Negroes, Indians, and the crosses and recrosses of the two with the whites were sufficiently numerous that the contact between the various strains did not need the assistance of class differences to ensure a large amount of mingling. However, the fact that the most relentless adepts at the hunting of wild Indians were themselves of mixed Indian and white descent, the mamelucos or sons of white fathers and Indian women, was not a retarding factor in the blending of the races. Nevertheless, in all of the racial mixing it is probable that the crossing involved comparatively little mingling of Indian and Negro ethnic strains, at least until they had both been diluted with those of whites. It is certain that the caboclos or mamelucos, crosses of Indian and white, and the mulattoes or *pardos* greatly outnumbered *cafusos,* or the offspring of Indian and Negro parents.[22] The factor responsible for the slight degree of Indian-Negro crossing seems to have been the culturally determined division of labor among the Indians which made agriculture a task for women. Because they viewed farming tasks as women's work, Indian men never made tractable slaves on Brazilian engenhos. Later on, the African's docile acceptance of work in agriculture caused the Indian to despise him, thus raising a great social barrier to the mixture of the red and black races.[23]

Finally, following the abolition of slavery and especially during the last quarter of a century, there has arisen in Brazil what amounts to a veritable cult of racial equality.[24] It numbers among its adherents most of the nation's leading scholars and many of its outstanding political figures. Although not formally organized and possessed of no written creed, two fundamental tenets, both designed to secure racial equality, seem to have general acceptance: (1) under no circumstances should it be admitted that racial discrimination exists in Brazil, and (2) any expression of racial discrimination that may appear always should be attacked as un-Brazilian. Undoubtedly this is effective, if not in securing complete racial equality, at least in preventing many of the grosser features of racial discrimination and in making for a freer legal blending of the races than otherwise could be possible. This, of course, has little effect on the racial composition of the elite class at the top of the social scale, for that matter is cared for by the strong Brazilian institution of the family and its system of consciously selective mating.[25] See Figure 9 for an indication of the relationship of color to social status in contemporary Brazil.

Before concluding this discussion of race mixture, a word is necessary about the Japanese population. Although the second and third generations of Brazilian-born Japanese have made their appearance, as yet these Japanese have mixed very little with other Brazilian racial stocks. There has been some crossing through the extramarital relations of Japanese males. Also, a handful of business and professional Japanese men, who set themselves up in business in São Paulo, have taken Brazilian wives. In this case the men found it more to their taste to cross racial lines in the selection of mates than to marry with their lower-class compatriots. However, this group is of little consequence numerically. The great mass of the Japanese in Brazil came to the country recently as agricultural

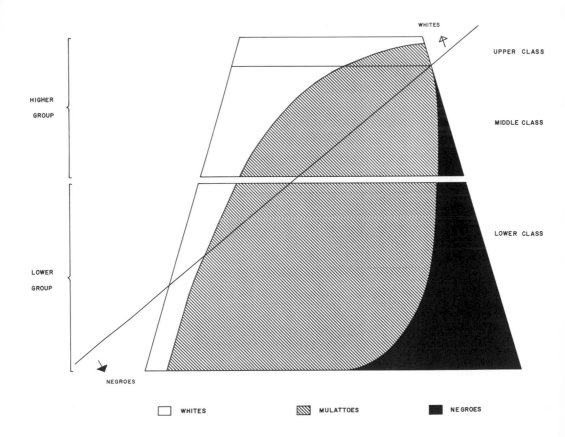

FIGURE 9.  Relationship between Color and Social Status in Brazil

laborers. For years they were carefully herded around by the various officials of the Imperial Company which introduced, installed, and worked them. Under these conditions they neither had the inclination nor the opportunity to mate with the Brazilians. Except for the insignificant number of offspring from matings between middle-class and upper-class Japanese men and Brazilian women, therefore, mixed-blood descendants of Japanese and Brazilian parents are neither numerous nor legitimate.[26] So little have the Japanese mixed and blended with the other racial groups in São Paulo, it has not been unusual for the Japanese element to be referred to as a "cyst" in the social body.[27]

## Present Racial Make-up

The task of evaluating the relative importance of the various racial elements in the Brazilian population was greatly facilitated by the 1940 and 1950 censuses of population. This is fortunate, for few subjects have received as much attention from foreigners and Brazilians alike as the absolute and relative importance of the various ethnic and racial strains that have contributed to the population composition as it is today.

According to the 1950 census the population of Brazil was constituted racially, or by color, as shown on page 30. These figures should be viewed with a considerable degree of caution. To begin with, the category designated as white should be thought of as designating those who are white or whitish. Not a few of them have a considerable admixture of Indian blood. In addition, Negroid ancestry in a limited degree, although not as prevalent as the Indian, is by no means lacking in many of those classified as whites. The number of those classed as black, or Negro, certainly is the absolute minimum. Any changes in the criteria used would inevitably have the effect of increasing their numbers. The use of the single category of pardos for all those of mixed ancestry, the crosses of whites and Indians as well as those of whites and Negroes, is to be regretted. Furthermore, few of those who use the data will realize that the census has actually included the Indians themselves in the pardo category. It is probable that the white-Indian crosses and the white-Negro blends are present in about the same proportions, but of course that fact cannot be established with any degree of certainty.

The data for the various states from the 1950 census, along with those from the 1940 enumeration, are presented in Table 2. They call for little comment. Obviously, in Brazil as in the United States, census procedures do not secure accurate anthropological classifications of the population. The apparent changes between 1940 and 1950 must be attributed far more to variations in the criteria actually applied in classifying the population than to any changes in the racial composition of the population. Nevertheless, the fact that the black, or Negro, population decreased in relative importance in most of the states probably is in line with the true developments. On the other hand there was a much greater tendency in 1950 than in 1940 to place the whitish elements in the mixed or pardo category. Those who have been most closely connected with the two censuses report that in some states the 1940 officials in charge were far too zealous in classifying persons in the darkest possible class.

## Distribution of the Racial Elements

Although throughout Brazil white, black, and red racial strains may be found in nearly every conceivable combination,[28] the relative importance of each race varies considerably from one part of the country to another. The 1940 and 1950 census data, as presented in Table 2, also supply the facts necessary for an understanding of these variations.

The white elements predominate to the greatest extent in Santa Catarina, Paraná, Rio Grande do Sul, and São Paulo (probably about in the order named) where the recent immigration from Italy, Poland, and Germany has contributed heavily to the populations of white racial stock. The city of Rio de Janeiro also contains large numbers of whites. Elsewhere throughout Brazil, the white elements are of less relative importance, although they seem to be concentrated in the coastal cities. Then, too, the whiteness of the population is largely dependent upon the social position of the group and to only a limited extent is related to the geographic space it occupies. However, in all parts of Brazil one will find some blond, flaxen-haired, blue-eyed persons, although they do not appear

**TABLE 2**

**Composition of Brazilian Population by Color, 1940 and**
**1950, by States and Territories**

| State | White | | Black | | Yellow | | Pardo † | |
|---|---|---|---|---|---|---|---|---|
| | 1940 | 1950 | 1940 | 1950 | 1940 | 1950 | 1940 | 1950 |
| Brazil | 63.5 | 61.7 | 14.6 | 11.0 | 0.6 | 0.6 | 21.2 | 26.5 |
| North | | | | | | | | |
| Guaporé ‡ | — | 28.5 | — | 8.1 | — | 0.0 | — | 63.0 |
| Acre ‡ | 54.3 | 30.0 | 14.2 | 5.2 | 0.2 | 0.0 | 31.1 | 64.6 |
| Amazonas | 31.3 | 36.9 | 7.2 | 3.4 | 0.2 | 0.1 | 61.1 | 59.4 |
| Rio Branco ‡ | — | 41.6 | — | 5.0 | — | 0.0 | — | 53.3 |
| Pará | 44.6 | 29.0 | 9.5 | 5.3 | 0.1 | 0.1 | 45.6 | 65.4 |
| Amapá | — | 27.1 | — | 8.1 | — | 0.0 | — | 64.5 |
| Northeast | | | | | | | | |
| Maranhão | 46.8 | 33.7 | 27.6 | 15.8 | 0.0 | 0.0 | 25.5 | 50.3 |
| Piauí | 45.2 | 28.0 | 31.9 | 12.9 | 0.0 | 0.0 | 22.6 | 59.0 |
| Ceará | 52.6 | 43.6 | 23.3 | 10.5 | 0.0 | 0.0 | 23.8 | 45.8 |
| Rio Grande | | | | | | | | |
| do Norte | 43.5 | 48.8 | 13.4 | 9.5 | 0.0 | 0.0 | 43.1 | 41.6 |
| Paraíba | 53.8 | 67.1 | 13.7 | 13.0 | 0.0 | 0.0 | 32.4 | 19.7 |
| Pernambuco | 54.4 | 49.6 | 15.5 | 9.3 | 0.0 | 0.0 | 29.9 | 40.9 |
| Alagôas | 56.7 | 40.5 | 13.8 | 7.4 | 0.0 | 0.0 | 29.3 | 51.9 |
| East | | | | | | | | |
| Sergipe | 46.7 | 49.7 | 18.7 | 14.2 | 0.0 | 0.0 | 34.4 | 36.0 |
| Bahia | 26.7 | 29.6 | 20.1 | 19.2 | 0.0 | 0.0 | 51.1 | 51.0 |
| Minas Gerais | 61.2 | 58.4 | 19.3 | 14.6 | 0.0 | 0.0 | 19.4 | 26.8 |
| Espírito Santo | 61.5 | 58.6 | 17.1 | 11.9 | 0.0 | 0.0 | 21.3 | 29.4 |
| Rio de Janeiro | 59.8 | 59.8 | 21.3 | 17.7 | 0.0 | 0.1 | 18.6 | 22.1 |
| Distrito Federal | 71.1 | 69.9 | 11.3 | 12.3 | 0.1 | 0.0 | 17.3 | 17.5 |
| South | | | | | | | | |
| São Paulo | 84.9 | 85.7 | 7.3 | 8.0 | 3.0 | 3.1 | 4.7 | 3.2 |
| Paraná | 86.6 | 86.4 | 4.9 | 4.4 | 1.1 | 1.9 | 7.4 | 7.3 |
| Santa Catarina | 94.4 | 94.6 | 5.2 | 3.7 | 0.0 | 0.0 | 0.3 | 1.5 |
| Rio Grande do Sul | 88.7 | 89.1 | 6.6 | 5.2 | 0.0 | 0.0 | 4.6 | 5.4 |
| West Central | | | | | | | | |
| Mato Grosso | 50.8 | 53.3 | 8.5 | 9.8 | 0.7 | 0.7 | 39.9 | 35.9 |
| Goiás | 72.1 | 57.9 | 16.9 | 10.1 | 0.0 | 0.1 | 10.8 | 31.6 |

Assembled and computed from data in the "Sinopse do Censo Demográfico: Dados Gerais,"
*Recenseamento Geral do Brasil, 1940* (Rio de Janeiro, 1947); and "Censo Demográfico," *VI*
*Recenseamento Geral do Brasil, 1950* (Rio de Janeiro, 1956).
†Includes Indians, mulattoes, mestiços, etc.
‡Territory.

elsewhere with the frequency that they do to the south, particularly
in Santa Catarina. In areas where new agricultural settlement is
being superimposed upon the old cattle-raising culture, as in western

São Paulo, it is interesting to see the intermarriage that occurs between the descendants of the German colonists from the south and the offspring of people of darker hue who have migrated to this promised land from the state of Bahia. This occurs where lower-class whites from the south meet their compatriots of a darker hue from the northeast. The meeting and blending of these two migratory currents is doing much to equalize the color content of Brazil's population, especially throughout the great newly settled areas of western São Paulo and northern Paraná.

Indian elements in the Brazilian population are of greatest relative importance in the Amazon Basin. Here, throughout the states of Pará and Amazonas, the territory of Acre, the northern part of Goiás, and the western portion of Maranhão, the Indian strain is predominant in a considerable portion of the population. Oftentimes in these areas people are encountered who show no evidences of either white or Negro ancestry. Other than in this immense region of sparse population and a collecting economy, Indian racial characteristics are most pronounced in the population of the great interior sertões. This is the heart of Brazil, away from the coast which has felt contact with the rest of the world, in the great open spaces where population is very sparse, where agriculture has hardly spread, and where cattle raising furnishes a meager livelihood for the scattered inhabitants. This area includes most of Mato Grosso, some of the more remote parts of western São Paulo, northern Minas Gerais, the western portions of Bahia, Pernambuco, Paraíba, and Rio Grande do Norte, and the southern two-thirds of the states of Ceará, Piauí, and Maranhão. The population of these parts, the sertanistas, shows evidences of long continued crossing and recrossing. No doubt all three of the principal racial stocks have left their imprint upon nearly every one of the inhabitants in this part of Brazil's vast interior. One great Brazilian scholar, Euclydes da Cunha, has emphasized the importance of the Indian racial heritage, while others, Gilberto Freyre and E. Roquette-Pinto, stress the Negroid contributions to the biological make-up of this population.[29] To choose between the two positions probably is unnecessary. One who visits these portions of Brazil will see many persons with unmistakable Negroid characteristics engaged in the care of herds of cattle, but also he will encounter even more frequently the high cheekbones and especially the heavy straight black hair that is a certain indication of a prevalence of Indian rather than Negroid blood.

Negroid elements, too, are much more prevalent in some regions than in others. Bahia and Negroid characteristics in the population are very closely associated in the Brazilian mind and properly so, since undoubtedly the Negro elements in the population of Bahia are more important than in any other state in the nation. Here too the survival of African cultural traits is easily observed. The dominance of black strains is greatest in the capital city, Salvador, where it seems to have filtered to a limited degree into the very elite, but Negroid characteristics have penetrated even the remote sertões west of the São Francisco River. About one-fifth of the great contingent of Bahianos who have moved to São Paulo during the last two decades, a very large share of whom came from the sertões of south-central Bahia, were classified as pretos when they passed through the hostel in the city of São Paulo.

Next to Bahia the Negroid elements in the population probably are of greatest relative importance in the state of Rio de Janeiro, whose sugar engenhos were almost as effective in introducing and perpetuating a host of black workers as were those in the sugar-growing *recôncavo* which surrounds Bahia's capital city. From the state of Rio de Janeiro and from Minas Gerais the granting of freedom to the slaves and the ability to move resulted in a great exodus to the national capital, Rio de Janeiro, so that what is now the state of Guanabara probably contains today about as high a proportion of Negroes, or people of mixed Negroid descent, as is to be found anywhere in Brazil outside of Bahia. In Brazil's former capital the people of darker hue are found to be concentrated in the poorer sections of the city, particularly in the *favelas* (slums) which overspread the numerous hills that contribute heavily to Rio's superb natural setting. On the other hand, the prevalence of the dark skin and other Negroid characteristics is not as great in Minas Gerais as one might be led to expect from a knowledge of the thousands of slaves who were imported to work the province's rich mines.

The capital of Maranhão, São Luís, and the coastal areas surrounding it, is probably the section which ranks next in importance of Negroid elements in the population. Sugar and especially cotton plantations were the factors that resulted in the introduction of a large slave contingent to this far northern or equatorial portion of Brazil. Here too, with the freeing of the slaves, there was a strong tendency for the darker racial elements to concentrate in the capital city, a trend similar to that which took place rather generally throughout Brazil. Today, as one witnesses a religious procession in São Luís, after the first few tiers of marchers have passed by, he sees for the most part a seething mass of black humanity. Among hundreds of faces, hardly one in which white features predominate will appear. On the outskirts of the city is the poorer type of dwelling, generally with wattle-and-daub walls, thatched roofs,[30] and dirt floors, from which these people have assembled.

Closely rivaling, or perhaps exceeding, São Luís and its hinterland in the relative importance of Negroid elements in the population are the sugar-growing, coastal sections of Pernambuco, Paraíba, and the neighboring states. Here, too, the engenhos and *usinas* of the sugar industry have counted on a mass of dark workers. In Recife, also, there is a large Negroid population.

## Bleaching

There can be little doubt that the Brazilian population is steadily becoming whiter in color. As compared with that of 1872 the censuses of 1940 and 1950 show—and correctly so—that the colored strains in the population are of much less importance than they were prior to the freeing of the slaves. It requires no reliance on mystical climatic influences, no belief in somatic changes induced by diet, nor acceptance of the idea that the genes of white people are more potent than those of their colored fellows to account for this tendency. A series of comparatively simple social and demographic factors seem sufficient to explain the change, and they should be given their proper weight before "open sesame" explanations of a highly questionable character are resorted to.

1. Through immigration a net contribution of several million European (white) people have been added to the populations of the city of Rio de Janeiro and of the four southernmost states—São Paulo, Paraná, Santa Catarina, and Rio Grande do Sul. Of these, the Italian and Portuguese immigrants formed the largest contingents, although Polish, Spanish, and German elements were also numerous. Minas Gerais and Espírito Santo have also received considerable immigration (white) since the freeing of the slaves.

2. But not all the bleaching of Brazil's population is due to immigration. This lightening of color also goes on in those parts of Brazil which have received few or no immigrants. In Brazil there is

little or no tendency towards a differential fertility favorable to the lower, which are also the blacker and redder, classes. Counting only legitimate offspring, the members of the upper classes probably produce as many children on the average as do those of middle-class and lower-class status.

3. Of the offspring produced, the children of the upper classes undoubtedly survive in larger proportions than the children of the lower and more untutored persons in society's lower strata. In other words, it seems also certain that the net reproduction rate increases as one moves up the Brazilian social ladder. This means that the whiter elements make a larger net contribution of legitimate children to the succeeding generation than do their darker fellows.

4. Upper-class (white) men continue to have ready access to women of the lower (darker) class. Thus, in addition to leaving more than their share of legitimate descendants, these men also contribute greatly to the increase, and consequently to the bleaching, of the lower classes. Neither the sex mores of Brazilian society nor the position of women in the upper-class family is sufficient to check the extramarital proclivities of the upper-class men. Even were immigration prohibited entirely, it is likely that Brazil's population would continue to lighten with each succeeding generation.

## Epilogue and Prologue

The materials given in this chapter are essentially the same as they appeared in the first edition of *Brazil: People and Institutions* in 1946. Even the proposition that a continuous "bleaching" or whitening of the population was going on has not needed revision; and in the 1970s there is every reason to suppose that the white and whitish components of the population continue to increase in relative importance, whereas the black and mulatto contingents annually make up smaller and smaller proportions of all Brazilians. But the portents seem to indicate that this state of affairs is coming to an end, and that within the next few decades Negroes and mulattoes will begin to increase more rapidly than their whiter fellows.

The reasons for this conjecture are somewhat complicated, but they correspond to a pattern that has already been traced in the United States. In this, as in many other features of Brazil's development, such as the date when the urban part of the population came to be more numerous than the rural, the course being followed corresponds rather closely, with a lag of about fifty years, to the one that formed part of the history of the United States. Thus in 1800 those classed as Negroes made up almost 20 percent of the population of the new nation called the United States. At that time the birth rate in the country was very high, and there probably was little or no inverse relationship between the rate of reproduction and the socioeconomic status of the families. Couples rich and poor, slave and free, all produced large numbers of children. There probably was, however, a tendency for the more affluent people to be able to save and rear larger proportions of their offspring than was true of the blacks who were almost exclusively confined to the lower levels of the socioeconomic scale. In any case, from 1800 on, with the passage of each decade, the proportion of Negroes in the population fell until in 1930 only 9.7 percent of the population of the United States was classified as Negro. And by that date a very strong inverse relationship between socioeconomic status and the rate of reproduction had come to prevail. By then the refrain in the popular song, "the rich get rich, and the poor get—children!" had become a highly accurate demographic generalization. Viewed in terms of the racial composition of the population, this meant that the Negroes continued to have a high birth rate whereas that of the whites higher up on the socioeconomic scale had been reduced to a mere fraction of its former level. Simultaneously the difference between the death rates of whites and Negroes had been greatly reduced. As a result, from 1940 on the proportion of Negroes in the population has been increasing, to 10 percent in 1950, 10.5 percent in 1960, and 11.1 percent in 1970. There are no indications that another reversal is in sight.[31]

In Brazil the birth rate in the 1970s probably is as high as it was there or in the United States in 1800; and there is a pronounced tendency for the color of the people to get darker and darker as one looks down the socioeconomic scale. But there is now strong evidence that the birth rate is beginning to fall. In Figure 3 it may be observed that in 1970 the number of children of less than five years of age was only slightly larger than the number aged five to nine, whereas in all previous censuses the very youngest age group was substantially larger than the one immediately above it in the age-sex pyramid. Moreover, as indicated in Chapter 3, the number of children under five per 100 women aged fifteen to forty-four was 68, whereas in 1960 it was 72.[32] Therefore it seems fairly evident that at long last the birth rate in Brazil has begun to fall. In all probability, the reduction is taking place to the greatest extent among the whites who now by the millions make up the rapidly increasing upper portions of the middle class in Brazil's cities and towns. It is unlikely that any substantial reduction in the rate of reproduction of the members of the lower socioeconomic strata has begun or that it will take place any time in the immediate future. My own guess is that this will produce within the next twenty-five years a pronounced inverse relationship between socioeconomic status and the rate of reproduction, fairly comparable to that which was an outstanding feature of society in the United States in the 1920s and 1930s. If this conjecture portends what actually is to come, well before the year 2000 the gradual "bleaching" of Brazil's population will cease, and, similar to what took place in the United States after 1930, a trend will develop in which Brazil's population becomes darker and darker.

# 5

## The Race between Population and the Food Supply

Brazil, the second most populous country in the Western Hemisphere, seems to be developing a population policy that is drastically different from the one that has guided its national endeavors for centuries. As I have indicated elsewhere and repeatedly,[1] all through the nineteenth and the first half of the twentieth centuries, *"falta de braços,"* literally lack of arms, which is the equivalent of the English "lack of hands," was the nation's theme song. Strenuous efforts were made and large sums of money were expended for the purpose of securing manual workers to man its huge sugar-cane and coffee plantations, and other agricultural enterprises. At first this was by the unobstructed importation of African slaves; later (from about 1850 to the abolition of slavery in 1888) by running them through the British blockade. And for about a century from 1860 on it was by subsidizing large contingents of immigrants from Germany, Italy, Japan, and other countries.[2] In the 1970s, however, after Brazil passed (about 1965) the mark at which the population became more urban than rural, and after it also became a member of the select 100-million club (along with China, India, the U.S.S.R., the United States, Japan, and Indonesia), the policy appears to be changing. At least some of Brazil's intellectual leaders appear to be adopting the view that Brazil should cease to worry about getting plenty of people and become more concerned that Brazilians of all colors and classes become a people of plenty. Such a policy is by no means established as yet but the drastic changes in immigration policy, the virtual cessation of immigration, and increased knowledge of birth control measures and family planning objectives seem to be generating a distinctly different outlook on uncontrolled increase of population.

In this paper attention is focused first on the growth of population in the huge country whose territory extends over fully one-half of the South American continent and contains one-half of all its inhabitants; and then attention is directed to the many effective ways in which the production of feed, food, and fiber is being increased even more rapidly than the population is mounting. These are matters that I have analyzed recently in considerable detail in the fourth edition of my book cited above. In this paper I draw heavily on those data. These are supplemented, however, by some of the more salient facts which have become available since that volume went to press, in the flood of information that now appears monthly about the life and labor of the people in that gigantic country.

## The Growth of Brazil's Population

Among the half dozen most populous countries in the world, Brazil is in a class by itself in the rapidity with which its population is growing. The population increase of 2.8 percent per year between 1960 and 1970 is about three times as fast as the growth of population in the U.S.S.R., the United States, and Japan; about double that in China; and substantially higher than the rates in India and Indonesia. In fact, it is keeping pace with the burgeoning of the populations of the remaining half of South America, and the countries that make up the other third of Latin America (Mexico, Cuba, Haiti, Santo Domingo, and five Central American countries). Brazil and the other Latin American countries together make up the great world region in which the growth of population is most rapid.[3] This statement is valid even though there still is some uncertainty relative to the actual number enumerated in Brazil's 1970 census. And it is valid even though reliable estimates of the size and changes in size of Brazil's population are more difficult to make and generally less reliable than those for most other parts of the Western Hemisphere or for European countries because of the lack of nationwide coverage in the registration of births and deaths.

For present purposes some of the most important facts to keep in mind about population trends in Brazil are the following.

1. By 1970 the population of Brazil had risen to about 95 million, up 24 million, or 34 percent, from the 71 million inhabitants enumerated in 1960. In the thirty years since 1940, when

the population was only 42 million and the huge upsurge was just getting under way, the number of Brazilians increased by more than 125 percent.

2. With the rates now prevailing the end of each year finds Brazil with about 3 million more people than it had at its beginning. At the present time Brazil's population is passing the 100-million mark, and she is becoming, after China, India, the U.S.S.R., and the United States, a member of the 100-million club. It is a matter of conjecture as to whether she joins this limited group before Japan and Indonesia, which also are at that important point in their demographic history, but the third rival for the distinction, Pakistan, recently dropped from the race for tragic reasons that are well known to everyone. Brazil quickly will outdistance her rivals, Japan and Indonesia, in population.

3. The birth rate in Brazil is still very high, probably more than 40 per 1,000, although it probably has begun to fall. If this hypothesis is borne out by developments in the immediate future, Brazil is on the threshold of an all-important demographic transition. A substantial fall in the birth rate of a country provides the thrust for a "shock wave" that eventually is felt in all aspects of life. Very quickly it produces a decrease in the demand for everything needed in the feeding and care of babies and their mothers. A few years later comes the falling off of kindergarten and elementary school enrollments, subsequently in the numbers of young people seeking entrance into the high schools, and a bit later in the sizes of the enrollments in colleges and universities. About eighteen years after a sharp fall in the birth rate gets well under way, the contingents of young men liable for military training begin to decrease, and almost simultaneously the numbers and proportions of young women in the ages in which their fertility is highest commence to fall off. This in turn generates another decrease in the crude birth rate over what otherwise would be the case. And so it goes, until eventually the proportions of those in the older ages, which at first were enlarged by the decreases in the relative importance of the younger age groups, are decreased by the fall in the birth rate that took place sixty-five years earlier.

4. The death rate in Brazil, which has been reduced substantially since 1930, or probably from a level of about 30 or 35 per 1,000 to no more than 15 by 1970, may be cut still further within the next decade. With birth rates of from 40 to 50 per 1,000, and the high

degree to which these produce a concentration of population in the ages from two to twenty-five, in which the age-specific death rates are very low, it is relatively easy for health and sanitary programs to reduce the crude death rate to considerably less than 10 per 1,000. Brazil very shortly may be reporting such encouraging indicators of social well being. However, since life expectancy at birth is the reciprocal of the death rate, so that in a stationary population a death rate of 10 would mean that the average baby born would live to be one hundred years old, neither Brazil nor any other country can long maintain death rates of less than two digits after the birth rate begins to fall substantially.

5. Brazil has moved well into the stage of its existence in which agricultural and pastoral activities have taken second place to industry, trade, commerce, transportation, and other nonagricultural forms of economic endeavor. This change will become more and more pronounced with every year that passes.

In brief, in the vitally important race between population and the means of subsistence, the increase of population in Brazil is a formidable contender. One hundred million people, annually adding about three million more to their number, with a birth rate that is near the maximum and only now beginning to fall, and with a death rate that almost surely will be cut sharply within the next decade, constitute a major feature of the dramatic contest between population and "the food supply" in the world as a whole. With this point in mind let us next direct attention to the second of the contestants, considering first the actual changes taking place and then analyzing briefly some of the principal factors that are producing the remarkable increase in the production of food, feed, and fiber in the Brazilian half continent.

## Spectacular Increases in "The Food Supply"

Since 1950 Brazil has taken gigantic strides in the production of the food, feed, and fiber for domestic consumption and for export. On this subject, however, the statistical data, even when they are available at all, are far less satisfactory than those on the population trends. In many cases the figures published are no more than educated guesses, and often they are not even that. Nevertheless the amounts of crops and livestock products secured from the soil are being expanded tremendously, even more rapidly than Brazil's population is growing, so that per capita production and consumption is increasing to some extent. To be specific, from the information available in the various issues of Brazil's *Anuário Estatístico*, one may observe that the index number showing the relative changes in the volume of agricultural products rose substantially from the 100 for 1955, the year used as a base, to 155 for crops and 151 for livestock products for 1968. During this period the population increased by 46 percent. This faster pace of the increase in agricultural products was registered despite the fact that it was greatly slowed by the temporary setback in the production of coffee occasioned by a severe freeze, which lowered the index for this, the most important Brazilian crop, from 239 for 1961 to 102 for 1968. For some of the other major crops the changes between 1961 and 1968 in the indexes of production are as follows: grains, from 124 to 165; roots and tubers, from 122 to 192; truck crops and vegetables, from 142 to 242; beans and other legumes, from 123 to 178; fruits, from 136 to 195; fibers and other crops for industrial purposes, from 141 to 172; and other crops, from 186 to 395. For livestock products, the increases for the same eight-year period are as follows: general, from 121 to 151; cattle, from 120 to 143; hogs, sheep, and goats, from 126 to 165; and poultry and eggs, from 126 to 185.[4]

Most of the activities through which Brazilians presently are increasing tremendously the amounts of products they are getting from the soil, gains which seem certain to be greatly expanded in the years immediately ahead, may be grouped into four large categories. These are: (1) the expansion of settlement; (2) the superimposition of farming as such upon the old, traditional, and rudimentary pastoral culture which has prevailed over much of Brazil; (3) great changes in the ways of farming; and (4) the implantation and promotion of new and improved types of farming. The remainder of this chapter is devoted to brief discussions of these four processes.

*Expansion of Settlement*

Brazil contains larger expanses of unsettled and sparsely populated land, much of it probably as responsive to human efforts as the areas already in use, than any other country in the world. For centuries this virgin territory has been viewed largely as a "land of the future," and settlements have remained hugged closely to its immense coastline. In recent decades this situation has been changing, and the pace is quickening at which the conquest of previously unsettled areas is taking place. This in turn is responsible for much of the nation's greatly increased amounts of food, feed, and fiber.

In the 1950s, along with the migration of about seven million people (one out of every ten enumerated in the census of 1960) from the farms to urban places, settlement was pushed rapidly into many previously unoccupied areas. The most spectacular of these migrations was the movement of hundreds of thousands of people into the northwestern part of the state of Paraná where a tremendous expansion of coffee culture in that highly favored area was taking place. At the same time other tens of thousands of families were occupying virgin lands in the northwestern part of the state of São Paulo and central Goiás to the northwest of the location of Brasília (the new national capital). Thousands of others were pushing into the Valley of the Rio Doce in northeastern Minas Gerais, and into the heavily forested area on the edge of the great Amazon rain forest in north-central Maranhão.[5]

During the 1960s these efforts, which may best be described as spontaneous colonization to distinguish them from the planned settlement projects carried on by governmental agencies, increased in volume and tempo. They took place at many, many places along the cutting edge of the immense frontier zones in the south, central, and northeastern parts of the immense country; but the most important of all were in the areas adjacent to and served by the great new road that was cut through the forest and the jungle to connect Brasília with Belém, the great metropolis of the gigantic Amazon region. Into these previously unoccupied territories several million people flocked in the decade between 1960 and 1970. A couple of quotations from Brazilian sources illustrate the importance of this development in relation to the race between population and the food supply.

The first of these is from a report titled *Transamazonian Highways* (pp. 21-23) presented by Brazil's Ministry of Transportation to the VI World Meeting of the International Road Federation, which met in Montreal, Canada, in October 1970:

Recent examples in the Brazilian economy have emphasized

that penetration roads have shown to be the decisive factors for the occupation of vast portions of the Brazilian hinterland, transforming virgin regions and deserts in[to] populated areas with immediate favorable responses in the economic sector.

One can take the Belém-Brasília Highway as an example. It is only ten years old, is already being paved, and will be completely paved from end to end within four years. The impact of the road is clearly shown in the following table: (The data in this table indicate that between 1960 and 1970 the population of the zone increased from 100,000 to 2,000,000; the number of villages, towns and cities from 10 to 120; the number of cattle from "negligible" to 5,000,000; farming activities from "subsistence" to "intensive" cultures of corn, beans, rice, and cotton; average daily traffic from "practically nonexistent" to 700 vehicles daily over one section, 350 over another, and 300 over the third; and feeder roads from "inexistent" to rapid expansion, with 2,300 kilometers to date.)

Only ten years have gone. He who had flown before over those desert places of the Central Plateau and that empty Amazonia, would be surprised today with the vitality of the continuous process of occupation and economic exploitation of the lands crossed by the 2,123 kilometers of the Belém-Brasília Highway.

To complement this macroscopic view of the immense zone as a whole, a translation of one perceptive observer's report on happenings in one specific município is offered. This seems especially significant because for centuries the inhabitants of the once sleepy small river town had languished in the desuetude of a little, almost hermetically sealed sociocultural world whose static condition resembled to a considerable degree that of a pendulum held at dead center by the force of gravity.[6] The fact that the area involved is located well within the limits of the Amazonian rain forest makes the development all the more significant. The analyst first describes the enormous increases in the production of rice, manioc, beans, and corn in Maranhão since the late 1950s and then he indicates that:

The tonic that led to this development was the opening of BR-10, Belém-Brasília, at the beginning of the decade. For example, the city of Imperatriz—[in the municipio] which produces the finest rice in Maranhão—experienced an increase of 67 percent in recent years, and presently is estimated to have 42,000 inhabitants. . . . The opening of new roads is the most important development. . . . The increase in the production of babassú and rice is due to the opening of new roads, which permit the establishment of new colonies, and form new fronts of agricultural production.[7]

The results of building the Belém-Brasília Highway were convincing to those responsible for Brazil's foreign and domestic policies, and in 1970 they launched the largest program of road building and agricultural colonization in the nation's history. The colossal undertaking has as its central feature the construction of a modern highway extending from the Atlantic Coast to the boundary with Peru. It is designed to link with modern means of land transportation the heads of navigation on all the southern tributaries of the Amazon River, and to establish settlements of farmers and stockmen along both sides of the lengthy new artery and its feeder roads. The results of this immense undertaking are still to be seen, but the work is being pursued feverishly and we have every right to expect that during the 1970s this huge effort to settle the Amazon Basin will do much to enable the increase in Brazil's food supply to exceed that in her population.[8]

*The Superimposition of Agriculture upon
the Traditional Pastoral Culture*

As the Portuguese colonists established their dominion over the half of the South American continent presently within the boundaries of Brazil, they devised a system of sugar-cane plantations and instituted their new creations in the more fertile areas near the coast, especially in what now are the states of Rio de Janeiro, Bahia, Pernambuco, and Pará.[9] Over most of their possessions in the New World, however, the Portuguese colonists merely established what may be described as the very thin veneer of a rudimentary pastoral culture over the territory they occupied and claimed. Subsequently coffee, sugar cane, and rice plantations, and especially the settlements of small general farmers in the three southern states (Rio Grande do Sul, Santa Catarina, and Paraná) have spread farming activities over areas once devoted exclusively to cattle ranching. Even the modernization of ranching activities involving the improvement of pastures, the production of forage crops, the introduction and spread of the practice of making and feeding silage, the use of corn and other grains for fattening cattle, and so on, is playing an increasingly important role in the spreading use of tillage.

All of these developments are going on so widely throughout Brazil that it would be far beyond the scope of this chapter to give the details about any of them. One careful and perceptive observer and painstaking analyst, Professor Harold M. Clements of the Stephen F. Austin State University in Texas, in his excellent study of the sociological aspects of the mechanization of agriculture in the massive state of Minas Gerais, however, formulated a generalization about the process that deserves the most careful consideration. As one ponders what this well-informed and objective sociologist says, it is well to keep in mind that Minas Gerais shares a long boundary with the highly advanced state of São Paulo, from whence a great many innovations in the fields of agriculture and animal husbandry are being spread to the less-advanced parts of Brazil. The following paragraph is from Clements's valuable monograph:

> Undoubtedly the most significant of the complex of factors that account for the variations in the importance of mechanized agriculture, and one closely related to all the others, is a highly important and long-continued trend in Brazil in general and especially in Minas Gerais. It consists of the gradual superimposition of an agricultural economy upon the old traditional pastoral economy of the nation. In such states as Rio Grande do Sul and São Paulo this process already is far advanced, whereas in others such as Goiás and Mato Grosso it is barely beginning. In Minas Gerais it already has made considerable headway, and it continues to progress. As things now stand, however, the extent to which agriculture has supplanted grazing is an important factor influencing the development—or retarding the process—of mechanization. Where the farmer now has control of the land, the tractor and the implements associated with it are coming into use; but where the huge grazing estates still reign supreme, the use of mechanized equipment is still a thing of the future.[10]

*Great Changes in the Ways of Farming*

One of the greatest problems I had when in 1939-43 I undertook seriously to understand the life, labor, and social organization of the people of Brazil was to convince myself that the ways in which the rural people of that nation were going about the process of extracting products from the soil actually were as backward or antiquated as they appeared to be. At first it was almost beyond belief that, near the middle of the twentieth century, such immense amounts of human energy and vast extensions of forests and other natural resources were being squandered needlessly for the production of niggardly amounts of rice, corn, beans, manioc, and other staples. In fact it was this Brazilian experience, coupled immediately thereafter with a comparable observation in Colombia that, after more than a decade of intense probing, reading, and cogitation, led me to classify all human endeavors to produce crops into six large categories. These are: (1) riverbank farming, in which nature's rivers alone are relied upon to produce seedbeds; (2) "fire agriculture," or felling and burning, in which through the expenditure of immense quantities of human energy, a "farmer" will spend months chopping down the trees in an acre or two of forest so that when the fallen timber is dry the immense bonfire he can make will create a soft, pliable seedbed into which he can dibble the seeds and thereby produce a few pecks of rice, corn, beans, etc.; (3) hoe culture, in which with an improved digging stick, sometimes supplemented with a crude variety of fertilization, the farmer, now entitled to be called a cultivator, can reduce his annual migrations and produce one crop after another from the same plot of ground; (4) rudimentary plow culture, where the forked branch of a tree, often much like the rude grubbing hoe that preceded it in the scale of cultural development, is converted into a plow by the application of the power of the domesticated ox or water buffalo to the tasks of farming; (5) advanced plow culture, or a highly perfected stage of tillage, wherein the central features of the highly integrated sociocultural system involved are the metal turning plow equipped with a mathematically designed mold board, drawn by even-gaited horses whose energy is efficiently applied by means of highly perfected harnesses and hitching equipment; and (6) mechanized or motorized farming, of which the central components of the system consist of the tractor and its associated implements, machines, and vehicles.[11] Moreover, as I weighed the evidence gathered by personal observations in all parts of Brazil and made painstaking analyses of available statistical data and of other observers' reports, I became convinced that in the 1950s fully half of all the Brazilians engaged in agriculture were using ways of getting products from the soil that were less effective or more antiquated than those in use by the Egyptians at the dawn of history.[12]

During the 1960s, however, great improvements in the ways of farming were introduced in many parts of Brazil and during the 1970s even greater advances are underway. The tractor and its associated implements, and the mechanized farming it symbolizes, is, of course, the portal through which Brazilian farming finally is entering the twentieth century; and volumes might be written about its role in the great changes in agriculture now under way. No such detailed analysis can be attempted here. It is interesting to note, though, that the authors of an official *Survey of the Brazilian Economy,*[13] written in English and prepared for circulation in the United States, indicate that 1939 was the date when these changes began. At that time they state "inferiority complexes . . . in Brazil were replaced by a sense of movement; [and] fire agriculture began to be replaced by the concept of mechanized agriculture."

This modernization of the ways of farming in Brazil is an excellent specimen of the transplantation of sociocultural systems and, as such, deserves the most painstaking study by all social scientists interested in the general process of social change. Therefore, it seems advisable to dwell for a moment on the developments elsewhere that brought to a high degree of perfection the extensive and intricate sociocultural system that for convenience is designated as mechanized farming. The system itself is readily available for transplantation, and fortunately the use of tractors and motor trucks is now so widespread in nonagricultural activities that all of the technical skills needed and the lines of supply for parts are readily available in all parts of Brazil.

The way of farming now being disseminated throughout Brazil was developed directly out of the most advanced stages of advanced plow culture as these had been perfected in the Midwestern sections of the United States and the adjacent parts of Canada in the period from about 1910 to 1920. There the tractor, the motor truck, and the automobile quickly replaced the horse as sources of power; the number of plow bottoms, cultivators, harrows, disks, and so on per implement, was substantially increased; attachments for performing various tasks (preparation of the seedbed, planting, the insertion of fertilizers, the application of herbicides and pesticides, and the making of furrows) during a single trip over the land were devised and tested; the principles of genetics were applied on a large scale in the production of seeds that would greatly increase the product per acre; the combine for harvesting and threshing grain and the corn picker were perfected, and the equipment for making hay and that needed in the preparation of silage were greatly improved; electricity was brought to the barns and milking sheds to power milking machines, water pumps, grinding machines, and other labor-saving equipment; and gasoline motors became the sources of energy used in the performance of a great many farm tasks. Perhaps the most revolutionary feature of all of these, however, was the attainment of the major objective of the entire search for improved ways of farming, namely, to enable one man, usually the farm operator himself, to perform any and all of the large and complicated processes. Simultaneously, the roads and highways were improved to the extent that even "farm-to-market roads" became "all-weather" arteries of transportation; and hundreds of other advanced features became integral parts of the remarkable mechanized way of farming. By 1950, this superbly effective sociocultural entity was almost universally in use throughout the United States and Canada, widely used in Europe, and readily available for implantation or transplantation in other parts of the world.

In recent years Brazil has become one of the chief beneficiaries of this ultramodern way of farming. Furthermore, unlike the situation in the United States, where in the most densely populated rural districts, such as the cotton belt in the South, the mechanization of agriculture has been a response to the flight of people from the land about as much as it has been a factor promoting rural-urban migrations, in the immense and sparsely populated pastoral regions of Brazil the introduction of the mechanized way of farming creates a need for many additional workers to assist in the cultivation of the soil. Certainly this metamorphosis in the ways of extracting products from the soil is, and for decades to come will continue to be, a major factor in the increase of food, feed, and fiber in Brazil.

### Changes in the Types of Farming

The fourth and last of the factors discussed here that presently are enabling the production of the means of subsistence to outrun the growth of population in Brazil is the substantial changes that are taking place in the type of farming. Type of farming denotes the enterprise or combination of enterprises that make up the economic activities on a given farm. Historically, various types of monoculture on large plantations (sugar cane, coffee, cacao, rice) and the "monoequivalent" in animal husbandry, the production of rangy beef cattle, have dominated rural economic activities throughout the immense half continent. Perhaps monoculture is the only thing feasible in a plantation system, a sociocultural system that depends upon a rigid regimentation of large numbers of slave or semiservile farm laborers and wherein there is a mere handful of persons in the managerial and supervisory roles. With the inputs of management reduced almost to the vanishing point, in combination with the use of large tracts of land and the lavish use of labor, it probably would have been foolish, from the pure economic standpoint, to complicate the tasks of management and administration by including multiple enterprises in the farm business. Be that as it may, educated Brazilians long have deplored the nation's dependence upon monoculture of one type or another. Furthermore, sometime ago I personally became convinced that Brazil (and most of the other Latin American countries as well) would never enjoy the productivity and levels of living to which the people aspired until the crop and livestock enterprises came to be combined effectively in highly symbiotic combinations such as the corn-hog-beef-cattle type of farming (this remarkable system was perfected before 1840, and from then until about 1960 it was responsible for the prosperity of the great Midwestern "corn belt," in the United States), the dairy husbandry of Great Lakes area of the United States and Canada, or the combination of dairying and swine husbandry featured in Denmark's remarkable farming activities.[14] Throughout the length and breadth of Brazil, however, I was able to find very few significant attempts to combine the crop and livestock enterprises in given farm businesses. The most important I did discover were among the small general farmers in the "colonial" zones of south Brazil; and especially noteworthy among these were those in the hills in the northeast of the state of Rio Grande do Sul where the system of growing and transforming substantial crops of corn into lard and other pork products was the basis for many fairly prosperous farming communities. Indeed, as decade after decade passed in which there was little or no visible evidence of substantial departure from monoculture of one kind or another, I almost abandoned hope that some day I would be able to observe significant improvements in types of farming throughout Brazil.

More recently, however, and especially in the 1960s and 1970s, changes occurred that are producing greatly increased symbiosis among crop and livestock enterprises on the farms in São Paulo, Minas Gerais, Paraná, Rio de Janeiro, and other states in the more densely inhabited parts of Brazil. Some of this represents an integration of swine, beef cattle, and poultry enterprises with the production of forage crops and grains, but by far the most important is the phenomenal rise of the dairy industry. In the latest edition of my *Brazil,* I have devoted a lengthy section (pp. 664-76) to the genesis and spread of this highly symbiotic sociocultural system and to an analysis of some of the principal factors that are responsible for these developments. Suffice it to say here, though, that in the areas near the great cities of São Paulo, Rio de Janeiro, Porto Alegre, Curitiba, and Belo Horizonte, dairy husbandry has become a major type of farming. The change is particularly striking in the area of the once-decadent old coffee zone in southern Minas Gerais, the state of Rio de Janeiro, and parts of the state of São Paulo. Among the factors providing the thrust for the tremendous change are: (1) the establishment since the end of World War II of a few colonies of European immigrants, and especially those of the Dutch and of the Mennonites from Russia, who transplanted highly perfected systems of dairy husbandry to locations near the cities of São Paulo and Curitiba; (2) the activities of Brazil's new and tremendously important agricultural extension service (the Associação Brasileira de Crédito e Asisténcia Rural), which combines adult education and supervised farm credit, in the service of the farmers who operate small and medium-sized farms; (3) the promotion of dairying by commercial firms that have mounted huge plants for the confection of chocolate candies and other sweets, for which the highly elastic demand in Brazilian cities is almost unbounded, which need the milk to combine with Brazilian sugar and cacao for the goods (or "goodies") they produce; (4) the tremendous demand for milk and milk products on the part of millions of persons, substantial numbers of whom are immigrants or the children of recent immigrants, who inhabit the cities of what now is a predominantly urban country; and (5) the decision by some of the proprietors of Brazil's great landed estates to establish huge, modern dairies, stocked with purebred dairy cattle which they import from the countries most noted for dairy farming.

Already Brazil, from a position that was invisible in world perspective as late as 1950, has moved to the forefront among the milk-producing countries of the world. Brazil still does not figure among the countries for which data are published in the U.S. Department of Agriculture's *World Agricultural Production and Trade* (July 1970 issue), which lists the leading dairy countries in order as follows: United States, France, West Germany, the United Kingdom, Italy, Canada, the Netherlands, and Australia. But by 1970 Brazil already outranked Australia in the production of milk, and it is almost certain that by 1972 it exceeded the Netherlands, Canada, and Italy in such production. Moreover, before 1980 Brazil seems certain to replace the United Kingdom as the world's fourth most important producer of milk. In any case the upsurge of dairy husbandry in Brazil is tremendous, the potentialities in this type of farming are almost unlimited, and both in recent years and in the immediate future the growth and spread of the almost new (to Brazil) type of farming is doing much to enable the increase of the food supply to outpace even the very rapid rate with which the population is growing.

In conclusion it seems important to stress that to date the accomplishments in increasing Brazil's production of "the means of subsistence" are relatively modest in comparison with the potential. Much of her territory is still to be brought into the service of mankind. Only a beginning has been made in the modernization of the ways of farming. And the possibilities of more effective types of farming are almost unlimited. One may confidently expect that within the next few decades the four great wonder crops (corn, alfalfa, soybeans, and the grain sorghums) will come to be the mainstays of Brazilian farming, and that the abundant harvests of these will be transformed into milk and milk products, beef, pork and pork products, poultry and eggs. These will be largely for domestic consumption in a rapidly expanding domestic market. In the great, drought-stricken, problem-ridden Northeast, for example, through which flow the potentially fructifying waters of the great

São Francisco River, in the years ahead immense fields of alfalfa and other forage crops, soybeans and milo sorghum, and corn, will be combined with greatly improved breeds of beef and dairy cattle, to transform that large area into one of the highly productive parts of Brazil. Elsewhere the modernization of the ways of farming used in rice culture and the combination of this crop in the same farm business with the production of beef cattle, often in rotation with soybeans, will bring prosperity to hundreds of thousands of farm families, and greatly augmented volumes of the necessities of life to millions of city people. Something akin to the combination of dairy husbandry and the production of bacon-type hogs, the basis of Denmark's enviable system of agriculture, may be developed at many places throughout Brazil. And such an enumeration of the possibilities might be extended at great length. It is hoped that enough has been said, however, to establish the thought that as yet the increase of population in Brazil is not pressing hard on the possibilities of expanding the food supply. Brazil is fortunate in that in her immediate future there is every reason to suppose that the production of her farms, plantations, and ranches will rise more rapidly than her population, so that she will have the time in which to develop and put into practice a population policy adapted to the realities of the problem of unchecked population growth.

PART III

# Social Structure
# and Social Institutions

Four highly important features of the social structure and institutions which constitute the anatomy of Brazilian society are analyzed and described in this section. Chapter 6 endeavors to give in capsule form some of the principal ways in which the patterns of living in Brazil differ from those in the United States. Then, inasmuch as the system of large landed estates was the great mold in which traditional Brazilian society was formed, and since the class system it generated still retains much of its strength even after Brazil has become predominantly urban, Chapter 7 is devoted to the place of the latifundia in Brazilian society. One of the most important trends in Brazil during the second half of the nineteenth century is the transition from a structural type of society in which the small neighborhood group almost completely enveloped the life and labor of its predominantly rural masses to one in which larger and more complex locality groups are the basic cells in social organization. Hence Chapter 8 deals with the organization and development of the rural community. Two aspects of Brazil's extremely significant religious institutions, namely religious differentiation and religious syncretism, are treated in Chapter 9.

# 6

## Patterns of Living
## in Brazil and the United States:
## A Comparison

This chapter will attempt to draw attention to major like and unlike elements in the cultural patterns of Brazil and the United States, with an eye to mutual understanding. Obviously, this constitutes a task of considerable magnitude, and much reflection was required in order to decide which of the many possibilities should receive attention. Finally, it was decided to center on the following four aspects of the general subject: (1) the diversity of patterns of living in the United States, and the even greater diversity of ways of life in Brazil; (2) the higher degree of social differentiation in the United States, in comparison with contemporary Brazil; (3) the similarities and differences in patterns of living which result from the class structures found in the respective societies; and (4) the effects upon general social and cultural patterns of the institutions which have played the most important roles in producing the distinguishing characteristics of each of the societies: in the case of Brazil, the great patriarchal family or kinship unit, and in the case of the United States, the public school.

### Diversity in Patterns of Living

Regional diversity in the ways of life found in the United States is proverbial. It is true that in recent decades automobiles, airplanes,

First published in the *Journal of Inter-American Studies* 3, No. 2 (April 1961): 187-94, and republished with the permission of the Pan-American Foundation, Inc.

radios, television, and other rapid means of communication and transportation have served to mix and blend the social and cultural traits of the inhabitants of various parts of the United States. Even so, the most superficial observer cannot fail to note the large and significant differences in patterns of living which are found throughout the nation. Consider for a moment the kaleidoscope of social and economic patterns which flash through the mind merely with the mention of the following: New York City, Vermont and New Hampshire, Detroit, Youngstown or Gary, Chicago, the Corn Belt, the Twin Cities, the northern plains, Seattle and the North Pacific Coast, the San Francisco Bay area, Southern California, the Spanish-American settlements in the Southwest, Salt Lake City and the irrigated portions of the Great Basin in which the Mormons live, Texas, New Orleans and the Louisiana French, the cotton plantation districts along the lower Mississippi, the Ozarks of Arkansas, the red hills of Mississippi and Alabama, Atlanta, the Southern Appalachians, Miami, the Piedmont, Charleston or Richmond, Washington, the Pennsylvania Dutch sections of Pennsylvania, and the coal-mining districts of West Virginia and Pennsylvania.

In Brazil, over an area still larger than that of the United States, one finds an even greater social and cultural diversity. Indeed, mutual understanding between the peoples of the United States and Brazil will be greatly enhanced when the items included in the following enumeration are as well known to well-informed people in the United States as the portions of this country mentioned above are known to their counterparts in Brazil. Be that as it may, the utmost in social and cultural diversity is suggested by the following indication of some of the social and cultural areas one encounters: moving northward from the Uruguayan border to the great Amazon Basin: the great cattle *estancias* on the *campina* of Rio Grande do Sul; Porto Alegre, bustling with commercial and industrial activity; the small farming districts, or "colonial zones" in the northern part of Rio Grande do Sul which are inhabited by the descendants of German and Italian settlers, those of the Germans in and around Blumenau and Joinville in Santa Catarina, and those of the Poles in Paraná; the mate producing districts of western Santa Catarina, western Paraná, and southern Mato Grosso; the new land of promise for coffee growers in northern Paraná; the city of São Paulo, Brazil's incomparable "melting pot," a gigantic industrial, financial, commercial, transportation, and cultural center; the

Japanese communities thickly dotted from the city of São Paulo over the northwestern part of the state and on into Mato Grosso, Minas Gerais, and Paraná; the tremendous coffee fazendas throughout central São Paulo, each with its large complement of workers who have been recruited from immigrant groups and from migrants from Minas Gerais, Bahia, and other still more distant states; the city of Rio de Janeiro, political and administrative center of the Republic, hub of the nation's transportation system, world-renowned as a tourist attraction, and rival of São Paulo for the position of chief metropolis in Brazil; the forested zone of Minas Gerais; Belo Horizonte, thriving new capital of Brazil's second most populous state, located near many fabulous mineral deposits, and into whose development the major efforts of the *mineiros* presently are directed; the immense cattle-ranching areas which fan out northwestward from Belo Horizonte to embrace the tremendous zone that extends from northwestern São Paulo to central Bahia and overspreads the southern part of Goiás and much of Mato Grosso; the cacao districts of southeastern Bahia; the city of Bahia or Salvador and the surrounding *recôncavo,* whose elite classes have contributed so much to Brazil's cultural tradition and whose Negroes have figured so heavily in culinary traditions, folklore, and in Afro-Brazilian religious cults; the São Francisco Valley; Recife, great port, and the rich sugar-producing districts from which it draws, the sections which constituted the chief laboratory from which Gilberto Freyre extracted the elements for his famed *Casa Grande e Senzala;* the great *sertão* of northeastern Brazil, which was the setting for the study of Brazilian patterns of living, *Os Sertões* by Euclides da Cunha, undoubtedly the greatest work to come from the pen of a Brazilian writer and hardly rivaled in the sociological literature of the world; Ceará, itself highly diversified, and which cannot be mentioned without bringing to one's mind such varied thoughts as large numbers of children per family, flights from the periodic droughts, great migrations to the Amazon and to São Paulo, Padre Cicero's New Jerusalem at Joázeiro, and the tremendous growth of Fortaleza; the babussú forests of Piauí and Maranhão; Belém, entrepôt and transportation hub for the entire Amazon Basin, and the Marajó Island on which so many of its leading citizens have cattle ranches; and Manaus, metropolis of the entire upper Amazon, and center about which are oriented the collecting activities of the highly nomadic population of the region. As in the case of the

United States, the areas enumerated by no means exhaust the list of those in which rather distinctive ways of life entitle them to specific mention in any comprehensive outline of the social and cultural patterns of the nation. It is hoped, however, that the enumerations given will emphasize the tremendous social and cultural diversity existing in the two largest nations of the Western Hemisphere and the need to know much about the various parts of both Brazil and the United States.

## The Extent of Social Differentiation

Social differentiation has developed to a high degree in Rio de Janeiro, São Paulo, and other great urban centers in Brazil, but throughout the vast rural sections of the interior in which the majority of the population resides, social division of labor and specialization have made relatively little headway. Herein lies one of the chief reasons for many of the most striking differences between the patterns of living found in the two countries.

Division of social labor, specialization, and the resulting interdependence of the parts are, of course, much more highly developed in the urban portions of any society than they are in the rural, and this is true in both the United States and Brazil. In the former, however, at the time of the 1950 census about two-thirds of the inhabitants were living in centers of 2,500 or more inhabitants or in the densely populated areas surrounding cities of 50,000 or more inhabitants, whereas in the latter at the same time less than 30 percent would have qualified as urban had the same criteria been applied. In other words, from the quantitative standpoint, Brazil's population then resided to an overwhelming degree in a highly rural environment.

Probably of even greater significance, from the standpoint of the patterns of living, is the extent to which from the qualitative point of view the bulk of Brazil's inhabitants then had been thought of as rural to an extremely high degree. This is because its 65 million people were spread throughout its enormous territory, with relatively few focal points of urban and industrial social and cultural influences, with high proportions of the population themselves engaged directly in agricultural and collecting enterprises, and with systems of transportation in much of the country still in a rudimentary form. Thus the resident of the typical Brazilian farm, village, or small town was conditioned to a far greater extent by cultural influences from the immediate rural environment, and less by those emanating from the large urban centers, than was the resident on a farm or in a village or small town in the United States. Several decades more would have to pass before good roads, automobiles, electricity, telephones, radios, television sets, newspapers, and other features which had come to be considered as the necessities of life in the average rural community in the United States would be found to any considerable extent in the rural districts in most parts of Brazil. Meanwhile the footpath, trail, or stream; the dugout canoe, pack animal, oxcart, and saddle horse; the homemade candle and lamp; and communication by word of mouth remained as basic elements in the rural Brazilian's way of life. Definitely, changes in rural Brazil during the last quarter of a century had not kept pace with those in her urban districts. Whereas Brazilian cities had moved ahead in the stream of modern progress, life in her rural districts continued decade after decade with little or no visible change. Cultural lag had been tremendous. Whereas in the United States since 1920, the trends had largely eliminated differences between rural and urban ways of living, in Brazil the changes had tended to accentuate to an extreme degree differences between the two.

Also of utmost importance in understanding similarities and differences in the cultural and social patterns of the United States and Brazil is the degree of specialization, or lack of it, on the part of political, business, intellectual, and other leaders of the two countries. In this connection it probably is valid to maintain that the Brazilian tends to be a generalist, whereas the North American is highly, one might very well say narrowly, specialized. Members of Brazil's upper classes tend to have a knowledge of business as well as politics, to excel in public speaking, to be prepared to assume diplomatic responsibilities, and to be at home in intellectual, literary, and artistic circles. In this connection it might be mentioned that the author, himself a university professor, has never met a Brazilian colleague who devoted himself exclusively to teaching and research. Nor has the author ever met one who seemed to be lacking in business acumen. As social differentiation proceeds, we may well expect greater specialization and division of labor in Brazil, even on

the part of those in the elite classes, but for the present the patterns
of life in Brazil and the United States differ considerably because of
the breadth of knowledge possessed by the members of the upper
classes in the former and the high degree of specialization on the
part of those in the upper ranks of finance, business, educational
activities, politics, and governmental service in the latter.

## Class Structures and Patterns of Living

The comparative roles of the upper, middle, and lower social
classes in Brazil and the United States also are closely related to the
similarities and differences in ways of life to be found in the two
countries. The large landed estate, with its host of slaves or other
laborers, generates, of course, much the same kind of class system
irrespective of whether it is located in the Hudson Valley, in
tidewater Virginia, in the Natchez area of Mississippi, or in
Pernambuco, the Recôncavo of Bahia, or the lower Paraíba Valley
in Brazil. In the United States, however, the historical sequences
were such that the persistence of the large estates and the high
degree of social stratification they engendered were limited to a few
sections of the nation, mostly in the South, whereas in Brazil, in the
words of the great sociologist and cultural historian, Oliveira
Vianna, they were nationwide. [See the paragraph from one of his
classic works quoted in Chapter 3 above.]

Today there are important middle-class elements in Brazilian
society, especially in the small-farming districts of Rio Grande do
Sul, Santa Catarina, and Paraná, and as petty bourgeoisie in the
cities and towns. Nevertheless the small upper class is dominant in
economic, political, governmental, and social activities throughout
the nation. Consider in this respect the eloquent testimony offered
by the following facts. In June 1958, following long months of
work and preparation, a group of far-sighted Brazilian intellectuals
published in the *Diário de Noticias* their analysis of the needs of the
country and their proposals for revolutionizing social affairs in
Brazil. They sought especially to resolve the hiatus between the *élite*
and the *povo* or common people. Agarian reform and the "Creation
of a Rural Middle Class" were key objectives in their manifesto.
The proposals were directed, however, neither to the government
nor the general public. Instead the closing words of the preamble in
literal translation are as follows: "We offer this study for meditation
by the nation's elite."

The patterns of living generated by a high degree of social stratification are to be found both in Brazil and in the United States. In the former, however, they prevail throughout most of the nation, whereas in the latter they are largely confined to the plantation sections of the South. In both cases some of the more important features are as follows: disdain for manual labor which stigmatizes the one who does it as belonging to a low social order, high proportions of illiteracy, a great deal of shifting about by the population from one place to another, lack of much in the way of material goods by the families of the workers and of respect for private property rights in general, and low aspirations on the part of the masses of the population.

On the other hand, patterns of life generated by a century or so during which the middle class has dominated a society are found only in some parts of Brazil, while they seem to prevail in most parts of the United States. Such middle-class patterns, though, are not those that develop when a petty bourgeoisie arises in towns and cities to form an intermediate stratum between the large landowners and the workers on their estates. Rather they are those that were produced by a strong family-sized system of farming through which, as the frontier was advanced from the Appalachians to the Pacific, the head of the typical household acquired the ownership of a farm, planned and conducted its management, and, with the assistance of the members of the family, did the manual labor needed in the various enterprises involved. As a result of the patterns and values which were formed in this crucible, it appears that North Americans wear a particular type of "spectacles" which give a peculiar slant to their evaluations of the patterns and values they observe in other countries. In brief, we North Americans tend to see everything, to evaluate everything, through a pair of "middle-class glasses." Indeed, the overwhelming importance of middle-class attitudes and activities has been the major factor in making United States society what it is, and a middle-class mentality is our most distinguishing characteristic.

## Institutions Most Responsible for Distinctive Features

With respect to the major social institutions, such as those regulating domestic, educational, religious, and governmental affairs, Brazil and the United States are similar in many ways. This is to say that the basic patterns of living in all these respects are a part of those developed in Western Christian civilizations. Probably if one evaluated the relative importance of the major institutions in Brazil, the United States, and other parts of the Western world it would be found that the family was by far the most important, and that the others ranked considerably below and in various orders in different nations. For the moment, however, attention is directed to the question: Which has been most responsible for giving to Brazilian society the features which do most to distinguish it from society in the United States on the one hand and from Spanish-American society on the other—the family, the Church, or the school? Simultaneously, the same question should be asked with respect to the institution that has done most to give the distinctive features to Spanish-American societies in comparison with those in the United States and with those in Brazil; and finally the same query with respect to which has done most to make society in the United States unlike that of Brazil in the first place and that of Spanish America in the second.

When the interrogations are phrased in this manner, it is the author's belief that the institution which has done most to give Brazilian society its own specific distinguishing characteristics is the large patriarchal family which has been so brilliantly analyzed and described by such sociologists as Gilberto Freyre and Antonio Candido. For Spanish America, which is important here for comparative purposes, the role of the Church is the factor which has done most to make it differ from Brazil on the one hand and the United States on the other. Finally, the author believes that the school and its role in giving universal education to the population of the United States, to the extent that in 1950 the average person of twenty-five years of age and over had completed 9.3 years of formal schooling, is the factor which has done most to make patterns of living in the United States different from those in Brazil and Spanish America. The overwhelming importance of the school in the United States perhaps is best indicated by the frequency with which the cynic links home, mother, and the little red schoolhouse in the verbal shafts he launches at our traditional ways of life.

It would be superfluous to attempt to offer evidences of the all-important role of the great patriarchal family or clan in Brazilian society, so well has this subject been documented in the studies of Gilberto Freyre, Oliveira Vianna, Antonio Candido, and Fernando de Azevedo, to mention only four names. Nor is it necessary to elaborate upon the comparatively weak role so far played by the school in establishing the characteristics of Brazilian society. But the role of the Church, and the reasons its influence seems to have been far less important than in Spanish-American societies, may call for a few words of explanation.

The following appear to be among the most important items involved: (1) Early in Brazilian history the tithes were secularized and the priests were paid by the state. As a result, the clergy suffered chronically from short allowances, and many of them in effect became merely retainers of the aristocratic landowners on whose estates they served. Indeed it seems fair to say that the Church, or perhaps it is better to say the chapel, frequently became merely an adjunct to the *casa grande*. (2) The religious beliefs and practices of the native American Indians survived among large sectors of the population and these were supplemented by the fetish cults brought by the African slaves. Even today, and despite the syncretism that has occurred, the Afro-Brazilian cults are important factors even in cities such as Rio de Janeiro, Bahia, Recife, and São Luiz. (3) Spiritualist bodies are a potent force throughout the length and breadth of Brazil. (4) In the southern part of the country several million Protestants are to be found. And (5) priests are lacking in many of the rural communities, and Church officials frequently state that the shortage of priests is a major problem. Perhaps there are other factors that should be mentioned, but there can be little doubt that the Church throughout much of Brazil's history definitely has occupied a secondary position in comparison with the large patriarchal family in establishing and maintaining the patterns of life throughout the nation.

Thus, for one who would appreciate the ways of life in the United States it would be well to focus attention upon the role of education and the school, whereas if one would understand Brazilian ways of life one must concentrate upon the large family. Even in cities such as Rio de Janeiro and São Paulo there are apartment houses inhabited entirely by those closely related to one another, and throughout the week family obligations may make it impossible for many professional and business members of such families to accept outside social engagements.

# 7

## The Dead Weight of Latifundia

In the 1970s Brazil is taking enormous and unprecedented strides in the production of food, feed, and fiber. Despite the fact that her population is burgeoning (probably at a rate of about 3 percent yearly), the increase in the means of subsistence is moving even more rapidly, so that per capita consumption gradually is moving upward. Nevertheless, the increases are reflected on a very low base, so that the bulk of her huge rural population is still very poorly paid, fed, clothed, and housed. (Or to put it in more common terms, hired farm labor is abundant, cheap, and widely used, even though many millions of humble country people recently have flocked into Brazilian cities and towns.) For an enormous number of rural Brazilians, whose aspirations (or standards of living) have risen tremendously since 1950, the improvements being accomplished are agonizingly small and slow; or, in brief, the difference or gap between their standard of living and their level of living—the zone of exasperation—is expanding greatly.

Attention is directed in this article to the institution that has been largely responsible for the unenviable condition of Brazil's rural masses in the past. I also contend that it continues to obstruct substantially the development of the nation's agriculture. Furthermore, it also continues to prevent an equitable distribution of the product that is obtained from the soil among all those who have a part in agricultural and pastoral activities; and in the last analysis, it precludes a substantial rise in the level of living, or improvement in the way of life, of a very large segment of the Brazilian population. This is the system of large landed estates, which in

First published in *Ceres* (FAO Review) 4, No. 5 (Sept.-Oct. 1971): 59-65, and reproduced with the permission of A. Biro, Editor-in-Chief.

Brazil is the equivalent of a system of very large farms, plantations, ranches, and largely unused private holdings which the Brazilians call latifundia. Any system of large landed estates means, of course, that there is a very high degree of concentration in the ownership and control of the land. It constitutes a genuine sociocultural system, i.e., a functional set of various human, social, and cultural components, and in this case, it influences drastically the life and labor of the men, women, and children who are involved in this large, extremely symbiotic and highly integrated arrangement.

With some notable exceptions, principally the areas in the three southern states (Paraná, Santa Catarina, and Rio Grande do Sul) inhabited by descendants of small farmers from Europe who were settled there in the latter part of the nineteenth century, Brazil's immense rural territory is dominated by the large landed estate. In some sections these huge properties are devoted to large-scale monoculture featuring the production of either coffee, sugar cane, or cacao; but for the most part the land is held in huge, very extensively used tracts on which an extremely rudimentary pastoral economy is the rule, so that the holdings qualify fully for the designation of latifundia, or great unused or poorly used properties, in the true Brazilian sense of the term. Such a society offers a rewarding specimen for study by a social scientist, such as myself, who seeks to determine what is actually responsible for the almost creature level of existence that has been the lot of the bulk of mankind from ancient times to the recent past and which remains the condition of a billion or so human beings in the 1970s.

Before proceeding with the analysis of the effects of the very high degree to which the ownership and control of farm and ranch land in Brazil is concentrated in a few hands, it seems advisable to present a few basic statistics that demonstrate conclusively the fact that the concentration still exists. One of the requirements of Brazil's new "Estatuto da Terra," put into effect in 1964, was that each proprietor supply the Instituto Brasileiro de Reforma Agrária with specific data about his holding or holdings. These data have been summarized and are available to the public in recent issues of the *Anuário Estatístico do Brasil*. They are far more satisfactory than earlier materials collected in the various censuses of agriculture, although few if any of the conclusions reached on the basis of the earlier materials have to be changed to be in accord with the data gathered in the recent nationwide inventory. The information is for the year 1967 and it shows the following: 36.4 percent of the proprietors have holdings of less than 10 hectares and these contain only 1.7 percent of the privately owned land; 41.6 percent of the proprietors, with holdings of from 10 to 49 hectares, have 10.1 percent of the land; 9.4 percent of the proprietors, with holdings of from 50 to 99 hectares, own 6.9 percent of the land; 11.2 percent of the owners, with holdings between 100 and 999 hectares, hold 32.4 percent of the land; 1.3 percent of the owners, with estates of from 1,000 to 9,999 hectares, possess 33.1 percent of the land; and 0.1 percent of the proprietors, whose holdings range upwards from 10,000 hectares, own 15.8 percent of the land. Few comments about these facts are needed, but it may be germane to state that in 1967 a mere 1.4 percent of those who by law were required to supply information on their landholdings possessed almost half (48.9 percent) of all the privately owned land in Brazil.

Also in accordance with the imperatives of the law promulgated in 1964, Brazil's Instituto de Reforma Agrária made use of a very complicated formula and classified the holdings into the following categories: minifundia; rural *empresas,* or farms on which the land is being used in an economic and rational manner in accordance with the economic possibilities of the region in which it is located and in accordance with norms established beforehand by the Executive Power; and two types of latifundia. On this basis over three-fourths (75.8 percent) of the landholdings in Brazil were classified as minifundia, only 2.4 percent as rationally conducted empresas, 21.8 percent as latifundia *"por exploração"* (i.e., the way in which the land was being used or unused), and only 279 (less than 0.1 percent) as latifundia on the basis of size alone. However, only 12.1 percent of the land was in minifundia, 4.7 percent in the empresas, 76.7 percent in deficiently used large properties, and 6.5 percent in the estates that were classified as latifundia solely on the basis of size.

To this starkly naked picture of the extent to which a few of the proprietors own and control the land, one must add the all-important detail that the bulk of the workers engaged in agriculture and pastoral activities are not farm owners or even tenants of any kind. They are landless agricultural laborers. The best estimates of this that I have been able to make indicate that three out of four of the Brazilian families that are dependent upon agriculture and stock raising for their livelihoods are headed by men who are not farm operators of any kind (owners, administrators, tenants, or even squatters) but are mere farm laborers dependent upon some kind of wage. This, of course, is merely one of the inevitable consequences of a system of *centrally managed* or administered large landed estates such as prevails in Brazil. (Quite a different picture holds in a country, such as England, in which the large estate is divided for purposes of operation among a number of renters, each of whom is responsible for the management of his farm.) Clearly the Brazilian scene is one in which a few people own large amounts of land and enormous numbers of people possess little or none of it. This I consider to be the fundamental cause of the slowness with which the great agricultural potentialities of a huge half continent have been utilized. Until the ownership and control of the land is transferred to a far greater degree to those who actually work it, Brazil's agricultural development is sure to be far less rapid than desired and the level of living of the bulk of her rural population far lower than is necessary.

My basic reasons for believing this can be stated very simply. I cannot accept in any form the idea that cheap labor of any type, be it that of slaves, serfs, peons, or any other kind of servile or semiservile workers, is an acceptable status for any part of the human race. In short I reject completely the idea that any variety of a two-class system (made up of a small elite at one extreme and the huge mass of the manual laborers at the other, with few if any persons of intermediate status) is to be desired or even tolerated. Therefore, I am fully convinced that any society should shun, as it would the plague, a system of large landed estates, since they almost inevitably generate and perpetuate such a two-class social structure. In other words, after almost half a century of endeavor to understand rural societies of the past and present, I am fully convinced that the most important factor in the well-being of those who live from agricultural and pastoral activities in Brazil, or elsewhere, is the degree to which the ownership and control of the land is vested in those who work upon it on the one hand or concentrated in the hands of a few large landed proprietors on the other.

The germ of such a conclusion began to emerge in my mind when I was a boy in southern Colorado. There I could not fail to observe the contrasts between the way of life of those in several small communities of middle-class operators of family-sized farms and the extremes of wealth and poverty characteristic of most of those who spent their lives on the huge ranches in the surrounding areas. The unenviable conditions prevailed on the large estates even though they monopolized the highly desired land along the streams. This idea was reinforced when, in the 1930s, professional responsibilities made it important for me to attempt to understand and explain the reasons for the extreme differences of levels of health, education, safety of life and property, and other aspects of the levels of living, in Louisiana and other parts of the Deep South. This came immediately after I had pursued studies of rural social organization leading to the Ph.D. degree in the "Corn" and "Dairy Belts" of the United States, both characterized by a sociocultural system in which the ownership and control of the land was in the hands of the actual middle-class farmers. In Louisiana, as in neighboring Mississippi and Arkansas, and other Southern states, I ran head on into the problem of "rich land, poor people." Here there was, for any who cared to see, undeniable evidence carefully assembled and analyzed by sociologists, economists, and home economists that the inhabitants of the unfertile, hilly sections of the region, where the farms were pitifully small, actually enjoyed substantially higher levels and standards of living than those of the rich, level lowlands where the members of the affluent planter class had installed their large cotton and sugar-cane plantations. As I searched for fuller comparative information about the effects of the large landed estate and the family-sized farm in other parts of the world and throughout history, every concrete case that could be brought under scrutiny made it clear that the effects of the two in the United States were by no means unique. Gradually I came to recognize that the history of mankind has been largely that of slavery and other forms of servile or semiservile labor—a situation due principally to the large landed estate and the sociocultural system it generates and perpetuates.

When, in the late 1930s, I had the opportunity of traveling widely throughout the Spanish-American countries, I already was fairly well prepared to anticipate what I would encounter in the vast rural areas extending from Mexico to Chile and Argentina, in which the hacienda system had dominated society for a period of four centuries; and as I visited hacienda after hacienda in Mexico, Peru, Chile, and the other countries, I found, in somewhat "enlarged prints," the same "two-class" system, a small handful of the elite and the masses of the people reduced to strictly lower-class socioeconomic status, that I had come to know far too well in the southern part of the United States. Hence it is not strange that in 1942-43, when it was my good professional fortune to travel extensively through Brazil, I sought to make use of that exceptional opportunity and endeavored to observe and analyze the nature of the great sociocultural systems based upon extreme concentrations of the ownership and control of the widely distributed land. By this time, too, it was possible for me to follow some of the footsteps and verify the accuracy of the conclusions of such noted predecessors as Richard F. Burton. For example, in my travels in southern Minas Gerais, I, too, was able to see far below me the Paraibuna River as it "brawled down its apology for a bed," and to observe that the "houses and fields became more frequent, and the curse of the great proprietors is no longer upon the land." Moreover, although I was far less traveled and also otherwise less prepared than Burton had been, still I could share his thoughts about the social and economic influences of the large landholdings in Brazil. Clearly "their effect is that which it has been in France, which was [and continues to be] in the Southern States of the Union, and which is in Great Britain. When will the political economist duly appreciate the benefit derived from the subdivision of the land!"[1]

As a result of this work, supplemented by observation in all parts of Colombia, and by a lengthy period of study in the Library of Congress, certain conclusions emerged. Therefore, when I published the first edition of *Brazil: People and Institutions* in 1946, I was prepared to state and defend the conclusion that "the size of the agricultural holdings, the concentration of landownership, or the distribution of landownership and control, is the most important single determinant of the welfare of people on the land."[2] Even then I had felt absolutely certain, theoretically and pragmatically, that in Brazil, the concentration of the ownership of the land "in the hands of a few and the reduction of the masses of the people to the position of landless agricultural laborers, is accompanied by: (1) a comparatively low average standard of living, although the elite landowning class may live in fantastic luxury; (2) great chasms of class distinctions between the favored few of the upper class and the masses who lack rights to the soil; (3) a comparative absence of vertical social mobility so that this chasm is perpetuated by caste barriers . . .; (4) a low average intelligence of the population because the high abilities and accomplishments of the few people of the upper class are greatly overweighed by the ignorance and illiteracy of the masses; and (5) a population skilled only in the performance under close supervision of a very limited number of manual tasks, and lacking completely in training and practice in managerial and entrepreneurial work.''

After a quarter of a century of additional endeavor (in all parts of Brazil and in all of the other Latin American countries, in some of the world's major libraries, and in classes and seminars with graduate students working for advanced degrees), I believe I have gained an understanding of some of the salient features of the sociocultural system involved. The names of three of the principal varieties of this are the hacienda system, the fazenda system, and the plantation system. Common features of all are as follows:

1. Wherever large landed estates monopolize the land a two-class social structure is generated and perpetuated. This consists of a small number of the elite in a small, highly elevated socioeconomic stratum and a huge mass of landless agricultural workers at a near-servile level, if indeed they are not actually unfree.

2. Practically no vertical social mobility. The elite families are able to keep their own offspring in affluent circumstances, irrespective of their personal characteristics, and it is practically impossible for anyone to rise out of the lowly position occupied by the masses.

3. Very low average levels of intelligence (or ability to adapt to new situations) prevail, because most of the potentials of the masses of the people are unrealized.

4. Likewise when a system of large estates relegates the mass of the population to a creaturelike existence, the personalities of most people are sadly undeveloped. They acquire some skills in executing under rigid supervision a few manual tasks but never acquire the characteristics that feature saving and investment or those connected with the multifarious mental activities involved in decision-making and management.

5. Personal relationships between those who own and control the land and their representatives and those of the workers are of the order-and-obey type, i.e., domination and subordination.

If space permitted, many other features of this sociocultural system could be identified and described, for in the highly integrated type of symbiosis involved, routine becomes all-important, manual labor comes to be considered degrading and demeaning, the average standards and levels of living are very low, and there is little or no incentive for most people to work and save. In fact, such a system often means that the worker best serves his own interests by doing everything possible to deceive the *majordomo,* overseer, or driver into thinking he is exerting himself while actually doing just as little as he can. It is hoped, though, that enough has been said to make clear why I consider the system of large landed estates a dead weight that Brazil must rid itself of before the bulk of its rural people can ever attain the levels of living and the way of life to which they are increasingly aspiring.

In conclusion, I desire to present brief quotations pertaining to the socioeconomic effects of a system of large landed properties from three of the most eminent sociologists who have ever lived, two of them Brazilians, and the other one of the founding fathers of American sociology. F.J. Oliveira Vianna, noted Brazilian lawyer-sociologist, whose ancestors must have included at least one slave from Africa, excellently summarized the idealist features (as seen from an upper-class vantage point) of Brazil's huge landed estates as follows:

> . . . we have been from the beginning a nation of latifundia; among us the history of the small farm can be said to go back only a century. All the long colonial period was one of the splendour of the immense landed estate. In this period it alone appeared and shined; it alone created and dominated; it is the central theme interwoven throughout the entire drama of our history for three hundred fecund and glorious years.[3]

At about the same time Edward A. Ross, one of the most widely traveled and perceptive men of his day, who wrote dozens of books about societies in all parts of the world, hit the nail exactly on the head in his well-founded generalization about Brazil and other parts of South America:

> Most travelers in South America have no eye for the fundamentals which make society there so different from our own. One may read a bushel of the books visitors have written on these countries without ever learning the momentous basic fact that *from the Rio Grande down the West Coast to Cape Horn, free agricultural labor as we know it does not exist.* In

general, the laborers on the estates are at various stages of mitigation of the once universal slavery into which the native populations were crushed by the iron heel of the conquistador.[4]

And, finally, Gilberto Freyre, the most noted Brazilian sociologist, culture historian, and writer of our day, who himself had idealized the old-style sugar-cane plantation in Brazil, describes the situation currently prevailing on the modern plantations as follows:

> In some areas, such as the sugar-cane plantation districts, the land serves only to provide what it can for industry, with the most archaic and anti-economic methods of production, by means of a poorly paid agrarian labour force and a rural population held as pariahs by the landowners. Not a few of these are absentees from the land which they have long owned and have little contact with their semiserfs, who live, it is well to repeat, in the condition of pariahs, while the urban workers and also the employees of the commercial establishments and banks and the public employees in the cities during recent decades have benefited from the legislation protecting labour and promoting social welfare. It was a situation in which the greater part of the rural population of Brazil was used on the rudest work on plantations and farms, on the estates of men with a mentality quite different from that which years ago characterized the relations between the landowners and their labourers, when the former were, most of them, a rural gentry: not only proprietors deeply attached to their estates but masters attentive to the needs of their workers in accordance with the patriarchal forms of association.[5]

# 8

## Rural Community
## Organization and Development

In this chapter attention is directed to some major aspects of rural community development in Brazil. Consideration is first given to the concept of community itself and to the new connotations of the term "development." Second, a few of the potent impediments to programs of community development are identified and analyzed briefly. Next, because the main tissues of community group solidarity are the features that must be dealt with in any realistic program of community development, four of these and the ways in which they have functioned are given special consideration. In order to do this, comparisons of the locality groups in the United States with those of Brazil are made to help bring out as clearly as possible the nature of Brazil's communities. Finally, four basic questions about community development, requiring decisions early in any substantial program of rural community development, are raised and discussed briefly.

### Basic Concepts

Anyone who endeavors to understand the proper specific meaning of the word "community," as it is used by persons in all walks of life, is dealing with a conceptual morass. Likewise one should not assume that those who make frequent use of the term "development" are agreed upon the connotations of the word, or

First published in *Luso-Brazilian Review* 10, No. 1 (1973), and reprinted with the permission of the University of Wisconsin Press.

that they are familiar with a connotation acquired since about 1950. In general, the term "community" is used in so many senses that it has come to signify all mutuality; hence now the sociologist who makes reference to a community has a heavy professional obligation to be precise and explicit relative to the sense in which he is using the word.

It also seems advisable to stress that in no other part of the world is the rural sociologist who speaks or writes about a community and community development under a stronger professional obligation to employ precise definitions of the terms than the one who works in Brazil. The guidance that can be derived from thorough familiarity with the works of Galpin, Sanderson, Taylor, Zimmerman, Nelson, Brunner, Loomis, Leonard, Sanders, Hillery, and others who have contributed to our knowledge of the community is essential if the need is to be met.[1] This is because in the assistance programs of the United States and other countries, the activities of international agencies, including the United Nations and the Organization of American States, and of many other private and public organizations, "community development" has come to denote nothing more than the promotion at the local level of social welfare activities and self-help programs of all kinds.

Consider briefly the nature of a community and an adequate definition of the term. First, professional sociologists agree that the community is a group, a social group. This at least tells us what a community is not; and it offers some bases for detecting some of the confused or unclear ways in which the expression is employed. For example, if a community is a group, it cannot be a "subculture." Of course it may *have* a subculture. Second, those sociologists who have considered the term most carefully also seem agreed that it is one of the groups in which the area involved forms an indispensable component, or, in brief, that it belongs in the category of locality groups. Those who go this far have taken the first step in the formulation of an adequate definition—they have referred the item being defined to a class, that made up of social groups, and even to the restricted category of locality groups.

The fundamental difficulty, however, is encountered when anyone in a strictly logical way seeks to take the second of the two indispensable steps in the rigidly demanding intellectual work of definition. Just as the precise criteria needed to differentiate mankind from the remainder of the animal kingdom are applied rarely if ever, so do many sociologists and anthropologists still have to demonstrate that they can formulate and apply consistently an exact means of distinguishing the community from other social groups.

Robert M. MacIver's proposal is, in my opinion, the most satisfactory of those made to date. Sometime ago, he wrote as follows: "Any circle of people who live together, who belong together, so that they share, not this or that particular interest, but a whole set of interests wide enough and complete enough to include their lives is a community."[2] This formulation is considerably more adequate than the one by Park and Burgess, which long weighed heavily in sociological circles:

> Community is the term which is applied to societies and social groups where they are considered from the point of view of the geographical distribution of the individuals and institutions of which they are composed. . . . An individual may belong to many social groups but he will not ordinarily belong to more than one community, except in so far as a smaller community of which he is a member is included in a larger of which he is also a member.[3]

Much of our inadequacy in dealing with the nature and definition of community arises because of the paucity of designations we have for the numerous societal entities which belong together in the category of locality groups. In this aspect of the building of our discipline we sociologists simply have not done our taxonomic "homework." In a certain sense, of course, the family, the state, and the administrative subdivisions of the latter all may be considered as locality groups. This, though, never is done. If it were the case, except for the family, the solidarity of most of the groups involved would be slight and ineffective. Likewise all hamlets, villages, towns, and cities might be considered as locality groups. In practice, though, other than in the cases of the hamlets and villages in areas where the farmers reside in small nuclei and commute to their plots of land in the surrounding areas, such a procedure would be roughly comparable to a classification in the field of biology that would place the nucleus of a cell in one category and omit the remainder of the entity from consideration.

We can put all such matters aside, however, and still have for consideration at least a dozen genuine social groups which belong together in a class or category of locality groups. About half of these are rural entities, but in my own search of the literature I have encountered only two designations for the variety of types involved. These are (1) neighborhood and (2) community. Unless one is inclined to dispute the validity of Cooley's basic thinking, and I personally am not, the term "neighborhood" should be restricted to denote only those locality groups that also qualify as primary groups, that is the ones characterized by frequent, intimate, and face-to-face contact and association.[4]

Everything else in the range, from the social entity consisting of a small hamlet plus the families living in its service area, to that involving the greatest metropolitan center and the hinterland tributary to it, may go under the name of community. The use of modifiers such as rural, urban, rurban, and metropolitan helps to some extent. But except for such combinations as "partial" community, "semi" community, and "incomplete" community[5] even they have little utility in our endeavors to know, understand, and describe locality groups which are too large and complex to be eligible for classification as neighborhoods, and too small and too deficient in ways and means for satisfying the needs of their residents to qualify even as rural communities. Between the neighborhood, at the lower end of the series, and the metropolitan community, at the upper extreme, there are about ten other clearly distinguishable groups in which area or locale is one of the indispensable components of the oneness and mutuality on the part of the members. Together the set constitutes a series in which $X_1$ is the neighborhood, $X_2$ the smallest locality group which is not also a primary group, $X_3$, $X_4$, and possible $X_5$ are still larger and more complete subcommunities, the X's next in order are rural and other still larger communities, and $X_n$ is the great metropolitan community.[6]

"Development" is another term to which the sociologist must attend, irrespective of whether it stands alone or is paired with others to form such widely used combinations as community development, rural development, social development, economic development, and agricultural development. The word development long has figured in the English language to denote such ideas as unfolding, unrolling, evolving, and so forth. Until recently it certainly has not been used to designate directed movement towards a consciously established goal. Similar was the practice in Spanish and Portuguese relative to its equivalents in those languages, *desarrollo* and *desenvolvimento,* respectively. In all three tongues the meaning which is equivalent to ''social telesis'' as developed by Lester F. Ward is a recent addition. Moreover, the manner in which this bit of growth took place simultaneously in the three languages is interesting.

Before the Second World War and the rapid improvement in the means of communication and transportation, contacts between persons from the four corners of the earth were minute in comparison with what they had become by 1950. In prior centuries there had been no particular reason for those from any one part of the world to tone down or conceal the well-known enthnocentric tendency for each people to consider itself as vastly superior to all others. Furthermore, during the first half of the twentieth century the rapid urbanization and industrialization that had been taking place in parts of some of the larger and more powerful nations had produced in them a system of values wherein a high degree of urbanization based upon industrialization represented an advanced stage in the scale of social and economic existence, whereas agricultural and pastoral activities were disdainfully considered to be outmoded and backward ways of gaining a livelihood. Indeed, as the desire to acquire automobiles, bicycles, radios, cameras, refrigerators, outboard motors, television sets, and thousands of other manufactured products rapidly spread to all parts of the globe, whether or not a given country was in a position to manufacture the articles needed to satisfy that desire, soon came to be a major criterion for distinguishing the ''have'' countries from the ''have-nots.'' All of this was at its maximum on the eve of the total collapse of the European colonial system, when industrialization was largely confined to Europe, parts of North America, and Japan. Before 1950 it was the rule of ethnocentric, patronizing representatives of urban and industrialized societies to refer to themselves as ''advanced'' nations and to designate as ''backward'' the peoples and societies whose economies were based on agricultural and pastoral activities.

The great confrontation took place soon after the end of the Second World War, when the representatives of people from all parts of the earth met in San Francisco to draw up a charter for the United Nations and to organize the specialized agencies. In these gatherings of people from all parts of the world the "advanced-backward" dichotomy suddenly ceased to be tenable. Under these circumstances "developed" quickly came to denote urbanized and industrialized and "underdeveloped" or "undeveloped" became a euphemism for backward. The next step was inevitable. "Development" was seized upon as the designation for the process of changing from the less desirable stage to the other, and this sense of purposeful change directed to previously established goals become the one with which social scientists came to deal. For present purposes it may be stated that rural community development either is a synonym for the organization of fairly large, strong, self-sufficient locality groups, or else it merely adds to the list of hazy, amorphous terms that clutter up the language.

## Hindrances to Programs of Community Development

Those interested in rural community development in Brazil are hampered by the paucity of serious, analytical studies of the nature, anatomy or structure, functions and roles, and so on, of the various locality groups in the large half continent involved. It is true that in recent years a flood of so-called community studies has appeared. Many of these contain interesting and significant information about segments of the cultures and societies of Brazil. However, even a cursory examination will show that most of what currently are labeled as "community studies" are in reality studies of society in miniature and that most of them deal very little or not at all with the fundamental aspects of the community as such. In its finest form, as exemplified by the works of such men as Willems and Wagley,[7] this approach contributes greatly to an understanding of society and social institutions in Brazil. This is especially true if care is taken to delineate and describe precisely the boundaries of the locality group being studied. However, the reports on many "community studies" are largely juxtapositions of items of information about various cultural features, social groups, social institutions, and so on, which are unified only by the bindings of the volume in which they appear. In not a few of them, one can strike out the word "community" every time it appears and insert some other noun such as "village," "settlement," "district," or the name of the countylike municipio involved, without in any way changing the meaning of the text. This means merely that attention has been focused upon certain social and cultural phenomena as these are found conveniently located in a given small geographical area, and that little serious effort has been made to ascertain, analyze, and set forth the salient facts about a community as such. Many of the so-called community studies of the type under discussion are little more than mere cataloging in its most superficial form, with the topics of greatest significance indiscriminately intermingled with hosts of trivia.

Except for the few efforts to delineate in a tried and tested manner the peripheries of certain locality groups, the study of the Brazilian community and its structure, functions, and differentiating characteristics is still to be done. Analysis is needed of the essential features of the Brazilian rural community, its structural types, its functions, its relationships to smaller locality groups, and the extent to which it complements or competes with larger communities (rurban, urban, and metropolitan). This must be done before we shall have the information essential for weighing the comparative advantages and disadvantages to it of any specific proposals for community development.

The wide variety of rural community types found in Brazil poses another large problem for those attempting to formulate programs of genuine community development for that country. From the point of view of structural types alone, almost every kind of community ecological pattern devised by the ingenuity of man will be found somewhere between Rio Grande do Sul and Roraima. The simplest form, i.e., the type involving the village settlement pattern (in which the rural community consists of the village nucleus where the farmers' homes and outbuildings are constructed, plus the surrounding area occupied by their fields, pastures, and woodlands), such as predominate in rural Mexico, however, is largely lacking. And in Brazil, as in the United States, the prevailing structural form of the rural community is that in which the entity consists of a village trade, service, and ceremonial center and a surrounding tributary zone. In this type, the agriculturists live either on single farmsteads or in small clusters of huts and houses that have been erected on the fazendas and plantations of the area.

But these arrangements are not stable, and this fact greatly complicates the work of producing and applying practicable and effective programs of community planning and development. As indicated elsewhere in this chapter, the equilibrium involved is an uneasy one, much resembling that of water that is heated to the critical point of 212 degrees Fahrenheit. The rapid construction of modern systems of communication and transportation is tumbling the barriers which not long ago limited the world of the rural Brazilian family to the area within a very short radius of its home. This enlargement of horizons is accompanied by changes and improvements in the ways of farming which, along with attractive forces in the cities, have produced an immense rural exodus. About 1965 the urban population of Brazil came to outnumber the rural. For present purposes the important thing about this is the fact of rural depopulation. This means that any realistic plans for community development plans and programs for many ·rural areas must be made for many fewer people than are now living in those districts. In areas where the structural type is based on agricultural villages, the best solution would seem to be to make use of one of the innovations introduced in Israel. This would involve (1) the development of one centrally located village as a fairly complete trade, service, and ceremonial center; and (2) the introduction of measures that would eliminate the necessity for each of the surrounding villages to maintain full community status. In realistic community development programs in these districts, many villages must be assisted to adjust to the role of satellite where each individually maintains only a part of the essential institutions and depends upon central village for the remainder.[8]

The uneasy and unstable nature of the equilibrium found at any stated time in the locality group structure of a nation or a region is another reality or impediment that must be faced by those in Brazil who are attempting to bring about directed social change of a type that would entitle it to be called community development. For example, rapid improvement in the systems of communication and transportation, such as those that have been introduced suddenly in many widely separated parts of the world during the twentieth century, may completely upset the tenuous balance existing between the hamlets, villages, towns, and cities of a given area. This is because the building of modern rapid and cheap means of communication and transportation promotes the growth of some population centers which form the nuclei of certain locality groups, partially at the expense of the others. This constituted a severely disrupting factor in the United States between 1900 and 1940 when the perfection of the automobile and motor truck, the slow acquisition of knowledge about road building, the development and dissemination of the radio, and so on, required several decades. Presently, however, all of the technology involved may be, and often actually is, applied almost overnight to bring about a complete metamorphosis in the systems of communication and transportation in specific parts of Brazil. In the nineteenth century the application of steam to move trains of cars and the building of the railroads in the United States profoundly affected the fortunes of many thousands of population centers. These railways sounded the death knell for some villages and towns and breathed life into others. Now this situation is being paralleled in Brazil by the manner in which the building of roads and highways, and to some extent the use of the airplane, is changing radically the comparative advantage of all types of population centers. The relatively stable equilibrium of the locality-group structure, long a feature of Brazilian society, is presently being upset by drastic changes and readjustments.

To foretell the exact ways and the full extent to which the disruption of the equilibrium will contribute to change in the sizes, importance, functions, roles, and mutual interdependence of neighborhoods, various kinds of subcommunities, and of rural, rurban, urban, and metropolitan communities throughout Brazil is impossible. It would be a mistake, however, to postulate any changes which would be based upon the assumption that, as the decades succeed one another, the social differentiation of a given society will tend to decrease. Nevertheless, it is fairly certain that in the years immediately ahead, neighborhoods, partial and incomplete communities, and even large numbers of the rural communities will lose ground in their competition with the larger communities. Many of the loyalties and attachments, and much of the patronage of the residents of villages and open-country areas of Brazil will be transferred from the smallest trade and ceremonial centers to the larger, more diversified and more completely equipped population, trade, and service centers.[9] In connection with rural community development, this change indicates that Brazil should concentrate upon the objectives of developing as fully as possible complementary relationships among the nuclei of the locality groups in a given region. It would be even better if each project were to concentrate upon the population centers which are tributary to a single great city. Irrespective, though, of whether the area involved is a region, on the one hand, or the part of the metropolitan community which is outside the limits of the central city, on the other, the course of action should be clear and definite. It would be the utmost folly to attempt to "organize" or to "develop" as strictly self-sufficient entities all of the locality groups involved.


## The Tissues in Community Solidarity

The major tissues in the webs of social relationships that constitute locality groups, communities, in many instances, and neighborhoods and other subcommunity units, in most cases, must be mentioned briefly. This is especially true in connection with the efforts of those reared and trained in the United States to observe, analyze, and describe the most salient features of the locality-group structure of Brazilian society. For example, in the United States the emphasis is upon the economic factors, with major attention in community delineation being given to interests and attachments involving commerce, trade, the market, transportation, processing of farm products, and so on. From about 1915, or the days of Galpin's pioneering work until the present, the terms trade and service center, trade zone, and banking zone have been major components of our concept of the rural community. In contemporary Mexico, however, the group of outstanding young professionals employed by the Instituto de Investigaciones Sociales—whom it was my privilege to have in a graduate seminar at the National University—convinced me that in all parts of Mexico it is more accurate to consider the ceremonial function as the primary one in community solidarity and to relegate trade and all matters pertaining to the market to a far less prominent place. This is in Mexico where, unlike the situation in Brazil, the Church was for decades a chief target of revolutionary activities. In Mexico after almost four centuries in which there was little or no differentiation between the functions of Church and state, the latter quickly assumed a dominant and repressive position and the former was forced to rely chiefly upon subterranean activities in order to carry on at all. These cataclysmic events suddenly modified basic Church-state relationships in Mexico, but even so, religious and ceremonial interests seem to play the primary role in locality group solidarity. Whether this operates largely in favor of neighborhoods and other small locality groups, or coincides with the administrative unit to promote the strength of the larger community is still to be ascertained. Probably, though, the first of these alternatives is the general rule.

The facts just mentioned pertaining to Mexico suggest that it is well to emphasize the significance of these three categories (economic, administrative, and religious) of social ties or bonds. Special attention should be given to the manner in which each of them functions to produce the social solidarity of the locality group in the United States, on the one hand, and in Brazil, on the other.

As consideration is given to the influences in community solidarity that are exerted by the religious congregations, governmental and administrative units, and trade and commercial zones of influence, one should keep in mind the fact that the range of none of these is constant. The area influenced by each of them in the production of the solidarity of the locality group varies tremendously from place to place and even within a given society from one period to another.

For example, trade and commerce as carried on by means of a country store may be a principal force in integrating and perpetuating a neighborhood or other small locality group. This economic institution, effective only within a short radius of its location, long was a powerful factor in shaping the locality group structure of the United States. In most parts of this country by 1900, however, small clusters of more specialized retail outlets situated in villages and small towns had become the major integrating force of a substantial rural community, one made up of the trade and service center and the open-country area economically tributary to it. This represented a drastic change in the role of a given factor, merely with the passage of time. In Brazil, in sharp contrast, the same economic factors, i.e., trade and commerce, in the form of a weekly market, and subject to little competition from established stores and shops, often operate over a sizable district to help produce the unity and solidarity of a rural or even rurban community.

Similarly, the religious congregation, if it is exemplified by the small open-country church such as has persisted in large parts of the United States wherein religious differentiations are extremely great, may be one of the chief causes for the continued significance of the neighborhood; whereas, if it is represented by the large parish or congregation, which is characteristic of the Roman Catholic Church, as is commonly true of Brazil, it may be the chief unifying force of the rural community. In view of the variation in the range over which the influence of a given factor is spread, it seems well to discuss briefly a few of the principal differences between Brazil and the United States in this aspect of locality group organization. In order to do so, attention is directed in turn to each of the following factors: (1) economic bonds; (2) the religious congregation; (3) the local governmental or administrative unit; (4) the school, public or private.

### The Economic Bonds

Trade and commerce long have been the major function of the small population center that is the nucleus of the rural community in the United States. Moreover, from the early 1930s on, the county seat has enjoyed so many advantages over its rivals that its trade and commerce have been powerful factors in the growth of larger rurban and urban communities. In Brazil, though, even now in most cases, the economic functions of the village or town are severely limited. Except for the feverish trading activities that take place weekly, when the open market is held in the central plaza, in many parts of the country merchandising is at a minimum. Only as roads are built and motor traffic increases do established retail stores become of any considerable importance in the places that form the centers of many locality groups. The weekly market strengthens to some extent the unity of the larger or municipio-wide community, whereas when specialized retail outlets that are open daily make their appearance they tend to promote the importance of subcommunity locality groups.

Trade and commerce also are among the first activities to separate or differentiate from the pattern in which the limits of all the fundamental community ties tend to coincide. Thus, a given family may begin to frequent the market in a fairly large center in the countrylike municipio adjacent to the one in which it lives without any notice being taken of that fact. The head of such a family must, however, meet the civil and legal exactions put upon him by the provincial and central governments in the seat of the municipio where he lives. Likewise, he must go to this seat in order to make his petition to the *prefeito* and await the decision of that august local representative of the law and the government. Similarly, his religious obligations must all be met there. Hence, in Brazil the economic factor seems to be becoming more important in determining the nature and solidarity of locality groups. It favors to some extent the smaller centers, and it is helping promote differentiation of a type that will enable a part of a family's interests and attachments to be extended beyond the limits of its own local administrative unit.

## The Religious or Congregational Ties

Consider next some of the essential facts with respect to the role of the religious bond in the solidarity of rural communities and the smaller locality groups. In the United States the high degree of religious differentiation and the persistence of the open-country church have made the religious factor one of the most potent agencies in the preservation of the neighborhood and various partial or semicommunities as significant structural features of our society. Indeed, they are likely to be fully as important as the rural community itself in the equilibrium to which we shall have moved by 1975 or 1980.

The situation is very different in the most tradition-bound parts of Brazil, especially those in which the cultivation of crops such as sugar cane and coffee bring about a relatively high density of population. In this case, the traditional estate was a little barony wherein the orders of the proprietor (the *senhor de engenho* or the fazendeiro) were the law and his decisions constituted the small realm's system of justice. This little dominion was a neighborhood (for it definitely was a primary group), and in many cases it also was a completely self-sufficient rural community. The chapel was an adjunct to the master's manor house and the priest was merely one of his assortment of lieutenants.

## The Bonds of Local Government and Administration

The local administrative or governmental unit in Brazil has a role in strengthening or weakening community solidarity that is quite distinct from the one it plays in the United States. It is true that the Brazilian town or village has a superficial likeness to the small population center located in the United States, and the municipio may appear at first glance to be a close counterpart of the county. But the Brazilian village or town is never a municipality, as that term is used in the United States, i.e., an entity empowered by charter to function locally and independently in order to meet certain needs of its residents. Instead, its officials are those who hold authority over all of the administrative district in which it is located irrespective of whether such authority is elective or appointive. Usually it is merely a convenient subdivision for administering the laws and policies of a state or the nation.

To differentiate the Brazilian municipio from the county in the United States, it is necessary to attend specifically to the proper designations for the types of administration or government involved. Both the county and the municipio are local governmental units, the smallest functional divisions into which the states (except in New England, where the "towns" are genuine entities) are divided. In the United States, though, it is common and also logically defensible to refer to the counties as entities of local self-government; and indeed the entire nature of our system of social organization would be radically different if the counties did not have and exercise the responsibility for primary and secondary schools, for the protection of life and property, for health and welfare services, and so forth. By no stretch of the imagination can they be thought of as convenient subdivisions for the purpose of carrying out at the local level the policies of the national government.

In Brazil, however, the "self-government" features of the local subdivisions are few and poorly supported. In fact they are so weak that the "debility of local government" must soon become evident to every serious student of the subject. The lack of authority and tradition in the local use of the general property tax is, of course, a major expression of this. It is indicative not only of the inapplicability of the expression "self government," but also of the resulting lack of schools, inadequate protection for life and property, and the slight effort devoted to construction and upkeep of local roads and trails. In Brazil, it is true, much authority is generated and applied locally, but this is largely the traditional "persuasiveness" of the large landed proprietor who owns and controls the land and all other means of production, and who is accustomed to govern a municipio as though it were still a little barony over which he exercises an exclusive right to rule. In contemporary Brazil this is commonly known, and with increasing frequency denounced as *coronelismo*. For present purposes, though, it is important to stress that in Brazil there is little in the way of local "self-government" unless "self" in the expression is limited so that it denotes exclusively the head of a powerful clan who rules about as he pleases over his small dominion.

From what has been said it should be evident that, from the standpoint of community solidarity, in Brazil the limits of the local governmental tie correspond closely with those of the religious bond. They both embrace all of the people in all parts of the countylike administrative subdivision. The local governmental tie is weak, and probably in most cases it is relatively ineffective in promoting community solidarity; but definitely it never fosters the unity of subcommunity groupings, not even that of villages or hamlets. In some cases the abuses connected with the subjection to the same overlord may give the people of the entire district a keen awareness of the tyranny of their master so that they may realize fully the fact that "they all are in the same boat." This is especially true in Brazil where the powerful families traditionally have lived on their estates.

## The Distinctive Role of the School in Community Solidarity

The role of the school in rural locality group solidarity is radically different in Brazil from what it is in the United States. The importance of the factor itself differs greatly. It is slight in many parts of rural Brazil, but of the utmost significance in the United States. In the former, the school does little to foster social solidarity of the neighborhoods, other small locality groups, or the rural communities. Some of the secondary schools located in major population centers help to polarize the social attachments of those living in the hinterlands, but as yet this is of minor importance. In the traditional patterns of rural social organization of the United States, however, the school (the one-room, open-country institution popularly known as "the little red schoolhouse") long rivaled the church congregation in effectiveness in keeping very small locality groups alive and functioning. Simultaneously, though, larger graded schools, generally with secondary work included, became key features of the village trade and service center which served as a nucleus for the typical rural community; and not infrequently in

recent decades the consolidation or centralization of high schools
(by tearing the educational hearts from existing rural communities)
has done much to reduce many locality groups to a subcommunity
level. At the same time they have helped elevate the towns in which
the new enlarged high schools are located to the status of nuclei of
rurban communities. In some states, such as Georgia and Texas,
school consolidation is combining with the influence of the
commercial factor to transform the county unit into something
deserving to be called a community. The experiences with schools
in the United States may be helpful in Brazil, as the development of
adequate systems of rural education becomes a key feature of
community development programs. In this aspect of rural
community planning and development, those in charge have the
opportunity of making a practically fresh start.

## Some Features of the Sociological Approach to Community Development

Finally, a few of the decisions of primary importance which must
be taken early in the process of a genuine community development
program in Brazil, elsewhere in America, or in any other part of the
world may be indicated.

1. First of all there is the problem of deciding whether, under the
name of community development, to go along with a set of
activities designed to foster self-help, engage piecemeal in rural
welfare endeavors, and so on, or to insist that the program must be
one which is designed to affect community entities and to make
them more effective locality groupings.

2. Providing it is decided that community development consists
of designing and putting into effect measures intended to develop
the locality groups known as communities, the next decision
involves the particular category or categories of those groups that
should be the objects of the program. Should it be the
subcommunities of various kinds, the rural communities, or the
rurban communities? To aid in the selection of the most appropriate
areas or units for the development programs envisioned, a thorough
knowledge of existing ecological arrangements, factors involved,
and nature and direction of societal trends is essential. Rarely is
such knowledge at hand. This is true even for Walworth County,

Wisconsin, and the Canton of Turrialba in Costa Rica, the two rural areas in the entire world that have been the objects of the greatest amounts of rural sociological research. A thorough understanding of the forces impinging upon the locality groups of a country, however, may be fully as important as a detailed knowledge of the "corpus societus" itself. For example, a rapid improvement of a country's systems of transportation and communication may checkmate a program of community development, or it might even make "directed social change" move in a direction exactly opposite from the one desired. This could easily take place where a development program was concerned primarily with small locality groups while the improvements in communication and transportation were enabling those living in the rural districts to visit easily, quickly, and economically the thriving little urban centers which are the nucleus of emerging rurban communities.

3. The third decision to be made in planning a community development program in Brazil is whether or not the territory involved should coincide with that of some governmental or administrative district which is empowered to assess taxes, collect them, and expend the funds secured for local purposes. In Brazil, as elsewhere, the requirements for community services are so numerous and so strong that they cannot be met with funds secured by purely voluntary contributions. When the community lacks authority to use the tax power, the essential services either are sadly neglected or the responsibility rests with some entity other than the community. The central government is most likely to retain this authority. This in turn means that bales of red tape ensnarl the efforts to establish and maintain schools in community X, to build a culvert on a local road in community Y, or to protect the coffee crop from thieves in community Z. Thus, whether or not the community unit is to exercise the power to tax may very well be the most important decision required in planning genuine community development programs. Moreover, if the decision is in the affirmative, then the units to be reorganized, reformed, strengthened, or vitalized necessarily must be the countylike administrative subdivisions called municipios. There are no others. In some parts of Brazil, such as São Paulo and Minas Gerais, however, the municipios already are of a size that would permit them to become genuine communities, and judicious consolidations in some cases and subdivisions in others could produce many more.

Fortunately, the community is such a resilient cell that given an opportunity it can adjust its size and shape to an extraordinary degree.

One other matter is related to this point. If administrative subdivisions larger than municipios are to be the units of community development programs, so that more developed rurban or small urban communities are the goals, the areas involved must consist of groups of entire municipios. This means the role of principal nucleus for the head town of the central administrative subdivision, and those of satellites for the head towns of the others.

4. The last of the decisions that should be made prior to embarking upon a program of community development in Brazil pertains to the relative importance of the two types of solidarity in the communities involved. Is mechanistic solidarity, that is, the mutuality generated because of the members of the community being alike in most important features, to be in the ascendancy? Or is it proposed to foster additional social differentiation, division of labor, and specialization, so that the resulting lack of self-sufficiency by any specific members of the community and mutual interdependence will promote solidarity of the organic type? It may be, however, that in our days the decision or choice is rather clear-cut. The choice may be between simply struggling against an overwhelming tide as expressed by the rapidly declining importance of mechanistic social solidarity (a primary-group relationship), and seeking to cooperate with the trend of the times by making the most of division of labor, specialization, commercialization, and all the other features of what now is considered as evidences of a "developed" society.

# Religious Differentiation and Syncretism

For all those interested in the genuine comparative method of study, Brazil offers a rich field for study in many aspects of society, especially in relation to the important religious institutions. By the true comparative method I mean procedures whereby a given social scientist, using exactly the same frame of reference and the same ways of getting and analyzing pertinent data, undertakes to compare and contrast features of the social organization and social processes in two or more societies; and the features of Brazil's religious institutions which I personally have spent the most time in studying and comparing with those in the United States are the processes of differentiation and syncretism. Consequently these are the subjects to which this exposition is devoted.

Before I began my extensive travels through the great rural sections of Brazil, where at the time of my first visits in 1942 and 1943 about 80 percent of all Brazilians were living, it seemed apparent that the religious homogeneity was very great. I took for granted that the rural Brazilians were almost exclusively adherents of the Roman Catholic Church, and that the relatively few Protestants in the country were concentrated in a few of the principal cities and towns. Then I could let my mind ponder the probable social effects of this homogeneity and how different life in the Brazilian rural community (with all of the people of one faith, members of one church congregation, and believers in a single set of religious ideas and practices) must be from that in the typical, highly differentiated rural community in the United States. However, the longer I remained in Brazil and the more familiar I became with religious thinking and practices, the less I was impressed by Brazil's religious homogeneity. The lack of other conspicuous church buildings and the prominence of the Catholic

Cathedral near the center of each village or town does not signify complete unity of religious belief and practice. In fact, a thorough knowledge of the richness of symbolism and belief of Catholicism gives only partial understanding of the religious beliefs, practices, and motivations of Brazil's people. As my close friend and associate, the noted Brazilian anthropologist Arthur Ramos, wrote: "The most advanced forms of religion, even among the most cultured people, do not exist in a pure state. Besides the official religion there are subterranean activities, among the backward strata of society, among the poorer classes, or, in heterogeneous peoples, among the ethnic groups, that are most backward culturally." Although the upper classes and the official religion of a society may have freed themselves to a considerable extent of animistic beliefs and magical practices, such is not the case among the less enlightened masses. "This fundamental form—incarnations of totemic, animistic, and magical beliefs—survives in spite of the most advanced religious and philosophical conceptions of the superior strata of societies."[1] From an intimate knowledge of the great cities of Rio de Janeiro and Bahia, more than a passing contact with many other parts of the country including his native Alagoas, and an acquaintance with Brazilian scientific literature, this eminent authority generalized as follows:

> We [Brazilians] still live under the full dominion of a magical world, still impermeable, to a certain extent, to the influxes of a true culture. . . . Brazil lives impregnated by magic. The medicine man, the fetisheer, has among our populations a prestige considerably greater than the directors of our destinies—it is necessary to have the courage to confess it. Because he is the image of the primitive Father, in the silence of the night there are elegant ladies and gentlemen of high rank who go to the *macumbas* [Afro-Brazilian religious cults and ceremonies of Bantu origin] to consult the invisible power of Pae Joaquim, Sezinho Curunga, or Jubiaba. Padre Cicero of Joazeiro dominates multitudes. Santa Dica is an inspired person [*illuminada*]. And any prophet with cabalistic formulas or medicine man with magical concoctions attracts a large clientele. A specter, the power of *mana*, dominates the festivals. . . . The Negro carnival is our great festival.[2]

The significance of the African religious heritage in contributing to the heterogeneity of religious beliefs and practices in Brazil is strongly evidenced by the materials on syncretism presented later in this chapter. However, before concentrating upon recent trends in religious differentiation in Brazil, it seems necessary to indicate briefly why the position of the Roman Catholic Church there has been much less strong than in most parts of Spanish America.

That the Roman Catholic Church never gained a control in Brazil comparable with the absolute sway it exercised in Mexico, Peru, and other parts of Spanish America is well established. More than a hundred years ago, Kidder summed up the situation as follows:

> On few subjects do Brazilian writers, of all classes, express themselves with greater unanimity of opinion than respecting the state of religion in the country. People and ecclesiastics, officers of state, men of business, and politicians, all agree in representing the condition and prospects of religion as low and unpromising.[3]

Then he documented his generalization with a lengthly translation of the report of the Minister of Justice and Ecclesiastical Affairs for 1843 which reads in part:

> The state of retrogression into which our clergy are falling is notorious. The necessity of adopting measures to remedy such an evil is also evident. On the 9th of September, 1842, the government addressed inquiries on this subject to the bishop and capitular vicars. Although complete answers have not been received from all of them, yet the following particulars are certified.
>
> The lack of priests who will dedicate themselves to the cure of souls, or who even offer themselves as candidates, is surprising. In the province of Pará there are parishes which, for twelve years and upwards, have had no pastor. The district of the river Negro, containing some fourteen settlements, has but one priest; while that of the river Solimoens is in similar circumstances. In the three comarcas of Belém, the Upper and the Lower Amazon, there are thirty-six vacant parishes. In Maranham twenty-five churches have, at different times, been advertised as open for applications, without securing the offer of a single candidate.
>
> The bishop of S. Paulo affirms the same thing respecting

vacant churches in his diocese, and it is no uncommon
experience elsewhere. In the diocese of Cuyaba, not a single
church is provided with a settled curate, and those priests who
officiate as state supplies, treat the bishop's efforts to instruct
and improve them with great indifference.

In the bishopric of Rio de Janeiro most of the churches are
supplied with pastors, but a great number of them only
temporarily. This diocese embraces four provinces, but during
nine years past not more than five or six priests have been
ordained per year.[4]

In fact it seems fair to generalize that in Brazil the priest often
was merely one of the dependents of the country squire and the
church an adjunct to the planter's palatial home. This is a far cry
from the situation in Spanish America where the *sacerdote* was
absolute master of all that he saw, and the church the repository of
all that was of value in the community.

It is an involved complex of circumstances that led the Portuguese
colonies to diverge so radically from those of Spain in this respect,
but one of the most important causes seems to be self-evident. As
described by Kidder:

The regulations under which the clergy of Brazil are now
suffering, were established as far back as 1752. By a royal
decree of that date, all the tithes of the Portuguese ultra marine
possessions were secularized, being made payable to the state,
while the state became responsible for the support of the
clergy. The obvious reason for this regulation was the
discovery that the state could support the church much cheaper
than the church would support itself, while the tithes remained
at the disposal of the priesthood. This was too fine an
opportunity for speculation to be neglected by a government
crippled and degraded for lack of funds, and, at the same time,
having the power to exercise its pleasure.

The arrangement proved no less profitable than convenient;
and once being established, could not be changed. The
government put the priests on short allowance, and fixed their
salaries at fifty, eighty, and one hundred milreis—sums which
have been lessening ever since, by a depreciation of the
currency. Efforts have been made in Brazil since the era of
independence, to raise the stipend of the clergy, and they have

been nominally successful, although the present salary of two hundred milreis, is scarcely more valuable than the sum of one hundred formerly was.[5]

The sociologists who have studied most intensively the social aspects of the Roman Catholic Church in Brazil have described the differentiation that is taking place among Catholics. Thus the able French sociologist, Roger Bastide, whose knowledge of Brazilian religious phenomena is second to none, indicated the differences between what he denoted as "rural Catholicism and urban Catholicism." The first of these he described as follows:

Rural Catholicism has remained very nearly the old colonial or imperial Catholicism, not only because the rural groups are essentially more traditional but because the lack of priests prevents a deeper education in the faith. It is more familial and more social, also more tarnished with superstitions. It is a religion that has remained in the *do ut des,* the promise made to a healing saint if he grants such and such a grace, a boon, a good marriage, an abundant harvest. The promise consists, if the saint responds to the prayer, of making a pilgrimage, of begging alms to provide a feast for the saint, or of depositing an ex-voto in such and such a chapel. Hence, there is an abundance of churches to which "miracle rooms" are attached, with legs, hands, or heads in wax or crudely carved in wood by some rural image maker. But if in spite of everything the grace is not bestowed, then the faithful turns against the saint. He is removed from the familial oratory in order to take him to another house, or is plunged head-down into a well and told that he will remain in that uncomfortable position until he grants the prayer.

But this Catholicism, utilitarian as it is, is sincere. It is like an integrating part of the personality. . . . Brazilian rural Catholicism is turned more to the worship of the saints and the Virgin than of God, and these saints vary according to the regions, as well as according to families. Bom Jesus da Lapa is especially adored in the São Francisco region as is Bom Jesus de Pirapora in the state of São Paulo. The rural families of Minas Gerais maintain the worship of the Holy Cross and plant one before the doors of their dwellings. . . . Religion cannot live without the rites where souls join. It has been indicated that the distances prevent the priest from officiating in the interior. Thus, in order to survive, this rural Catholicism is obliged to create its own institutions and to invent its own chiefs. Nearly everywhere one finds *resadores,* sometimes an old Negro, sometimes a *Caboclo,* or a more or less literate white, who gathers some countrymen around a little private chapel and there recites the litanies and celebrates novenas. Thus, in the absence of the priest, faith, which feels the need of spiritual nourishment, elaborates its own means of conservation. But the layman who celebrates the rites often has only an elementary knowledge of dogma, when he has any at all, and one now understands why superstition can so readily graft itself on the Catholic trunk. The *resador* is not always and necessarily the *benezedor,* he who cures the disease of beasts as well as of men by making the sign of the cross and mumbling some Latin words—but very often he is.[6]

In sharp contrast are the essential features of what Bastide calls urban Catholicism. These he summarizes as follows:

Urban Catholicism is purer. It rests on a population that is perhaps more restrained but in any case more instructed in its duties. It binds the people together in its brotherhoods, its patronages, its confessional associations. The clergy there is closer to the faithful and thus the control of the Church over its members is stronger in the cities than in the rural zones. It follows the individual from childhood with the catechism to the most advanced age with Catholic Action, in order to educate and support him. The urban clergy is bound to the rest of universal Catholicism by the Catholic hierarchy of which it is a link. Thus it is the bastion of Romanism in Brazil. A complete strategy has been worked out to develop the inclination for communion by organizing paschal days, officers, functionaries, bankers, professors—and, in order to fight immorality, by organizing, for example, retreats during Carnival, Brazil's great pagan feast.

Urban Catholicism is, however, in great contrast to rural Catholicism, for it is necessary to take account of the heterogeneity of the urban population and the diversity of social classes. There is, however, even in the cities and especially in their lowest strata, a popular Catholicism, characterized by miraculous revelations and cures, and despite the orders of an always prudent clergy, by the extraordinary and the supernatural. This leads to the flourishing of more or less heterodox cults, such as that of Antoninho in São Paulo.[7]

More recently, an illuminating study of the religious institutions of São Paulo was made by Candido Procopio Ferreira de Camargo. He distinguished between the rural and urban variations of "traditional Catholicism" along the same general lines as Bastide; and then he went on to identify three varieties of a newer type which he calls "internationalized Catholicism." These three new types he designated as "traditionalistic," "progressive," and "modernized," respectively. All of them consist of persons faithful to the Church and general Church doctrine, but they are differentiated from one another by specific sets of religious values and norms of conduct to which the adherents of each subscribe.

Unlike "traditional" Catholicism, the "traditionalistic" form places no overwhelming emphasis on the continuity of tradition. Instead, it tends to reinterpret and idealize the past. Its values and norms favor the preservation of theological order, and the application of the idealization of the past to the social and economic affairs of the present. It strongly opposes proposals for change such as agrarian reform.

Those in the faction Camargo calls the "progressives" give primary importance to the values of social justice. They try to apply Christian values combined with concrete beliefs about the needs of Brazilian society that are derived from the social sciences and from the doctrines of populist and leftist political movements. In this group as a whole, the degree of radicalism varies greatly.

"Modernized" Catholicism, as described by Camargo, is the faith of those who try to unite Catholic doctrine and its values and norms with the theories of the behavioral sciences so as to produce a model society that is Catholic and also modern. Its advocates place great emphasis upon the need for religious behavior and instruction that is attuned to the needs of the family in modern urban society. It is doubtful whether Camargo or anyone else can give any accurate estimate of the absolute and relative importance of traditional Catholicism, rural and urban, and the several varieties of international Catholicism as they are in the 1970s in São Paulo and elsewhere in Brazil. Nevertheless, the mere fact that an accomplished scholar attempts such a classification itself is an evidence of considerable differentiation within the body of adherents to Roman Catholicism. That such developments also are taking place within the ecclesiastical hierarchy itself is evidenced by the published extent of the differences of thought and action between such high churchmen as Dom Helder Camara and his fellow bishops of the Brazilian Church.[8]

Religious developments connected with the various Protestant religious bodies are among the most striking changes in Brazilian religious life and culture since 1960. And of all the features of this part of religious differentiation that command the most attention, and justly so, is the phenomenal spread of the Pentecostal faith. The official statistics give no materials for the Pentecostal bodies as such, but both Camargo and Willems, who have made intensive study of the subject, are convinced that the upsurge of Pentecostalism is by far the most important feature of recent changes in Brazilian religious life. The major denominations involved are the Assemblies of God, the Christian Congregation, the Pentecostal Evangelical Church, and "Brazil for Christ." Camargo estimated that in the 1930s the members of these bodies made up no more than 10 percent of the Protestants in Brazil, and that by 1968 the proportion had risen to 60 percent. At the time he wrote, the "Brazil for Christ" organization was building in the city of São Paulo "the largest Christian temple in the world" with a capacity to seat 25,000 persons.[9]

Accompanying these developments are numerous other patterns of religious differentiation. The waxing importance and diversification of the spiritist or spiritualist movements is one of these. The proliferation and increased toleration of the Afro-Brazilian cults is another. The growth of the Umbanda groups, combining many elements taken from spiritist groups and African fetish cults is a third. And with the growth and spread of the Japanese population, the increased importance of Shinto and Buddhist beliefs and observance is a fourth. And the process is by no means slowing down. During the final quarter of the twentieth century, the student of religious differentiation and syncretism should find Brazil to be an ideal site for his studies.

## Syncretism

Syncretism, or the mixing and blending of the sociocultural components of religious systems, has been studied extensively by specialists who have sought to determine the relationships between the great religions in remote historical periods.[10] For significant materials on this important process in contemporary societies, however, one searches largely in vain. In the results of the sustained work of Arthur Ramos, a great Brazilian psychiatrist-anthropologist-sociologist, though, one finds a remarkable exception. Ramos spent his highly productive scientific career in helping to develop a systemized body of knowledge pertaining to the Brazilian Negro. In common with his teacher and mentor, Dr. Nina Rodrigues of the Medical School in Bahia, he early became convinced that he would never be able to understand, diagnose, and treat the mental illnesses of his Negro patients until he had become thoroughly familiar with their trances and other intense emotional religious experiences. Accordingly, for years in Bahia and subsequently in Rio de Janeiro he devoted his efforts to the study of the Negro, his cultural heritage, and above all to his religious cults and activities. In order to do this, almost inevitably he also had to train his perceptive mind on the relationships between the Afro-Brazilian beliefs and (1) the practices of the Roman Catholic Church, (2) those of Brazil's heterogeneous Indians, (3) those of the sizable numbers of spiritists and spiritualists, and (4) those of various groups of theosophists. In brief, Ramos spent an unusually brilliant scientific career in the study of a rich variety of religious institutions and activities. To a far greater extent than any other careful, objective observer, he sought to determine, analyze, and portray the process of syncretism in a modern society. It was my own good fortune to be closely associated with him during the period of his most fruitful studies from 1939 until his untimely death in 1949.[11] This came while a chapter on "The Negro in Brazil" which I had solicited, translated, and edited, a presentation in which he gave in summary form the principal results of his studies, was in press.[12] The contents of the following paragraphs are taken in slightly abridged form directly from the aforementioned chapter.

Consider first the beginning of the study of syncretism and the African cultures involved.

It fell to Dr. Raymundo Nina Rodrigues, professor of legal medicine in the Faculty of Medicine of Bahia, at the turn of the century to develop a method which was to revolutionize the studies of the Brazilian Negroes. This method consisted of the comparative study of the African cultures and of their survivals in Brazil, in an attempt to reconstitute the ethnic groups of the Negroes representing these cultures. This procedure, which was adopted much later by anthropological students of the Negro in other parts of the New World, permitted a general study of the Negro cultures in a way which corrected the deficiencies of the historical method.

Another result of the studies of Nina Rodrigues in Bahia was the demonstration of the phenomenon of the cultural syncretism, which modern anthropologists call acculturation. He studied the phenomenon in its religious aspect, demonstrating the fusion of African cultures with Catholicism, the dominant religion of the Brazilians, and also in other phases of the Negro cultures such as art, culinary practices, language, and folklore.

In these works of comparative ethnology Nina Rodrigues was able to demonstrate the cultural predominance of the Sudanese groups in Bahia, principally of the Yoruba Negroes, in contradiction to the assertions of the authors cited relative to the Bantu predominance. It is regrettable that Nina Rodrigues' studies were limited to the Bahia area, in which, at least culturally, the groups of Sudanese origin actually predominated. But by comparing his studies with others of the Negroes in the southern part of the country, and by continuing with direct investigations, today we have a more complete view of the ethnic groups of Negroes that were transported to Brazil.

In his attempt to reconstruct the African Negro cultures of Brazil, the contemporary scholar must try to overcome the historical difficulties through the direct study of the surviving Negro cultures. On the basis of the original researches of Nina Rodrigues in Bahia, those now being conducted by a number of investigators, and as a result of my own personal observations and researches, I propose the following provisional classification of the Negro cultures surviving in Brazil:

A. *Sudanese groups,* represented principally by the Yoruba

of Nigeria (Nagô, Ijêchá, Eubá or Egba, Ketu, Ibadan, Yebu or Ijegu, and lesser groups); by the Dahomans (the Gêge group—Ewe, Fon or Efan, and minor groups); by the Fanti and Ashanti from the Gold Coast (the Mina group proper); and by minor groups from Gambia, Sierra Leone, the Grain Coast (Liberia), and the Ivory Coast (Krumano, Agni, Zema, Timini . . .).

B. *Mohammedanized Guinea-Sudanese groups,* represented by the Peul (Fulah, Fula, etc.); by the Mandinga (Solinke, Bambara . . .); by the Hausa of northern Nigeria; and by lesser groups such as the Tapa, Bornu, and Gurunsi.

C. *Bantu groups,* made up of the innumerable tribes of the Angola-Congolese, and of those from the East Coast (Mozambique).

It must be emphasized that these cultural groups, identified by the survivals of their cultures in Brazil, no longer exist in a pure state, and are not even easily distinguishable. The work of acculturation has proceeded continuously. The Sudanese groups have mixed among themselves with a strong predominance of the Yoruba culture in Bahia, and their influence has been predominant among other groups of Negroes in other states. The Negro-Mahometan cultures were polarized about the Malê Negroes, and they also were preserved in Bahia. Dahoman survivals can be identified in Maranhão and in Bahia, alongside other Sudanese traditions. And the Bantu elements are dispersed throughout the agglomerations of Negroes in Minas Gerais, Rio de Janeiro, and, on a lesser scale, in other parts of the country.

We shall examine briefly these survivals, referring the reader who desires more of the details to the first volume of our work *Introdução a Antropologia Brasileria.*

Then for each of the three great Afro-Brazilian religious cults, in turn, Ramos described the salient features of the system and indicated the essential nature of the process of syncretism that was taking place. Consider first the Sudanese groups and their cults or *candomblés.*

At the opening of the nineteenth century the Kingdom of Dahomey dominated the entire Slave Coast of Africa and São João de Ajudá (Whydah) had been converted into the great slave emporium of the African West Coast. In this period the commercial relations between Whydah and Bahia were intensive, and from it dates the great flow of Yoruba Negroes, along with others from Dahomey and the Gold Coast, to Brazil. For this reason the generic denomination *Minas* was employed for all of the slaves coming from the Slave Coast, Dahomey, and the Gold Coast, when, strictly speaking, that designation should have been reserved for the Negroes from the Gold Coast (Fanti, Ashanti).

After Lagos lost its supremacy as a center of the slave trade, the traffic in Yoruba Negroes still went on and it continued even after the prohibition of the traffic. The great mass of the Yoruba Negroes was landed at Bahia, where they were known by the general designation of Nagôs, a name which the French gave to the Yoruba-speaking Negroes from the Slave Coast. Some tribal names such as Egbá and Yebu were also applied to the entire group.

Naturally the Yoruba Negroes were preferred in the Bahian slave markets. They were tall, strong, valiant, industrious, good-natured, and the most intelligent of all. Anthropologically, they were of two distinct types. The first of these were of a heavy black color, dolichocephalic, and had thick, drooping lips and very kinky hair; the second had a lighter skin and the other Negroid characteristics less pronounced. The Nagô in Bahia were also distinguished by their tribal tattooings, which consisted of three lines on each cheek. As time passed and mixing took place, the physical differences among the various groups of Negroes were eliminated, and tattooing was abandoned. They preserved only with tenacity a few of their cultural traits.

The Negroes from Dahomey received the general name of Gêges. The introduction of this group began very early, for the Portuguese supremacy in São João de Ajudá dates from remote times, and the traffic in slaves in this region was intense from the beginning of the colonization of Brazil until the nineteenth century. Already in the eighteenth century the Gêges were important in Bahia, and Dahomans from Ardra, or Allada—called for this reason Ardra Negroes—played a distinguished part in the war against the Dutch invaders of Brazil.

In the nineteenth century the supremacy of the Dahomans

over the other peoples of the Gulf of Guinea was established. Whydah, or São João de Ajudá of the Portuguese, became the principal port on the slave trade. From there were dispatched to Brazil not only the Negroes from Dahomey but also those from the Gold Coast and Nigeria. In Rio de Janeiro and other parts of the country they were known under the general name of Minas Negroes. The relations of Whyday with Bahia, with which the traffic was most intense, were so frequent that various merchants in Bahia were the recipients of distinctions conferred by the king of Dahomey.

The great majority of the Gêge Negroes were landed at Bahia, but some also were disembarked at Maranhão and Rio de Janeiro, where, as we have seen, they received the name of Minas. But their number was small in comparison with that of the Nagôs. They came from the central and coastal portions of Dahomey, from Ajudá, from Grand and Little Popo, from Agbomi, and Cotonou. They were of olive color, some groups of them being weak and idolent, and others such as the Fon (Efan in Bahia) ferocious and turbulent. Their culture was almost entirely absorbed by the Nagô group; but a few groups, as in Maranhão, still preserve their Dahoman traditions.

The Sudanese Negroes, predominantly Yoruban, were responsible for introducing into Brazil, and especially into Bahia, a body of cultural traits relating to religion, dress, the preparation of food, and folklore, which entitles us to speak of the Gêge-Nagô cultural survivals. These survivals are most readily distinguishable in the realm of religious culture. There has been preserved a Gêge-Nagô cult, which is predominantly Yoruban in Bahia and mainly Dahoman in Maranhão. In other parts of Brazil such as the Northeast, Rio de Janeiro, and Minas Gerais, it is greatly mixed with other African cults and with Indian elements. These cults, called *candomblés* in Bahia, *macumbas* in Rio de Janeiro, and *xangôs* in the Northeast are religious survivals left by the Sudanese Negroes.

The Bahian Negroes pay homage to a genuine pantheon of *orishas,* or Negro saints, all of them originating on the Slave Coast. In the line of orishas the most important is Obatalá, the "greatest of the saints." Xangó is another orisha, also possessed of great power. He is the god of lightning and of the storm. His cult is expremely popular throughout all Brazil, and for this reason his name has come to be used by extension in the Northeast as the designation of the Negro religious cult.

Ogun, another orisha much revered and feared, is the god of conflict and war. Exú is the personification of the powers of evil, but as frequently is the case in primitive religions, he is honored in the cult. The Brazilian Negroes fear and respect him, and nothing is done in the religious ceremonies without first making a *despacho* to Exú. The despacho consists of magical acts designed to bring about the retirement of Exú, in order that he will not disturb the religious ceremonies and the profane activities.

Among the feminine orishas are a number of water deities, goddesses of the sea, the lakes, and the rivers—Yemanjá, Oxun, and Yansan. The ceremonies of their cult attain poetic expressions of great lyrical intensity. These orishas are merely incarnations of the mermaids, with the ceremonial activities and divinations of a mystical nature that are widely distributed in folklore throughout the world.

The worship of Yemanjá became very popular throughout Brazil, based on the reminiscences of the mermaids in European folklore and of the *yaras* of the Brazilian Indians. For this reason, in the Brazilian macumbas the mermaids are given the most unexpected names: *mãe d'agua* (water mother), *sereia do mar* (sea mermaid), *rainha do mar* (queen of the ocean), and Dona Janaina. It is the universal cult of the waters, in accordance with the conceptions and predilections of the Negroes in the macumbas of Brazil.

The series of orishas is enormous. In addition to those carried over from Africa, the Negroes in Brazil have created many more, a result of the syncretism with the saints of the Christian tradition and with the supernatural beings of the American Indian religions.

This syncretism is a phenomenon which has been carefully studied since the time of Nina Rodrigues. It is sufficient to recall that in Bahia, Oxalá has been identified with Jesus; Xangó with Saint Jerome and Santa Barbara; Ogun with Saint Anthony and Saint George (in Rio de Janeiro); Yemanjá with our Lady of Rosario and Nossa Senhora do Piedade;[13] Oxun with Nossa Senora da Conceição and Nossa Senhora das

Candeias; Nanamburucú with Santa Ana; Oxóssi with Saint George; Omolú with São Bento; Ibeji with Cosme and Damion; and Exú with Satan. The identifications continue, with variations from state to state, and even from one locality to another.

In Bahia the worship of the orishas takes place in special temples called *terreiros*. In each terreiro there are the altars—the *pegis*—of the orishas. It is in the terreiros that the orishas are "prepared" by the Negro priests *(pais de santo* or fathers of the saint). It is also in the terreiros that the acolytes of the cult, the *filhos* and *filhas de santo* (sons and daughters of the saint) are initiated. Finally, the ordinary worship and the great religious festivals dedicated to the orishas take place in the terreiros.

Among the Afro-Brazilians the religious and magical functions of the *pai de santo* have undergone some alterations. In Brazil the magical practices, which were inseparable from the religious cult in Africa, gradually were differentiated from the cult proper and came into competition with it. Later they developed into witchcraft in the popular sense, medical quackery, etc.

The principal function of the pai de santo is the preparation of the orishas and the direction of the activities of the cult in the terreiros. The preparation of the orishas is a complex function which includes many various parts—animal sacrifices, the beating of sacred drums, and dances and songs by the filhos de santo.

The orisha requires persons, the filhas de santo, to be consecrated to his worship. In Brazil the initiation of the filhas de santo has lost much of its primitive character. The taboo restrictions are not as firm as they were in Africa. Today only a few of the Bahian candomblés preserve all features of the sacred initiation.

In the ceremonies dedicated to the orishas the filhas de santo dress and paint themselves in the colors corresponding to each of the saints: white for Obatalá, white and red for Xangó, and so on.

On the occasions of the periodic ceremonies dedicated to the orishas large assemblies gather in the terreiros. The pai de santo (and in some cases the *mãe de santo* or mother of the saint) assembles the filhas de santo and begins the solemnities. Animals such as the rooster or the hen, depending on the orisha being honored, are sacrificed to the beat of the drums.

When all are properly arranged for the ceremony in the principal room of the terreiro—the filhas de santo in a circle, the pai and the mãe de santo in the center, the drummers on one side, and the spectators in the back of the room—the pai de santo begins the sacrifice to Exú. After this *despacho* come the songs and dances dedicated to the various orishas. These continue until late in the night, the rhythm marked by the beat of the drums. It is a choreography hallucinating to the filhas de santo, with the total participation of the body—arms, hands, legs, and head—in movements and contortions, rhythmic at first and progressively intensified and violent, unceasing until the onslaught of the spasmodic manifestations and the final phases of the *queda no santo* (falling into the saint, or trance). It is an exhausting performance, a pandemonium, which defies all attempts at description. The filhas de santo then seem to be completely dominated by a furious insanity, leaping about, giddily hallucinated by the monotonous and deafening noise of the drums and by the refrains of the magical songs. The most resistant sing and dance in this manner the whole night through, unless they "fall into the saint."

The queda no santo is a special psychological state to which I have devoted much study from the medicopsychological point of view. The bodily weariness produced by the dance, the fatigue brought on by the attention devoted to the endlessly repeated songs—all this produces the phenomenon of the queda no santo, from the simple, transitory swooning to the most violent muscular contortions with their famed convulsions.

For the Negroes these phenomena indicate the entrance of the saint, or orisha, into the body of the believer, to whom, from then on, are paid all the homage and reverence of the terreiro. In this case one is dealing with the phenomenon of possession by the spirits, the common base of all primitive religions.

Among the Brazilian Negroes, as in Africa, possession is still a phenomenon of the culture. It is the manifestation of the "saint" who appears on the special occasions. But in certain aspects the queda no santo in Brazil has other causes, of a psychosocial nature, such as the profound sentiment of frustration among the Negroes. This has been accumulating since the period of slavery and it still continues to grow out of the vicissitudes and deficiencies of an economic and educational nature. The abuse of stupefying drugs helps complicate the picture, and everything burst forth in the highly emotional act of possession, the causes of which, therefore, are much more complex than a purely cultural conditioning.

The Afro-Brazilian cults of Muslim origin are far less important than either the gêge-nagô groups just discussed, or the Bantu peoples treated below. Ramos gives the following information about them.

As a group the Mahometan Negroes, of Sudanese origin, were designated as *Muçulmis,* or *Malês,* in Bahia, and *Alufás,* in Rio de Janeiro. The origin of the term Muçulmi is clear; it is a corruption of Mussulman. *Malê* is a small modification of the terms *mel, melat, malel,* which the Semites and the Arabs applied to the Malinke peoples, and which later came to designate the African Negroes who had experienced some contact with Islam. *Alufá* signifies doctor or theologian and it came to be applied, in Rio de Janeiro, to the ceremony itself or to the religious group of Islamized Negroes.

The Malê Negroes of Bahia belong to the group of Islamized Sudanese. They had almost entirely disappeared by the close of the last century. Today it is impossible to reconstruct their ethnic characteristics. And even the identification of the survivals of their culture is a difficult task, because the Malês are being acculturated rapidly.

In Bahia the Malês always lived apart from the other Negroes, and they preserved the prerogatives of an aristocratic caste. Formerly they had austere habits and sought to follow exactly the precepts of their religion. In their homes they used the typical dress of the Sudan Mohammedan: the white tunic and the cap, from which hung a long white streamer. The priests (*lemanos* or *alufás*) also wore suspended from their belts a rosary, about 18 inches long, made up of 90 large wooden beads and terminating with a ball in place of the Christian cross. The women used elegant turbans and "handkerchiefs of the Coast," lace stockings, and little slippers, a garb which blended with other cultural traits from the Slave Coast and came to be the costume of the present-day "Bahiana."

The Malês spoke the languages of their respective groups, the Hausa, the Tapa, the Kanuri, etc., onto which corrupted Arabic terms had been grafted. Many expressions survive in the formulas and prayers of the cults and in the "mandingas" or magical practices. The Islamism of the Malê Negroes of Brazil always had an effect upon the African-Negro religious practices, a phenomenon which began in the Sudan itself.

Today Malê survivals are found diluted in the gêge-nagô and bantu practices and cultures in the macumbas and candomblés of Rio de Janeiro, Bahia, and other parts of Brazil. The so-called "lines" of the Muçrumi, Muçuruman, or muçurui, etc., evident corruptions of Muçulmi, are common in Rio de Janeiro. The "pais de santo" of these lines are still called alufás and some of them take the name of Pai (father) Alufá or Tio (uncle) Alufá.

The Malês have almost entirely disappeared. Their cultures have amalgamated with others of Sudanese and Bantu origin, giving rise to blends of the most unexpected kinds. In the religious realm their practices are diluted in all degrees of syncretism.

During the last ten years of his life Ramos was working intensively in the study of the cults of the Bantu peoples in Rio de Janeiro. Unfortunately, much of the knowledge he had attained was never written down and published. The last paragraphs he wrote on the religious institutions and syncretism of these groups are as follows.

The traffic in Bantu Negroes commenced early in the sixteenth century, when Portuguese sovereignty already had been established in Benguela and Mozambique. The Congo kings agreed to supply the Portuguese with Negroes for the trade, and thus by 1547, and perhaps earlier, ships loaded with slaves sailed from the Congo for Brazil.

The founding of São Paulo de Loanda made the capital of Angola into the principal center of the traffic in Bantu peoples, who were recruited in Angola, in the Congo, and in Mozambique on the East Coast. The Negroes from Angola, who embarked at São Paulo de Loanda, São Felipe de Benguela, and Novo Redondo, were called Angolas. To the north of these places, the traders sought slaves in the Congo—in Loango, Cacongo, and the ports of the Zaire and Congo rivers. The Negroes from these sections were called Cabindas and Congos. Finally, from the east coast of Africa came the Negroes captured there, and even in the interior, who were embarked at Mozambique or sent overland for loading at the western ports mentioned above. They were the Macua and Angico Negroes, also known under the general denomination of Mozambiques.

In Brazil most of the exact tribal names of the Negroes of Bantu origin have been lost. It is true that there are innumerable references to these names in various documents. However, some of them were greatly altered, and there are various names applied to the same tribal group; or, on the contrary, the same name is used for peoples of diverse origins. The Brazilian Negroes of Bantu origin belong to two general groups: (a) the Angola-Congo Negroes; and (b) the East-Coast Negroes. For the Negroes of the first of these groups we can take present-day Portuguese Angola as the ethnic center of reference, and the Ambundo and Congo peoples as representatives. For the second group we can recognize Mozambique as the ethnic center of reference.

These Negroes were introduced principally in the markets of Rio de Janeiro, and from there they were distributed to various parts of the country, chiefly for work in the mines of Minas Gerais which were opened in the eighteenth century. But as a matter of fact Negroes of Bantu origin are found throughout all of the Northeast, in Bahia, and in other parts of Brazil.

The survivals of their culture are encountered in the fields of language, the preparation of food, music and the dance, musical instruments, folk tales, and religion and the cults. The large group of religious practices which are called macumba in Rio de Janeiro was strongly influenced by the Negroes of Bantu origin, just as we have seen that the Bahian candomblés reflect Sudanese predominance through the Yoruba cult.

In the macumbas of Rio de Janeiro and some of the southern states, the Bantu religious tradition comes from the Negroes of Angola and the Congo. The high priest *Embanda,* or

*Umbanda,* is the one who evokes the spirits and directs the ceremonies, aided by an assistant called *cambone,* or *cambode.* The head of the macumba is also called *"pai do terreiro"* as in the Bahian candomblés.

The terreiros of the macumbas in Rio de Janeiro are rude and unpretentious. Nearly always they take the name of the protecting saint or familiar spirit, who is evoked successively by the various generations of "pais de santo." The ritual ceremony is called *linha* (line) or *mesa* (table) by the Negroes.

The filhas and filhos de santo are also called mediums through the influence of spiritualism. In addition to Ogun (Saint George), one of the most common protectors of the terreiro in Rio de Janeiro is Xangó, identified here with São Miguel. Another is the powerful and influential Oxóssi, the hunter, identified in Rio de Janeiro with a caboclo[14] spirit (syncretism with the American Indian culture). The characteristic of the macumba of Bantu origin is not the protecting saint but a familiar spirit who, from time immemorial, invariably was come forth to incarnate himself in the Umbanda as "Pai (Father) Joaquim," or Velho (Old) Lourenço," etc.

Groups of spirits appear in phalanxes. These belong to various "nations" or *linhas.* The greater the number of linhas with whom he works, the more powerful the high priest. There is the linha of the Coast, the linha of Umbanda and of Quimbanda, the linha of Mina, of Cabina, of the Congo, the linha of the Sea, the linha of the Cross, the linha of the caboclo, the linha Muçurumim, etc.

At the ceremonies which open with an invocation to the protecting spirit by the high priest, the mediums are arranged in two rows, the women on the left and the men at the right. The filhas de santo wear stockings and dresses of white cotton, and the men brimmed hats and shoes of the same color. The Umbanda stands upright in front of the altar, stretches his arms to the front, and pronounces an unintelligible prayer. Then he turns to the worshipers and cries, "Ogun!" The filhos de santo clap their hands, bow their heads and raise them, and respond in a chorus: Ogun! Then the *cambone* enters to begin the singing.

Time is kept with the hands and with percussion

instruments, tambourines, drums, and others. The songs vary according to the protector, Xangó or another, giving rise to the improvisation of curious verses, so fertile is the imagination of the Brazilian mulatto. And these verses—this characteristic music—already have come down from the hills and taken the city of Rio de Janeiro by storm.

In some of the macumbas of Rio de Janeiro, the *pai do terreiro* begins the ceremony with the song of the *defumador* (fumigator) for the cleansing of the terreiro. It is a purifactory rite which resembles the *despacho* of Exú in the Bahian candomblés. In this fumigation the pai employs a kind of censor in which grains of incense, rue, etc., are burned. Evidently a liturgical practice, an imitation of the Catholic rite, is involved.

Following the invocation of the protecting spirit, the worship proper commences: the invoking of the ancestral spirits, the familiar spirits, and other friendly divinities.

A little later the pai de santo undergoes a transformation. He stands perfectly rigid, and then advances with hesitating steps, muttering as he goes. "Pai Joaquim has descended!" cry the Negroes. "Pai Joaquim" salutes the linhas in his African tongue, and the chorus responds, keeping time by the clapping of hands.

"Pai Joaquim" draws near. As he passes, everyone bows and requests a blessing. He embraces his old acquaintances, as if he has just returned from a long trip. He inquires about the health of each one, gives advice, and solves problems, exactly as the familiar spirits in Angola intervene in order to solve domestic difficulties with judicious counsel.

The activities of "Pai Joaquim" become more inclusive. Now it is not only his intimate friends who receive the words of wisdom but the others as well, the bulk of the congregation who have come from afar to hear him. There is a charge for these consultations. Numbers are distributed, and "Pai Joaquim" retires to a room and receives in order those who wish to consult him. While the consultation proceeds the whole night long, the macumba continues under the direction of the cambone.

One linha succeeds another. Among the most important of these is the black one of the malevolent spirits. The invocation is made with a circle of powder, which is lighted, and the spirits descend amid the dense smoke which shoots up. A strong linha is that of the ocean, which "Pai Joaquim" returns to direct after the consultations are finished.

The spirit or angel of the seacoast descends into one of the mediums. The latter advances slowly through the hall, her long hair falling down in front and concealing her face, while "Pai Joaquim" sprinkles her with drops of water from a cup in his hand. She is the "Queen of Guinea," a kind of water goddess, called also the Queen of the Sea. This is a survival from the Angolan cult of Calunga. She sings with a voice that is slow and mournful.

In the macumbas of Rio de Janeiro, the phenomena of possession rarely have the degree of intensity that characterizes the state of the santo in the Bahian candomblés. Many of the effects are conscious and sought after. At a certain point in the ceremonies, in a kind of collective imitation, the filhas de santo believe themselves to be possessed by old African spirits. Then they stoop over, converse among themselves, smoke pipes, and go about in little circles while uttering unintelligible phrases. After a ceremony I asked one of them what they were talking about. She responded vaguely, "things of the Coast," but she did not recall more of what was said. The ceremonies end as they began, with an invocation to the protecting spirit.

Following this, they repeat the songs to Ogun, with the same exclamations and the clapping of hands. Umbanda gives a blessing to all and finishes with a Catholic prayer: "Blessed be to God!" which is immediately answered by the audience with a "Blessed be forever!"

Brazilian macumbas and candomblés are undergoing rapid changes. There is a curious fusion, as has been pointed out in passing, with other religions and cults, especially with Catholicism and spiritualism. It is the phenomenon of syncretism which continues in its work of diluting the original cultural traits. The linhas of the macumbas in Rio de Janeiro are now sessions and tables of low spiritism, with an infusion of theosophical elements, which are disseminated through popular books and pamphlets. Hence the attendance of whites and mulattoes daily becomes greater. In Brazil the Catholicism of the masses absorbs in its immense womb the old religious cults and religions, here fragmented and diluted.

## From the Shadows to the Spotlight

One of the most remarkable changes in Brazilian religious organization and behavior in recent decades has been the extent to which the various Afro-Brazilian religious cults have been enabled to bring their beliefs and ceremonies out of the shadows to which they long were confined, into the glare of the daylight. This seems to be especially true in the cities of Rio de Janeiro and São Paulo, and other highly urbanized areas in southern Brazil. In the years 1942 to 1946, when I spent many interesting hours accompanying Arthur Ramos in his penetrating studies of the African religious heritage in Brazil, one could not even dream of the time when the macumba and the candomblé would occupy the spotlight before an overflow crowd in Rio de Janeiro's gigantic Maracanã stadium; nor did I think the day would ever come when data on the still furtive practice of *Umbanda* would appear in Brazil's official *Anuário Estatístico*. My recollections of those days are of the great difficulties encountered in attempting to inspire enough confidence in the informants that they would consent to answer questions about their religious beliefs and practices, allow some of their religious songs to be recorded, and so on. Ramos himself, along with other well-established white men, was serving as an *ogan,* or intermediary with more esteemed portions of society, for one of the cults; and my files include clippings from newspapers, featuring the visit to Rio de Janeiro of a celebrated Pai do Santo from Bahia. For example, on August 7, 1942, *A Noite,* widely circulated evening newspaper, announced above a picture of "The King of the Macumba," João Alves Torres, the arrest of the king and that he was going to be sent back to Bahia immediately. In the *Diario da Noite* of the same date the story, also accompanied with a picture of the *macumbeiro* who had been arrested, played up the fact that he was a teacher of African dances who had trained some well-known Brazilian ballerinas. In this case the headline, "O 'rei da macumba' veio ao Rio em viagem de recreio," perhaps would be most accurately translated as "The 'King of the Macumba' *Says* He Came to Rio on a Pleasure Trip." In any case, there could have been little doubt in the minds of the readers that he was not welcomed by the authorities in the

This section is from T. Lynn Smith, *Brazil: People and Institutions,* fourth edition (Baton Rouge: Louisiana State University Press, 1972), and is reproduced with the permission of the Louisiana State University Press.

nation's capital and that he was being sent back to Salvador with dispatch.

Some years later, in 1956, it was my good fortune to be in Salvador on the occasion of the 100th anniversary of the birth of Nina Rodrigues, noted physician who pioneered the study of Afro-Brazilian religious cults in Bahia, and teacher and mentor of Arthur Ramos. At that time by special invitation I attended a gala occasion at the medical school of the University of Bahia in honor of Nina Rodrigues. All of the notables in the city were present, with the exception of the Roman Catholic clergy; and the guests of honor were four noted *mães de santo* bedecked in their best ceremonial attire. This convinced me that things were changing, yet I was somewhat surprised when I read stories in Brazil's great newspapers such as the one featured in the *Journal do Brasil* of Rio de Janeiro for May 13, 1965, well illustrated with photos of prominent orishas, from which the following opening paragraphs are translated:

> The Maracanã stadium will be transformed today, beginning at 6:00 P.M. into an immense candomblé terreiro, when to the sound of 500 sacred African drums, the folkloric festival Night of the Macumba will be opened. This is organized by the Spiritist-Umbanda Confederation in commemoration of the abolition of slavery and in honor of the 400th anniversary of the city of Rio de Janeiro.
>
> The ceremonies will be opened with an address by Governor Carlos Lacerda, and presided over by Yialorixá Ilê Afonjá, Dona Maria Bebiana, and great mãe-de-santo of the candomblés of Bahia, who, symbolizing all Negro mothers, will be crowned as Black Mother of the Year.

Finally, the 1969 issue of the *Anuário Estatístico do Brasil* carries statistical data about the *Umbandistas* on a par with the data for the Catholic, Protestant and Spiritist *cultos*. The tabulation indicates a total of 280 buildings dedicated to cult purposes, the use of 1,332 halls for religious meetings of the adherents, and the use of 590 rooms in private homes for religious assemblies of the Umbandistas. They are credited with holding 217,399 worship services during the year, of admitting 101,022 new members and excluding 46,376 former members in 1967, and of having a total membership of 240,088 persons at the end of the year. Rio Grande do Sul, with 59,552 reported members of the cult, São Paulo with 57,663, Guanabara with 45,100, Rio de Janeiro with 29,442, and Minas

Gerais with 24,055 are the states in which the bulk of these identified as adherents are located.

These data alone are evidence that only a very small portion of those fully imbued with the Afro-Brazilian religious beliefs are figuring in modern *Umbanda*. Only 332 members are reported for Bahia, where the actual numbers of those participating in the candomblés must run into the tens if not the hundreds of thousands.

It also should be indicated that the process of syncretism with Spiritism and Catholicism has gone on sufficiently, and the process of giving respectability to Umbanda beliefs and practices has gone on to the extent that it may not be accurate to characterize Umbandistas solely as the members of one of the Afro-Brazilian religious cults. When Ramos was fully conversant with affairs in the macumbas of Rio de Janeiro, in the years immediately before his untimely death in 1950, Umbanda or *Embanda* was the name of the high priest of an African cult of Bantu origin. Since then substantial changes have occurred. Wagley states that the African fetish cults, "once very discreet in Rio de Janeiro," now are found in every part of the city and in the suburbs. He also indicates that the most famous leaders of the cults in Bahia now have residences and "branches" of their temples in the city of Rio de Janeiro. Moreover, "there are innumerable pseudo-African fetish cults in São Paulo, Rio de Janeiro, and other large cities which practice a watered-down version of the traditional ceremonies."[15] But he does not specifically mention that the name Umbanda is given to any of these. Finally, Renshaw, who studied the Umbanda cults intensively, especially in São Paulo, first indicates that the macumbas of Rio de Janeiro, xangós of Recife, and so on, are popularly referred to as *baxio espiritismo* or "low spiritism," and then adds, "Another cult commonly included in this category is that of *Umbanda,* for under casual observation it appears to be similar to the above-mentioned Afro-Brazilian rites. Nevertheless, Umbanda, referred to as white magic by its sympathizers, claims to be motivated by the virtue of Christian charity and to seek only to help those in need."[16] However, on another page he indicates that the terms "macumba" and "umbanda" are frequently used interchangeably in Rio de Janeiro.[17] Thus, we probably are not greatly in error in thinking that the appearance of statistical data on the Umbandistas in the *Anuário Estatístico* is eloquent evidence of the emergence of certain parts of the Afro-Brazilian religious heritage from the shadows into the light of day.

# Sociocultural Change
# and Development

In the two decades of the 1960s and 1970s, Brazilian society underwent, and is still undergoing, a metamorphosis from a so-called underdeveloped society into one of the world's more developed areas. The five chapters comprising Part IV deal with various aspects of this striking change.

No small part of the transition in Brazil is due to the initiative and hard work of its large colony of Japanese immigrants and their descendants, presently numbering well over 500,000. Chapter 10 is a study of the acculturation and assimilation of this group, based almost entirely on Japanese sources.

At long last, millions of Brazilians who depend upon agricultural and livestock enterprises for a livelihood are learning to use modern, effective ways of getting products from the soil. This indispensable feature of "modernization" is the subject of Chapter 11. In Chapter 12 the attempt is made to use a "broad lens" in picturing general social trends in Brazil. And the two concluding chapters, 13 and 14, portray the role of urbanization in the metamorphosis of Brazilian society. Chapter 13 concentrates upon the changes in Brazil itself, and Chapter 14 deals with a comparison of several of the more significant features of urbanization in Brazil and the United States.

# 10

## The Assimilation and Acculturation of Japanese Immigrants

The first Japanese immigrants to Brazil left Japan under a contract between the government of the state of São Paulo and the Kokoku Emigration Company. The group, consisting of 781 persons (158 families), arrived in Brazil on June 18, 1908. This first migration gave rise shortly to bitter complaints about the intolerable conditions encountered by the immigrants.[1]

Before continuing with the account of the migration of Japanese to Brazil, it is well to consider briefly Brazil's motives for promoting immigration. Among the first of these was the desire on the part of some leaders to develop or create a small-farming class in the population, to offset and change in part the large-scale monoculture of the tremendous Brazilian estates. Another motive was that of securing persons to serve as poorly paid manual laborers on the nation's coffee, cotton, and sugar plantations. These two major motivating forces were intensified by Brazil's granting of freedom to the children of slave mothers in 1871 and freeing the slaves themselves in 1888.[2] Brazil's far-flung activities in the recruitment of labor caused the Italian government (in 1902) to prohibit the recruitment and granting of free passage to Italian workers destined for São Paulo. As a result, shortly thereafter Brazil looked to Japan for immigrants to help supply the labor for her plantations.

On the other hand, the Japanese had their own motives for

Selections from Yukio Fujii and T. Lynn Smith, *The Acculturation of the Japanese Immigrants in Brazil*, Latin American Monographs No. 8 (Gainesville: University of Florida Press, 1959): 3-8, 25-51. Republished with the permission of the Pan American Foundation.

migrating to Brazil. First, there were the interests of the Japanese emigration companies whose business was almost destroyed by the Gentlemen's Agreement between the United States and Japan in 1907 which stopped the importation of Japanese laborers into the United States. Simultaneously the owners of Brazilian plantations, and especially the coffee fazendas, sought manual laborers to substitute for the Italians. As a result, business activities of Japanese emigration companies received a new lease on life by the migration to Brazil.[3]

The second principal motive grew out of the economic prosperity in Japan which followed her victory in the Russo-Japanese War. But in 1910 the wage levels in Brazil and Peru were not very different from those in Japan. The wages paid to Japanese immigrants in these countries were less than one-fifth of those received by the Japanese in Hawaii during the same period. In addition, the lesser spatial and social distance between Hawaiians and the Japanese was more attractive that the status accorded the latter in Brazil.[4]

In spite of this, however, the desire for labor in Brazil and the need for business by the emigration companies in Japan boosted the promotion of the Japanese migration to Brazil. Consequently, Japan became one of Brazil's greatest sources of agricultural workers, most of whom settled in the state of São Paulo.

During the period from 1908 to 1923 a total of 32,266 Japanese immigrants arrived in Brazil, most of them landing at the port of Santos. (See Table 3.) In these years, the total number of Japanese immigrants made up only 2.5 percent of all the immigrants to Brazil. Despite socioeconomic difficulties, however, the Japanese made a relatively successful beginning in permanent settlement in Brazil.

Late in 1917, Japanese immigration gained impetus through the organization of the strong Kaigai Kogyo Kabushiki Kaisha (Overseas Development Company), or K.K.K.K. Before this company was established, several similarly organized emigration companies in Japan had introduced the Japanese to Brazil. Beginning in 1923, the government made budgetary provisions for "emigration publicity," and Japanese legations and consulates were instructed to furnish information on immigration. In 1924 the Emigration Council, headed by Minister of Foreign Affairs Shidehara, sent a new mission to South America, and as a result Japan concentrated her emigration efforts on Brazil. As soon as this

**TABLE 3**

**Japanese Immigration to Brazil**

**1908-23**

| Year | Number of Japanese | Percentage of All Immigrants | Year | Number of Japanese | Percentage of All Immigrants |
|------|------|------|------|------|------|
| 1908 | 830 | 0.9 | 1916 | 165 | 0.5 |
| 1909 | 31 | * | 1917 | 3,899 | 12.9 |
| 1910 | 948 | 1.1 | 1918 | 5,599 | 28.3 |
| 1911 | 28 | * | 1919 | 3,022 | 8.4 |
| 1912 | 2,909 | 1.6 | 1920 | 1,013 | 1.8 |
| 1913 | 7,122 | 3.7 | 1921 | 840 | 1.9 |
| 1914 | 3,675 | 4.6 | 1922 | 1,225 | 1.1 |
| 1915 | 65 | 0.2 | 1923 | 895 | 2.8 |

*Source:* Compiled and computed from Conselho Nacional de Estatística, *Anuário Estatístico: 1954,* Ano XV, Rio de Janeiro: Instituto Brasileiro de Geografia e Estatística, 1954, p. 59.
*Less than 0.1 percent.

decision was taken, the Japanese government established the Overseas Development Company, a centralized and highly rationalized management of migration to Brazil, and this agency organized the intercontinental transportation of human beings on a large scale. A governmental subsidy was given to the K.K.K.K. from 1924 on.[5] In 1927, when the Minister of Interior was president of the K.K.K.K., a special colonization bank was established. By the end of 1930, the K.K.K.K. had handled over 96,000 emigrants of whom 73,000 went to Brazil, 14,000 to the Philippines, and 3,000 to Peru.

Many of the Japanese in Brazil finally achieved their goal and became small independent farmers. This stimulated the bulk of the Japanese immigrants not merely to go to São Paulo but also to establish themselves in the areas along the Noroeste railway in that state.

At about the same time, contracts were made for migrants to go to the Amazon area. A small number of the Japanese who had entered Peru prior to 1923 had been induced to work in the Brazilian Amazon during the rubber boom—hence their name *"Peru Kudari"* (Down from Peru). There is no accurate information on the number of *Peru Kudari,* but some of them were interviewed by Japanese investigators.[6]

After 1925, colonies on the land concessions which were privately managed by Japanese companies became active. Consequently, the Instituto Amazonia and Amazon Kogyo KK., supported by the Japanese government, were founded. However, the enterprises of these overseas companies were not successful.

During the three years from 1932 to 1934, approximately one-half of the total immigrants to Brazil were Japanese. (See Table 4.)

Early in the 1930s the great flow of Japanese to Brazil came to be viewed adversely by the Brazilian government. The immigration legislation of July 1934, voted by the Government Assembly under the influence of opposition started by Dr. Miguel Couto, restricted the annual entry of immigrants to 2 percent of the total entries of the past fifty years. This famous Article 121 affected Japan more than any other country, despite absence of explicit anti-Japanese discrimination.[7] This law seems to have been an effort to rescue many Brazilians from the economic effects of a rapid decline in the price of coffee. In any case, Japanese immigration decreased until, in 1938, the number of immigrants was less than the quota.

TABLE 4

**Japanese Immigration to Brazil**
**1924-41**

| Year | Number of Japanese | Percentage of All Immigrants | Year | Number of Japanese | Percentage of All Immigrants |
|------|------|------|------|------|------|
| 1924 | 2,673 | 2.8 | 1933 | 24,494 | 53.2 |
| 1925 | 6,330 | 7.7 | 1934 | 21,930 | 47.6 |
| 1926 | 8,407 | 7.1 | 1935 | 9,611 | 32.5 |
| 1927 | 9,084 | 9.3 | 1936 | 3,306 | 25.9 |
| 1928 | 11,169 | 14.3 | 1937 | 4,557 | 13.1 |
| 1929 | 16,648 | 17.3 | 1938 | 2,524 | 13.0 |
| 1930 | 14,074 | 22.5 | 1939 | 1,414 | 6.2 |
| 1931 | 5,632 | 20.5 | 1940 | 1,268 | 6.9 |
| 1932 | 11,678 | 37.1 | 1941 | 1,548 | 5.6 |

*Source:* Compiled and computed from Conselho Nacional de Estatística, *Anuário* Estatístico: 1954, Ano XV, Rio de Janeiro: Instituto Brasileiro de Geografia e Estatística, 1954, p. 59.

The decline in immigration continued until the outbreak of World War II. The percentage of Japanese among all immigrants in the entire period from 1924 to 1941 was 16.8 percent, as compared with 2.5 percent in the preceding period. (See Table 5.)

**TABLE 5**

**Number of Immigrants to Brazil by Country of Birth**

**1924-41**

| Country of Birth | Number | Percent |
|---|---|---|
| Total | 930,728 | 100.0 |
| Portugal | 307,820 | 33.1 |
| Japan | 156,349 | 16.8 |
| Italy | 81,605 | 8.8 |
| Germany | 79,579 | 8.5 |
| Spain | 57,543 | 6.2 |
| Russia | 8,228 | 0.9 |
| Other countries | 239,604 | 25.7 |

*Source:* Compiled and computed from Conselho Nacional de Estatística, *Anuário Estatístico: 1954,* Ano XV, Rio de Janeiro: Instituto Brasileiro de Geografia e Estatística, 1954, p. 59.

Following 1942, Japanese immigration to Brazil ceased entirely. Indeed, Brazil received a total of only 5,326 immigrants during the war years. Right after the war, a few Japanese were permitted to enter Brazil, the first of whom were fifty-four persons who left Kobe on December 28, 1952. This immigration was arranged by Kamitsuka and was intended to help stimulate the production of jute. After 1952, Japanese immigration became substantial (see Table 6), with the Amazon region receiving a fairly large proportion

**TABLE 6**

**Japanese Immigration to Brazil**

**1945-56**

| Year | Number of Japanese | Percentage of All Immigrants | Year | Number of Japanese | Percentage of All Immigrants |
|---|---|---|---|---|---|
| 1945 | . . . | . . . | 1951 | 106 | 0.2 |
| 1946 | 6 | * | 1952 | 216 | 0.3 |
| 1947 | 1 | * | 1953 | 1,928 | 2.4 |
| 1948 | 1 | * | 1954 | 3,119 | 4.3 |
| 1949 | 4 | * | 1955 | 4,051 | 7.3 |
| 1950 | 33 | * | 1956 | 4,912 | 11.0 |

*Source:* Compiled and computed from Conselho Nacional de Estatística, *Anuário Estatístico: 1955,* Ano XVI, Rio de Janeiro: Instituto Brasileiro de Geografia e Estatística, 1955, p. 59; and *Anuário Estatistico 1957,* Ano XVIII, Rio de Janeiro: Instituto Brasileiro de Geografia e Estatística, 1957, p. 54.

*Less than 0.1 percent.

of the total. Although the number of persons involved is not comparable to that during the decade of the 1930s, the proportion of the Japanese among all immigrants currently is increasing at a rapid rate. For the entire period 1908 to 1956, the number of Japanese immigrants amounted to 202,947, or 4.3 percent of all immigrants to Brazil during the 49 years.

## Adjustment to Physical and Agricultural Environments

In analyzing stages of social and cultural contacts, it is necessary to consider differences between the physical environments in the homeland and in the country of destination. Also, the new agricultural structure becomes a part of the environment of the immigrants and helps to change their consumption habits. These differences in physical and agricultural environments have much to do with changes in the people's dress, housing, and diet.

### *Dress*

In the 1930s, the straw sandals worn in Japan were seen in many shops in Registro, São Paulo, whereas Japanese wooden shoes were found only in one house, solely as a keepsake. Dress was almost entirely occidental, except during festivals or other special occasions.[8]

Use of the Japanese *kimono* seems to be retained to a greater extent by females than by males, for they display their beauty by wearing it. In present-day Japan, most urban women keep a kimono to wear on such special occasions as New Year's Day and wedding anniversaries. In 1954, Izumi investigated the extent to which Japanese Brazilians retained an interest in their native costume. No native costumes were found in colonies of the Japanese Brazilians. In farming areas, the males wore working clothes similar to those of other Brazilians, and they wore ordinary western suits and ties when they went to official functions. When at work, the women wore a loosely fitting dress over pantaloons, a mode of dress that was not used by other Brazilians. The summer kimono was used in place of pajamas by some of the first generation.[9]

Because of the high prices of textiles in Brazil, most of the post-war immigrants have tried to bring enough clothing from Japan to last for a couple of years of hard wear under laboring conditions.[10] Even though the dress of Japanese Brazilians generally is western in style, its mode and fashion are actually from Japan where occidental dresses soon became Japanese even in farm villages. Working clothes of Japanese women in Brazil, that is, a loosely fitting dress under which pantaloons are worn, are similar to the working attire, or *monppei,* in the rural districts of Japan. Thus, apparently the Japanese experience no serious acculturation difficulties in connection with dress.

## Food

Rice, prepared and served in Japanese fashion, is the most important element in the diet of Japanese immigrants, although the newcomers' desire to eat Japanese rice is often restricted by natural scarcity and economic disadvantage. In the south, however, rice is a staple food for upper-class Japanese Brazilians, while in the Amazon region, *farinha do (agua)* or *mandioca* flour is one of the main staples. In general, both wheat bread and rice are commonly used throughout the Japanese-Brazilian colonies; and the rice is cooked in both Brazilian and Japanese ways. Brazilians fry the rice in fat with hot water added, whereas the Japanese ordinarily boil the rice and use no grease. Other minor dishes are seldom distinguishable, since both Brazilian and Japanese elements of cooking exist in various combinations.[11] In the 1930s, black beans, one of the Brazilians' staples, were already used in considerable amounts by Japanese immigrants.[12]

Distinctive Japanese foods are readily obtained in such cities as São Paulo where many Japanese Brazilians are clustered. However, their cost is generally so high that they are used only on special occasions, such as weddings and Japanese festivals. Even for a wedding party, the dishes are not completely Japanese, although pork and poultry dishes are essential at any special parties. Frequently both chopsticks and knife and fork are employed.[13]

Acculturation in diet and eating habits is remarkably complex. To Izumi's question, "Which do you like better, Brazilian or Japanese dishes?" the most common answers were: "I like Brazilian dishes but sometimes I like Japanese ones," and "I like Japanese dishes but sometimes I like Brazilian dishes.'' Extremely infrequent were the answers: "I like only Japanese dishes," or "I like only Brazilian dishes." With respect to food habits, men seem to acculturate more rapidly than women.

There are some interesting data on the importation of Japanese foods to Brazil. This commerce is called the *takuan* trade, which means literally the "pickled radish trade," because the pickled radish is relished to such an extent by the Japanese that general exports of Japanese cigarettes, edible oils, medicines, foods, and other miscellaneous goods are so designated. In 1954, the volume of the takuan trade with Brazil amounted to 323,942,000 yen ($955,290). Despite the large number of Japanese in Brazil, however, the volume of this trade was less than comparable commerce with the mainland of the United States and Hawaii. This is due to restrictions on imports to Brazil. However, large amounts of miscellaneous goods from Japan have been and will continue to be consumed by Japanese in Brazil and in other foreign countries.[14]

Immigrants require a few years in which to substitute new foods for their traditional ones. *Mandioca,* black beans, fats, and meat are foods least relished by the Japanese in Brazil.[15] Of course, the dietary habits of postwar immigrants may be different from those of prewar ones, for the impact of industrialization and urbanization upon rural Japan has changed food habits in the homeland to some extent. In Brazil, the immigrants first attempt to raise enough rice to meet their own needs. Then other minor food crops are planted which may involve some adaptation to Brazilian foods. If the Japanese hire Brazilian laborers, substantial modifications are necessitated in the foods prepared and served. It is, of course, hard for newcomers to change their appetites and to acquire a taste for the greasy foods which are little used in rural Japan.


*Housing*

The most prominent features in the furnishings of the Japanese house are the thick straw *tatami* (mats), on which the people sit or recline. These convenient articles are radically different from the furniture of westernized houses which persons may enter without removing their shoes. Indeed, it appears that the most lingering nostalgia on the part of the immigrants is for tatami.

Except on the southern coast and in the Registro district where the houses of some wealthy people showed Japanese architectural traits, Willems and Baldus found no Japanese-style architecture. However, a great many houses in Registro, as elsewhere in Brazil, have the mud walls which were adopted by the Japanese from the Brazilians. Almost all the houses of the immigrants had smoothly plastered walls, and a wattle which supports the mud was superior to that in the native or *caboclo* house.[16]

In the Amazon region, two types of architecture are employed. A commonly accepted mode of housing is of the type in which a person may enter without removing his shoes and where beds are placed on wooden floors. The other is a type of house one may not enter without removing his shoes and in which the *futon* (a sleeping mattress) is used on the floor instead of beds. The former type, with wooden walls and a tile roof, is frequently found among upper-class people. In it tatami are not found at all and hammocks are used by Japanese Brazilians only for lounging and napping.[17]

The housing of Japanese immigrants, as well as their clothing, seems practically adjusted to the environment. Traditional features of the Japanese house are of secondary importance for the people. However, it is interesting that most houses include a bathtub made from a large oil drum. The Japanese tenaciously adhere to a love of hot baths, open scenes of which sometimes become topics of lively Brazilian commentary.[18]

Generally, the material aspects of housing are gradually undergoing acculturative change.[19] On the whole acculturation in clothing, food, and housing is going on smoothly and producing little or no tension among Japanese immigrants. The direction of acculturation, however, can hardly be called Brazilian. Rather the changes affecting both the Japanese and the Brazilians are oriented toward European patterns, which trend Gamo noted in connection with housing, clothing, food, and other sociocultural aspects and in both Brazilian and Japanese-Brazilian communities.[20]

As far as household matters are concerned, Japanese-Brazilian women tend to be culturally more conservative than men, probably because women have less frequent contact with other ethnic groups.

## The Institutionalized Relationships of Man to Land

The Japanese, who in their homeland are confined to such small islands, have paid much attention to matters of land tenure. Their serious attitudes regarding land scarcity are entirely different from the Brazilians' somewhat indifferent approach to land.

Japanese farmers may be classified into five tenure categories. Highest in the scale is the independent owner-operator. Next comes the *jikosaku* (owner-tenant), who owns more land than he leases, followed by the slightly lower *kojisaku* (tenant-owner), who owns less land than he rents. Next in rank is the *kosaku* (tenant), who is entirely dependent upon land leased from others. The lowest category of farmers consists of those who are landless and who work for others. In 1941 the proportions of Japanese farmers falling into each of these five categories were 31.2, 20.7, 20.0, 27.7 and 0.4 percent, respectively.[21]

The rent on rice and other crop land varied from 40 to 50 percent of the product. In Japan the economic subordination of tenants to landowners amounted to a servile relationship of the former to the latter. This important characteristic of rural social organization in Japan has been greatly fostered by familism. Indeed it should be stressed that the tenants' relations to landowners are familistic rather than feudalistic.

Izumi's study of 116 farmers in Avares Machado indicated that a half of them had been owner-operators in Japan. This figure is much higher than that for the homeland as a whole.

A majority of Japanese immigrants entered Brazil as agricultural laborers *(colonos),* intending to become independent farmers as rapidly as possible. After 1940, the Japanese were seldom found working as *colonos,* a fact which makes it evident that the immigrants quickly became renters or land owners.

For the Japanese to be an independent farmer is the most attractive status in the land of ''opportunities,'' although the Japanese immigrants' aspirations sometimes led to derogatory Brazilian commentary. Under a São Paulo rental system,[22] Japanese tenants with their strong desire for the status of independent farmers became infamous for their soil mining practices.

Of the 347 farmers in Izumi's sample drawn from throughout Brazil, 76.6 percent were owner-operators (see Table 7), 15.9 percent were renters, and only 7.5 percent laborers. Most of their holdings were between 29.5 and 118 acres in size, whereas the average farm in Japan in 1938 consisted of 2.6 acres.[23] Under these conditions, the social organization of Japanese immigrants quickly changed. The tenant's loyalty to the landowner, the services rendered by the tenant, and other aspects of the paternalistic system rapidly disappeared. Most of the tenants retained few relations with or obligations to landowners other than the obligation to pay the rent.

In Brazil, vertical mobility of the immigrants is rapid and internal migration is considerable. The immigrants have great faith in the ability of the individual to climb the social scale by his own effort. This free individualistic competition and independent pursuit of economic improvement by Japanese immigrants represent personal and group aspirations substantially different from those prevailing in Japan.

In Japan, the typical rural community is of the nucleated structural type in which farmers' houses are grouped together in a village. Dispersed settlements of single farmsteads are very few. Even the few communities of dispersed settlement are closely related to the history of land tenure in villages, and functionally are not very different from nucleated settlements.[24]

**TABLE 7**

**Distribution of the Japanese-Brazilian Farmers According to Tenure and the Size of Their Farms**

| Tenure | Size (Alqueires)* | Number | Percent |
|--------|-------------------|--------|---------|
| Owner-operator | | 266 | 76.6 |
| | 0- | 42 | 12.1 |
| | 5- | 51 | 14.7 |
| | 15- | 99 | 28.5 |
| | 20- | 65 | 18.7 |
| | 50- | 4 | 1.2 |
| | 100-over | 5 | 1.4 |
| Renter | | 55 | 15.9 |
| | 0- | 37 | 10.7 |
| | 5- | 9 | 2.6 |
| | 10-over | 9 | 2.6 |
| Laborer | | 26 | 7.5 |

*Source:* Compiled from Seiichi Izumi, ''The Japanese Brazilian Colonies,'' p. 48.
*One alqueire equals 5.9 acres.

In Brazil, however, the line-village type of settlement is the one in general use in Japanese colonies. It is significant that use of the river-front system of land division gives all of the farms access to the stream; that a road encircles the valley in which such a settlement is located; and that line-village arrangement of the houses on both the land and fronting on the road, results in compact, efficiently serviced settlements.[25] Except in jute-producing areas of the Amazon, the well-planned colonies of Japanese immigrants make for fairly uniform settlement patterns.

The farmsteads usually are rectangular in shape. For example, in the colony of Dourados, Mato Grosso, one farm is 250 meters wide and 1,220 meters long.[26] In Vale de Ribeira de Iguape, lots are rectangles 100 meters wide and 200 meters long.[27]

The ways of farming of the Japanese immigrants differ sharply from those of the native Brazilians. Brazil's traditional system of ''fire agriculture''[28] has not been adopted by the Japanese immigrants. They brought with them an elementary type of plow culture in which oxen serve as draft animals, and this probably has contributed substantially to the dissemination of the plow culture in Brazil. At the same time, commercial fertilizer, rarely used in most parts of Brazil, was distributed to the Japanese farmers by agricultural cooperatives; and these and other agricultural practices were borrowed from them by the Brazilian farmers.[29] However, many of the Japanese in Brazil have come to use mules instead of oxen, and they have adapted the native Brazilian's large axes to help in clearing the forest.

A variety of crops were either introduced or promoted by the Japanese, with the list of such including peppermint, silk, ramie, strawberries, persimmons, peaches, and pears. Jute and pepper should receive special mention, for the production of these is highly important to the prosperity of the Amazon region. In addition, the introduction of diversified farming was fostered by the Higashiyama farms.[30]

## Changes in Community Structure

One of the more important ways of obtaining an understanding of rural society is through study of the forms of human interaction which constitute its social organization. The fact that most Japanese immigrants came from rural districts suggests investigation of their community organization in Brazil. In this section, however, only the structural aspects of the community as a whole are of major concern.

## The Structure of the Japanese Village

In Japan, villages *(sonzaku)* differ administratively from cities, and in fact may be considered as rural communities. However, the term *mura* (village) most commonly refers to a local administrative unit and not to a community as such.

Most Japanese villages are based on the large kinship unit or clan, and Suzuki, applying Sorokin's theories of cumulative social relationships, has classified them into two types: the natural village and the administrative village. In addition, Suzuki insists that a natural village is an entity in which village and community boundaries coincide, whereas an administrative village is less integrated.[31] It is rather difficult to distinguish a natural village from an administrative village. As time passes, the functions of a natural village decline, and the distinction between it and the administrative village no longer is made, because such differentiating features as communal lands have been lost. Sometimes a community consists of subvillages *(burakus)* which appear to be natural villages.

One must also understand the relation of family and the neighborhood to a village community. An especially important structural relationship is that between a main family and its branch families. The relation of a main family to a branch family usually is consanguineal, but the spatial distance between the main and branch families is of importance. The tie between a main family and one of its branches in the same village is much stronger than when the two are in different villages. Therefore, both consanguinity and spatial distance are major determinants of intensity of the tie. Sometimes the nonconsanguineal family located in the same village as a main family has more effective interaction with the latter than has a consanguineal branch located farther away. Thus, the Japanese kinship group is based both on proximal variations in residence and on descent. The classic relation of a branch family to a main family is one of subordination of the former to the latter, in both economic and social matters. The economic dependence of the branch family on a main family is strong, and the relationship of a tenant to a landowner frequently is of this type. However, the paternalistic aspect of this relationship is a feature of familistic society of this form. Of course, the classic relationship between the main and branch families is in reality modified by many variations of the "ideal type," and may appear differently in different villages.

There is also an extreme type of village structure which contrasts sharply with the one based on the clan that has just been discussed.[32] Fukutake calls it the village community of the *kogumi* type,[33] and it is composed of families which interact on a plane of equality. The hierarchical system characteristic of main and branch families is less apparent in the kogumi type of village in which the various component families are approximately equal in socioeconomic status. This is quite different from the clan-type village, where control over most of the social institutions is monopolized by the main family. Kogumi villages are associated with a monetary economy, and each of them is made up of equal and independent families with mutual aid systems, although there is less group solidarity in a kogumi village than in a clan village. Small clans are present in kogumi-type villages, but their existence in the community is not strong enough to change the basic structure of kogumi. Ceremonial events are conducted by the households in rotation, and democratic administration is practiced to some extent in the family unit.

Fukutake's working hypothesis holds that the kogumi type of village prevails in southwestern Japan and the clan type of village in northwestern Japan, although mixed types also exist.

In general, Japanese neighborhoods are distinct in their widely varied functions and sizes. To avoid a complicated discussion of neighborhoods, the present writers prefer the name of kogumi, because *kumi* and *ko* overlap in their functions and characteristics. Suzuki meakes the following statements about the ko: (1) it is a locality group or territorial unit; (2) it has communitylike characteristics; (3) its relationships are highly rationalized; (4) each family pays an equal amount for its maintenance; and (5) in it, all family members have equal rights.[34] These features of the ko are among the most prominent characteristics in the Japanese village, although there are numerous types of the ko. To some extent, its functions in urban areas are similar to the European guild system of the Middle Ages, while a voluntary association composed of individuals is not found in the Japanese village community.[35]

Important is the fact that the ko has developed as a religous group, changing its main function, and frequently duplicating functions of the neighborhood *(kumi)*. Therefore, kumi and ko are often confused, which is why the term kogumi is best used to analyze the basic organization of a Japanese village community. For example, Embree's study discloses the system of kumi as a cooperative unit of neighbors.[36] A few closely grouped households make up a kumi, which is really a neighborhood united in emergencies by mutual aid.

In 1955 one of the present writers investigated the community organization of an island off western Japan. The kogumi system was found to be functioning in funerals, festivals at the village shrine, and in other community events requiring mutual aid. The kogumi's most important function was in the funeral service, including cremating, burying, and other ceremonial arrangements. The development of technology and a monetary economy is replacing the kogumi's functions in the repair of roads, roofing houses, and mutual aid and interaction of all types. Equalitarian systems of mutual aid are more predominant in kogumi villages than in clan villages.

## Changes in the Japanese Village Community in Brazil

The changes in physical environment and man-land relationships which were discussed above have brought about drastic alterations in the traditional relationship of Japanese tenants to landowners in Brazil. In addition to this destruction of traditional human relations, the functions of the traditional cooperation of kogumi have been greatly modified, because the members of the new community lack primary contacts. A further obstacle to the transplantation of kogumi is the diversity of mutual aid systems taken from different regions in Japan. This does not mean that cooperative systems have disappeared, but that they have been modified considerably.

Observation of changes in social organization requires a time perspective. The relatively short history of the Japanese immigration to Brazil makes it impossible to determine a decisive moment of acculturation in social organization or to clearly identify its stage. Nevertheless, the present aspects of acculturation may be described. First, in certain colonies, the immigrants are from different villages, even though they are from the same region. Hence, traditional homogeneity of the community is lacking. The planned-colony policy was a tremendous step in liberalizing land tenure. The master-servant relationships of land tenure prevailing in Japan could not survive in Brazil. At the same time, the relationship between a main family and a branch family lost the basis whereby the latter was subordinated to the former. Even though a father may not have enough land to divide among his children, the latter have many opportunities to buy land cheaply, and this makes them far less dependent upon the father and the family. Furthermore, since the spatial distance between kin groups is no longer important, children can readily seek better conditions.

In such a situation, the old paternalistic relations of Japan lost much of their effectiveness. On the other hand, kinship groups related by marriage overlap locality groups in such isolated Brazilian colonies as Tome Asu, Amazonas.[37] The social solidarity of this kind of group becomes stronger through mutual aid in productive activities.

According to Izumi, social organization of Japanese Brazilians in rural areas is based largely on territorial proximity. The village, *buraku,* consisting of less than a hundred families, is often called *nihonjin kai* (Japanese association) and in this territorial group there are neighborhoods called *kumi* or *ku*. Each territorial group has a head chosen by the people of the community who sometimes also select councils which are in charge of such activities as civil engineering and education. The budget of the nihonjin kai is based on a regular fee paid by each family, but extraordinary expenses, such as those for schools or roads, come from special assessments on all members of the nihonjin kai. The local nihonjin kais are, in turn, organized into a nihonjin kai which is municipio- or countywide. Only rarely are rural people not organized into a nihonjin kai. The nihonjin kai and such associations of both girls and boys as exist in Japan help integrate communities with Japanese tradition.

The organizations of nihonjin kai have no place in the social organization of the urban Japanese Brazilians. Urban Japanese-language schools are more likely to be managed by private individuals, whereas maintenance of rural Japanese-language schools is through the nihonjin kai. In urban areas, the associations of both young women and men are more voluntary in their membership than those in the rural districts.[38]

In Assaí, São Paulo, with a population of 7,600, there were about 3,000 Japanese Brazilians in 1955. Here the social organization is the same as in Japan. The system of buraku (subvillages) is employed, although expansive territory and racial mixtures make for substantial differences.[39]

It is likely that the quality of group feeling among Japanese Brazilians is somewhat different from that among the people in the village community in Japan. Among Japanese in the suburbs of São Paulo, many first-generation farmers maintain the same sort of consciousness as exists in the Japanese village community, even though they are independent and their involvement in the economic structure is not paternalistic.[40]

After World War II, in Dourados, Mato Grosso, 28 of the total of 80 lots were assigned to Brazilians, so as to promote contacts between the natives and the immigrants. In distributing the remainder, the colonists decided to promote neighborhood groupings through the distribution program. Nine groups were devised, four of which consisted of persons who had formed close friendships while on the ship which brought them to Brazil. One group was of kinfolk, and each of the others was limited to families who came from the same prefecture. All nine were merged into five administrative groups.[41]

In another new colony in Boa Vista, Rio Branco, mutual aid systems were relied upon in building houses and exchanging labor.[42]

An example of a disintegrative form of social organization is found in the colony at Monte Alegre, Pará. The entry of the immigrants at different times to the colony divided them into three groups. Consequently, since group activities are not common, the establishment of the cooperative society in the colony as a whole was postponed.[43]

There are no organizations "typical" of all the Japanese colonies, for each is differently influenced by time, population, natural environment, and economic organization. Almost every old Japanese colony has nihonjin kai, which is an organization limited to Japanese Brazilians and is strongly oriented to the traditional Japanese culture. In addition, the administrative divisions of the colony are similar to those in Japan, but the degree and quality of the community solidarity in the New World do not resemble those in the traditional Japanese communities. The symbolic village shrine does not integrate the members in the community as it does in Japan. Economically, a majority of Japanese Brazilians have more freedom than do farmers in Japan, and even though some immigrants rent land in Brazil, paternalistic relations with the landlord seldom prevail. Also, the subordination of a branch family to a main family is much less than in Japan. The importance of belonging to "good, old families" is considerably depreciated by Japanese immigrants in Brazil. But in the future, family status may contribute to the position of the wellborn.

Opportunities to obtain factors of production give second and third sons a basis for economic independence. Hence, the clanlike system which prevails in some villages in Japan has more or less disappeared in Brazil, even though interaction by members of kin groups continues. The main point is the fact that the generation which holds the leadership in the community is being replaced by a younger one less bound by Japanese tradition. Of course, there are colonies in which the population consists of postwar immigrants who also have a differing ethos than do prewar immigrants.

## Changes in the Basic Social Institutions

In comparison with the modern family in Europe and the United States, the Japanese family is larger, more complex, and is conscious of a greater number of generations. In addition, the Japanese family is distinguished by the following features: (1) it is conceived of as existing continuously from the past and indefinitely into the future, quite independent of the birth or death of individual members; (2) each family is centered about a household shrine where its gods are worshipped; and (3) property is owned by the family, although an individual member may occasionally be allowed by the patriarch to hold minor personal property. This last feature illustrates the extent to which family affairs are managed by the patriarch, who has authority over all the members.[44] However, all of these distinguishing features are losing their strength, especially since World War II.

### Marriage and the Family

Family members may be classified into two categories: (1) persons socially recognized as direct descendants in the family line and their spouses, and (2) more distant relatives and servants socially recognized as being outside the direct family line. The former enjoy a higher status than the latter. Even brothers are assigned status in accord with the relative likelihood that each may acquire the headship of the family.[45] As the family divides, adopted sons, servants, and others establish new families each of which is subordinate to the main family.

Izumi studied the heads of 346 Japanese families in various parts of Brazil. Almost all of them (98 percent) were born in Japan and their mean age was forty-six years. About one-half (47 percent) of the households were still headed by those who held this position when they entered Brazil, 21 percent were newly established families, 17 percent were those whose head had been changed by succession, and 15 percent were new branch families.[46] These facts suggest that changes are operating slowly, and the leadership of families is still held by persons born in Japan. In other words, in the first generation the general tendency to change is not great.

The size of families in Brazil is much larger than that in the rural areas of Japan, owing to the large number of unmarried children in the Japanese-Brazilian family. Thus in south Brazil there is an average of 7.7 persons per family, and in the Amazon region one of 6.7 persons, in comparison with only 4.7 persons per family in rural Japan.[47] However, Izumi found that in Brazil, the nuclear family and conjugal family are increasing in importance; and this seems to be the most important change in the family system in Brazil. On the other hand, some families are dependent upon family labor, and the adage that "good family composition is an easy way to success" is still relied upon by the immigrants. When questioned by Izumi, more than half of the heads of families in the sample answered that they wished to have at least six children, so that their family labor supply would be increased. This is related to the fact that parents wish to get wives for their sons from other farm families. Most of the mothers and the fathers desire to live with their children after the latter are married.[48] The large family is also characteristic of the independent farmers in Assaí, São Paulo.[49]

From Tome Asu in the Amazon region comes the report that a new house and one thousand pepper trees are given to a second or third son when he marries. In such a colony, economic prosperity provides the basis for second and third sons to become independent. Accordingly, the branch family and the main family establish a relationship quite different from that prevailing in Japan.

Regarding property inheritance, Izumi found that a large proportion of the people favor the equal division of property, but that a substantial group favors primogeniture. With reference to mate selection, the greatest proportion of people in the sample allow their children to find their own spouses, and the next largest proportion wish their children to consult with them on the matter.[50] Izumi states that in the rural districts in Brazil the custom of making betrothal presents and the selection of mates by parents or a go-between still prevails.

Wedding ceremonies in Tome Asu are partly Japanese and partly Brazilian. The couple is accompanied by the sponsor or patron, a priest, a clerk in the registration office, and relatives. After registration of the marriage, a party is held at the home of the bridegroom, but the wedding feast is far less lavish than that in the rural areas in Japan.[51] Marriage customs in urban districts are further different, and children are free to select their own mates. In fact, about 50 percent of the Japanese-Brazilian graduates from the medical and law schools of the University of São Paulo are married to Caucasian women from prosperous families. In Alvaro Machado, 97.0 percent of the Japanese-Brazilian men and 97.8 percent of the women are mated with other Japanese Brazilians. Oriental husbands have wives who are either Oriental or Caucasian, whereas exogamous Japanese-Brazilian wives usually have mates of a darker color than their own.[52]

Izumi also compiled data showing the mean age at marriage in Alvaro Machado, São Paulo, of Japanese immigrants in Brazil, their Brazilian-born children, and other Brazilians. For males the averages were 30.0, 24.8, and 24.9 years, respectively; and for females the corresponding indexes were 24.0, 21.4, and 20.4 years.[53] It is evident that the mean age at marriage of Japanese immigrants is higher than that of Brazilian-born Japanese and that of other Brazilians. This, Izumi explains, is the result of the failure of the Japanese prior to 1941 to register their marriages. Marriages between the Japanese immigrants and Brazilian-born Japanese in Brazil are relatively harmonious, although the cultural difference between the two is recognized to some extent.[54]

Generally, the close tie between the main family and the branch family is being weakened by the disappearance of primogeniture and the independence of the second and third sons. The patriarchal family system also is on the wane, and the conjugal family has become most typical in the new homeland.

Data are not available to show the extent to which birth control is practiced. Saito states that as the immigrants stopped practicing the birth control to which they were accustomed in Japan, the birth rate during the second year in Brazil rose considerably.[55]

Striking differences in the social status of the sexes is still a primary characteristic of Japanese Brazilians, but such also is the case among other Brazilians.

## Religion and Religious Institutions

As indicated above, the Japanese family system is based on lineage from the past, and this is closely associated with ancestor worship, usually through Buddhism. Relative to religious acculturation, Willems mentions syncretism and cultural change in Registro during the 1930s.[56] Almeida studied the Japanese in the same districts in the 1950s and indicates that the Japanese Brazilians are not preoccupied with religious problems. The *bustuda* (a Buddhist altar) and *tokonoma* (alcove) are infrequently seen.[57]

In Izumi's study, 40.6 percent of the households in south Brazil had no Shinto altars, while in the Amazon areas, the corresponding percentage was 78.3. His material indicates that formal faith in Buddhism has been abandoned by 26.1 percent of the people in south Brazil and 53.9 percent of those in the Amazon region. His data also indicated that 6.2 percent of those in the sample in the south and 28.0 percent of the Amazon residents are affiliated with Roman Catholic churches. Thus, religious acculturation is more advanced among the people in the Amazon region than among those in south Brazil.[58]

There are many cases in which the children of non-Catholic parents have been converted to Catholicism. In addition, dual affiliations of the Japanese with both Buddhism and Catholicism presents evidence that a Japanese attitude of indifference toward religion is common. It is important to note that about one-fourth of those under twenty-five years of age are Catholics, whereas over 90 percent of those aged fifty or more are Buddhists. The middle-aged, on the other hand, are affiliated in somewhat higher proportion with the newly established religions. *Seicho no Ie* (a new sect, especially popular in Japan after World War II) is gaining new members and believers at a rapid rate, although conversion data are to be interpreted with caution because the religious affiliations of children who have little or no consciousness of religious meanings are often determined by their parents. Many of the children who go to *groupos* (Brazilian schools) are baptized because of pressures from Brazilian teachers and pupils. The parents' attitudes toward children's religion are complicated through the ethos inherent in Japanese culture. However, religious acculturation of the Japanese Brazilians has been facilitated by their flexible and indifferent attitudes toward religion.

*Education and the School*

Appraisal of Japanese culture is more effectively made if one has an adequate command of the Japanese language. The easiest course for immigrant parents in Brazil is to establish an environment in which they are not forced by necessity to use Portuguese. This is one of the greatest *raisons d'être* for the Japanese-language schools which function as cooperative and integrative agencies in the colonies. In addition, many others of their aspirations may be accomplished through education.

In 1938, when Brazilian legislation nationalized education, there were 260 Japanese-language schools in São Paulo, employing 335 Japanese teachers who were registered by the state's Department of Education.[59] The legislation nationalizing teaching prohibited all foreign-language schools of any kind; nevertheless, some secret Japanese schools continued to be maintained. In the rural districts there are presently two schools in a community—a Brazilian school and a Japanese-language school in which the textbooks are those supplied by the Japanese government prior to the end of World War II.

In the Suzano area, where about one thousand Japanese Brazilians are clustered, the children attend Brazilian schools. But some secret contracts between policemen, Brazilian teachers, city officers, and the leaders of nihonjin kai resulted in the opening of Japanese-language schools. The management of these schools is entirely controlled by the nihonjin kai.[60] On the other hand, in Tome Asu, in northern Pará, where the Japanese Brazilians are a small minority, a school was opened in 1952, but soon was discontinued.[61]

There are some indications that the Japanese in the Amazon area use Portuguese more frequently than do those in the South. Conversations between children are mostly in Portuguese, although they use Japanese when talking with their parents. Apparently the ecological isolation of the Japanese in the Amazon is a factor in promoting the rapid acquisition of a knowledge of Portuguese.

It seems necessary to conclude, therefore, that marginal persons are being formed through the dual educational orientations and dual language system. In contrast with religion, the language used is a serious matter, for the Japanese eagerness to adhere to Japanese culture is most frankly manifested in their attitudes toward the use of the Japanese language.

## *Economic Institutions and Agricultural Cooperatives*

The integrative functions of economic institutions in community organization deserve particular emphasis. Here, the analysis of economic institutions is mostly concerned with agricultural and industrial cooperatives.

In 1936 there were in Japan 357,628 agricultural associations, having a membership of 24,937,534. The major functions of these were connected with credit and the improvement of production.[62] Thus from experience, the Japanese immigrants knew the value of cooperatives, and the people in the newly established settlements attempted enthusiastically to found economic cooperatives, as a basis of successful living.

In rural areas, the Brazilians were excluded from membership. Thus, the nihonjin kai and the Japanese-language school are closely related to the cooperatives which frequently contribute financial support to both the nihonjin kai and the Japanese-language schools.

In Suzano, São Paulo, there are three large agricultural cooperatives: Cooperativa Agrícola, Cooperativa Agrícola Mogi das Cruzes, and Cooperativa Central Agrícola, the members of which are spread widely throughout the state.

Saito conducted an intensive survey of the cooperatives in the Cotia area near the city of São Paulo. The prosperity of the Cotia Agricultural Cooperative is partly indicated by its membership, which was 4,868 in 1954. The racial composition of the members is as follows: Japanese, 2,670; Brazilian-born Japanese, 238; and Brazilians, 1,960. The increase in the number of native Brazilians is remarkable, whereas membership among the Japanese is increasing at a decreasing rate. This tendency to open the cooperatives to the public is evidenced by the fact that in 1954, eight of the officers of the Cotia Agricultural Cooperative were Brazilians.[63]

The agricultural cooperatives contribute in various ways to the integration of the community. Moderate-sized cooperatives in the Japanese-Brazilian colonies overlap considerably with the nihonjin kai in enhancing group solidarity among the Japanese. The larger and statewide cooperatives, such as the Cotia Cooperative, orient members to stress economic gain and promote little group consciousness.

*Political Organization and Government*

The Japanese Brazilians are still a small minority in political affairs in Brazil as a whole. Indeed, there is no formal political organization among them. In order to understand the association as the controlling power in Japanese communities, the nihonjin kai requires analysis. In the urban areas there is less social pressure to join the nihonjin kai. In fact, Japanese Brazilians in a city with a diversified racial composition hesitate to organize their unified nihonjin kai.[64]

When a community composed largely of Brazilian-born Japanese is controlled by the nihonjin kai, this association becomes a significant political pressure group. At present, it appears that Japanese Brazilians do not usually enjoy preference in Brazilian political parties.[65] The prewar Japanese immigrants were politically dependent upon Japanese governmental agencies and colonization companies, and disregarded Brazilian politics. Since they have come to recognize Japan's defeat, their attitude toward Brazilian politics is shifting.

*Play and Recreational Associations*

In the city of São Paulo, Japanese recreational facilities are available to the colonists, much as they would be in Japan. In the rural districts, most of the recreational activities are arranged by the nihonjin kai or by the associations of girls and boys. In an integrated Japanese-Brazilian community such as Assaí, there are clubs of kendo (Japanese fencing), judo, Japanese chess, and 4-H. Furthermore, *kinjin kai* (a group of persons from the same prefecture in Japan) is commonly organized.[66] The present writers have been unable to secure data on the dissemination of baseball in Brazil, although it is the most popular sport in Japan. The discrepancy between generations in types of recreation should not be overlooked. It may be true that Japanese festivals or other special occasions retain ways of celebration more familiar to older members of the community.

In the colony of Assizal in the Amazon area, where the youth association is not active, contact is frequent between the Japanese and Brazilians through informal dancing parties. In urban districts, voluntary associations are found to a greater degree in sports clubs and dancing parties which are often held for the younger generation. Thus, voluntary recreational associations and clubs prevail in the cities where the nihonjin kai or the association of the young men are not integrative forces in the community. On the other hand, the characteristics of exclusiveness and cohesiveness prevail in rural districts where basic institutions are more likely to be Japanese. Social pressures in the community make for almost involuntary alliance with the integrative nihonjin kai.

## Changes in the Ethos

If the ethos were an actual and valid identification of the distinctive features of a particular culture, we would still need to use great caution in generalizing about it. But as Ogburn and Nimkoff state, such an attempt to single out any one dominating characteristic for a comprehensive culture is merely impressionistic emphasis.[67]

In this section, some aspects of Japanese-Brazilian cultural conflicts from prewar times to the present are discussed. Some of these already have been touched upon. The main concern is to examine their attitudes toward their mother country.

It is a well-known fact that Japanese patriotism was great and that loyalty to the family, community, nation, and Emperor as a social symbol was manifested in many ways. Most of the Japanese immigrants were conscious that they were Japanese, and ''do not disgrace Japan'' was a particularly effective slogan. Of course, most of them were imperialistically oriented by Japanese policy. After the *Estado Novo* was established by Getulio Vargas in 1938, political pressures from the Brazilian government became strong. In 1942 *Doko kai* (a kind of totalitarian association) was organized to denounce the Japanese who were engaged in producing silkworms and peppermint plants for export to the United States. The people in this association damaged the silkworm sheds and peppermint fields, in order to decrease production.[68]

Even after August 14, 1945, many Japanese in Brazil refused to believe that Japan had been defeated. The totalitarian *Shindo Renmei* was then established, and had as its main purpose fostering the spirit of Japanese nationalism to help in building a greater Japan. At the same time, recognition of the defeat was becoming widespread among the colonists; however, even by the end of September 1945, the demagogism that Japan had been victorious and that Japanese ships were coming to Brazil to carry immigrants back to Japan brought more than 2,000 people from the interior to the city of São Paulo.

At about this time the Japanese Brazilians came to be divided into the two groups: the "victory group" who believed that Japan had been victorious in World War II, and the "defeatist group" who believed that Japan had lost the war. The conflict between these two groups horrified all Brazilians. The terroristic activities of *Shindo Renmei* started with the assassination of the president of Bastos Industrial Cooperative on March 7, 1946, and during the following year about fifteen persons who were supposed to be leaders in Japanese-Brazilian communities were killed and attempts were made on the lives of others.[69]

Izumi found that the Japanese in the Amazon region were more prone to recognize Japan's defeat than were their fellows in south Brazil. About 28 percent of the people in south Brazil were classed as fanatics on this topic, in comparison with only 3.7 percent of the residents of the Amazon area.[70] However, part of the misinformation was due to the lack of reliable communication media during the war.

The people's reaction to the horrible conduct of *Shindo Renmei* and the "victory group" is evidenced by their replies to the question: What was the most regrettable attitude of the Japanese Brazilians? Approximately three-fourths of the persons in the sample named the conflict between the "victory group" and the "defeatist group."[71]

These events promoted by the "victory group" and *Shindo Renmei* have shaken Japanese Brazilians; and the pride of Japanese Brazilians in their mother country accompanied by its decline as a first-rate world power has made for numerous conflicts. Yet ideological backgrounds and basic beliefs were so deeply rooted that they did not disappear, and of those questioned, about 90 percent of the people indicated that Japan must regain worldwide strength.[72]

It is significant that there are great differences between the ethos of Japanese in Brazil and those in Japan. Also, the cultural differences between generations are important. If they are to become thoroughly attuned to life in Brazil, the people must abandon their former mystic confidence in Japan, which was called "God's country." They must not rely on their mother country, but must shift their allegiance to the Brazilian culture and state.

# 11

## The Improvement of
## the Ways of Farming

In a few selected parts of the world such as Canada, northwestern Europe, and the United States, agriculture and animal husbandry have been perfected to an amazing degree during the last one hundred years. The quantities of food, feed, and fiber produced by given amounts of human energy and fixed acreages have been multiplied time and time again. The ways of extracting products from the soil are being improved with remarkable rapidity. Nevertheless, in a world in which the majority of mankind still is directly dependent upon agricultural and pastoral enterprises, and in which hunger is the daily lot of hundreds of millions of people, the slowness of general progress along these lines is dismaying. Indeed, in some of the largest and most densely populated sections of the globe the failure to effect substantial improvements in the growing of crops, the management of livestock, and the transporting of farm supplies and products still dooms large segments of humanity to lives that are only slightly above the mere creature level of existence. Even at a time when mankind is well along into the nuclear age and when billions of dollars are being spent on space exploration, much of the world's agriculture is woefully backward. In fact, it probably is fair to say that at least one-half of the earth's farmers continue to use methods that are no more advanced than those employed in the Tigris-Euphrates or Nile valleys in ancient times. Millions of these culturally handicapped farmers are in Brazil. Surely no more than 50 percent of all the agriculturists and herdsmen there are using any but the most antiquated procedures.

This exposition first appeared in the *International Review of Modern Sociology* 2, No. 2: 190-96, and is reproduced with the permission of the editor of that journal.

They still depend upon ways of preparing the soil, sowing the seeds, fostering and protecting the growing plants, taking in the harvest, transporting farm supplies and products, breeding cattle and sheep (and goats), maintaining pastures and ranges, and so on, that are hardly more modern than those of Abraham, Isaac, Jacob, and their contemporaries in the "Fertile Crescent." Therefore, for all genuinely interested in the well-being and advancement of 100 million Brazilians, the question that follows is of overwhelming importance.

Is it going to be possible for Brazil to quickly replace deeply rooted systems of agriculture that for the most part are antiquated and inefficient, and not infrequently even demeaning to the workers, with modern and efficient ways of extracting products from the soil? The future of most of the great half continent involved depends to a high degree upon the answer that can be given to this query. If the average Brazilian farmer were equipped with the knowledge, skills, and managerial proficiency more or less equal to those possessed by the agriculturists of such Canadian provinces as Manitoba and Saskatchewan as early as 1910, Brazil already would be the envy of most Spanish-American countries and other "developing" societies as well.

I feel fully justified in making such generalizations, even though I personally have been privileged to observe the highly perfected systems of agriculture in selected portions of Brazil. I am acquainted with the modern ways of farming that European immigrants and their children have superimposed upon the traditional methods in southern Brazil. I have visited and admired the magnificent coffee, sugar-cane, cotton, and rice plantations in São Paulo; and I know some of the ultramodern cotton plantations and dairy farms in the same great state. I have observed with intense interest the effective ways of producing crops and livestock that are employed by the Japanese colony in Brazil and by recent Dutch colonists at Holambra, São Paulo; and I have watched with fascination the development of highly mechanized agricultural establishments in a few other parts of Brazil and the emergence of other modern examples of farming as they have been implanted elsewhere between Uruguay and Venezuela. On the other hand, however, I have also personally seen throughout the most heavily populated portions of Brazil tens of thousands of tiny subsistence tracts, thousands of small and moderately sized farms, and many hundreds of large estates on which the prevailing systems of agriculture are no more advanced than those in use during Old Testament times. Moreover, for Brazil, as also is true for Colombia, I have myself been able to assemble the statistical data to show that the majority of all the agriculturists are lacking any agricultural implements whatsoever other than the ax and the hoe; and that most of them are able to make use of no power, animal or mechanical, except that supplied by their own arms and backs. Such antiquated systems of agriculture are prima facie evidence that human labor is being wasted to an appalling degree and that the input of management in the various agricultural enterprises is extremely meager.

## Ways of Farming: A Sociocultural System[1]

The concept of ways of farming as used in this article requires careful definition, although its general connotations are reasonably self-evident. As is true of any other system, the sociocultural system we designate as the ways of farming involves an ordering or organization of constituent parts into a functional entity, or a unity that is vastly different from a mere aggregation of the components. Thus, the significance of the term "system" in the conception is similar to what it has in other contexts such as organic system, mechanical system, weather system, and so on. In addition it is, of course, essential to distinguish this specific sociocultural system from all of the other entities in the category to which it pertains. This we do by specifying that the term we are defining involves an integrated body of practices, culture traits and complexes, customs, ideas, skills, techniques, prejudices, habits, implements, machines, domestic animals, scientific knowledge, seeds, and so on, as they are used by the members of a specific society in order to carry on the various enterprises connected with the growing of crops, the care of livestock, and the transportation of things on the farm and between the farm and the market. Moreover, this part of the socioeconomic order is highly institutionalized, so that among the farmers and herdsmen of any given region or community the prevailing methods of preparing the seedbeds, sowing and cultivating the crops, animal husbandry, poultry management, harvesting, and transportation are highly standardized; and in general the social and cultural values of the rural society involved are oriented towards the preservation of the traditional forms of life and labor.

Throughout Brazil there is the utmost variety with respect to the kind and amount of scientific knowledge, skills and practices, implements and machines, domestic animals and harnessing equipment, and so on, which serve as components of any given system used in the extraction of products from the soil. Thus the system used by a village of Indians on the upper reaches of the Amazon or one of its tributaries may have as its central features the digging sticks manipulated by the women of the tribe and a set of magical and religious practices thought to have utility in fostering the productivity of the soil; whereas that used on a large, modern sugar-cane or cotton plantation in São Paulo, or a large rice plantation in Rio Grande do Sul, may consist of an intricate and integrated combination of the most modern practices, well-established scientific principles, highly perfected machines and implements, and thoroughly rationalized principles of management. In Brazil, as elsewhere throughout the world, the crux of the matter of agricultural productivity and development involves rapid and general adoption of ways of farming for which many of the central components were unknown at the opening of the twentieth century.

## The Six Principal Ways of Farming

The basic ways of farming can be classified into the six following categories: (1) riverbank plantings; (2) what is known as *rozar* in Spanish, and *derrubar e queimar* in Portuguese, all of which might be translated into English as *felling and burning;* (3) hoe culture; (4) rudimentary plow culture; (5) advanced plow culture; and (6) mechanized farming. All six of these systems are to be reckoned with throughout Brazil, although each of them except hoe culture and rudimentary plow culture has a rather limited distribution. The first four, and especially the third and the fourth, are the ones which are responsible for the utter waste of astounding proportions of the time, energies, and resources of the Brazilian people. The fifth is practically impossible to propagate in any "underdeveloped" country, except by means of the actual transplantation of colonies of farmers from northwestern Europe or Japan, apparently because few people recognize that the steel plow, mathematically balanced and equipped with a moldboard, is only one of the central components of an intricate and highly interdependent system. Hence the keen disappointment of those who have attempted to introduce this instrument (without at the same time transplanting along with it the appropriate draft animals, harnesses, hitching equipment, and even an experienced plowman) in the years since Brazil and the other Latin American countries gained their independence.

## Improvement of the Ways of Farming

As mentioned above, huge contingents of Brazil's rural population remain enchained by the gross inadequacies of their traditional ways of growing crops and managing livestock. In order to set forth more clearly the nature of the problem and the possible solution for it, each of the four traditional ways of farming is considered in turn. This then is supplemented by a few comments about advanced plow culture.

### Riverbank Plantings[2]

Agriculture (as distinguished from the mere collection of nature's gifts of seeds, fruits, and tubers) began when woman saved a few seeds or tubers from the plants which she had learned to rely upon for bounteous quantities of foodstuffs and deposited them in locations suitable for their growth and development. Among the places which early came to be known as being the most propitious for such purposes are the soft, loamy surfaces along the banks of a stream such as the Nile, the Tigris or Euphrates, or the Amazon, as the waters recede in the course of their annual cycle. In its earliest and simplest form, the weight of the body placed upon the ball of the foot as it is used to press the seeds into the spongy surface of the soil is the manner of planting and no cultivation whatsoever is involved. Many thousands of people in Brazil's great Amazon Basin still rely for much of their foodstuffs upon this primitive procedure; and others who make their plantings along the dry beds of streams and washes in Brazil's great problem-stricken Northeast and along the banks of such streams as the São Francisco are employing methods that are only a step removed from these rudimentary practices. Fortunately, improvements in this elementary system are the easiest to implement, for the use of a digging stick or a crude hoe can be incorporated in it to effect radical transformations; and this innovation need not produce any highly offensive disruptions in the prevailing sociocultural equilibrium.

Along the banks of the great São Francisco River, as it flows through the highly arid portions of the Brazilian states of Bahia and Pernambuco, I have observed the women incorporating the crudest type of irrigation into this primitive manner of growing crops. There I noted women carrying water in old five-gallon gasoline tins from the stream up to the spots on which they had made their plantings. Then, the water was poured into large, hand-shaped wooden bowls or troughs; and from these with their cupped hands the women scooped it up and on to the plants in a manner roughly designed to simulate rainfall. Obviously, as I attempted to explain to these industrious farmers during a single brief conversation, this "sprinkling" type of irrigation could be greatly improved and a given amount of labor made to serve a garden at least twice as large as the tiny plot each of them was using, merely by making the discarded oil or gasoline container into a crude sprinkler by punching a few holes into one side of its top, thus eliminating completely the need for the wooden trough and the scooping operation. Moreover, even a doubling of the area used for plantings would hardly be noticed on the almost totally barren inner slope of the riverbank, nor would a doubling or quadrupling of the amount of beans, melons, corn, and other products greatly exceed the dietary needs of the families involved although hopefully small quantities might begin finding their way to market. Of course, now that technical assistance on a large scale is being directed to the area, perhaps it is not too much to hope that this riverbank gardening can be facilitated, greatly expanded, and even commercialized to a considerable degree, by the introduction and widespread use of small gasoline pumps, plastic hoses, and metal nozzles and sprinklers. Surely however, the general practice of employing the hoe would be among the innovations made in any such development program, and this would mean the transformation of the way of farming we have been commenting upon into the more advanced system of hoe culture.

## Felling and Burning

Throughout the huge, warm, lowland expanses which extend from southern Brazil to the boundaries with Peru, Colombia, and

Venezuela, the second of our ways of farming is indigenous and widely used even today. Indeed, the lack of any less primitive and antiquated manner of getting products from the soil is responsible for the useless expenditure of the bulk of the energies of millions of humble rural Brazilians on the one hand, and the almost wanton destruction of immense expanses of forests on the other. Its replacement by ways of farming which involve tillage and cultivation, permanent use of the same pieces of land, the application of fertilizers, and so on, offers one of the major opportunities for increasing production and feeding the masses presently concentrating in the nation's cities and towns. This system of production has been observed by me in the course of the last quarter of a century in nearly all parts of Brazil, and also in extensive portions of Bolivia and Peru, in Colombia and Venezuela, and in many lowland portions of Central America. The exact procedures involved are generally about as follows: (1) at the beginning of the dry season the countryman begins felling the virgin forest or the great second growth on the tract he has selected for use that year, and this he continues until the signs indicate that the rainy season is about to begin; (2) fire is put to the entire mass of fallen timber; (3) amid the tangled mass of unburned trunks and limbs—and frequently while the fires are still smoldering—seeds of beans, corn, or other plants are deposited in the opening made by a swipe of the big toe, a crude digging stick, or in rare cases, by a hoe; (4) there is no cultivation to destroy competing plants, although now and then the machete may be used to cut back the suckers that sprout out from the abundant stumps; (5) in many instances some of the unburned branches are used to build a crude fence about the small clearing in order to keep out animals of various kinds; and (6) eventually the harvest is taken. The following season, or at most after a second planting of this primitive type, the process will be repeated in another place where the trees are large and plentiful; and the "old field" that is left will revert to forest until after the passage of several decades when the second growth may be sufficiently large and abundant to attract another family that is seeking out a favorable location of a new *roça* or "field."

Apologists by the thousands, including not a few agricultural scientists, have defended this system (in Latin America, Africa, and Asia) on one ground or another; but its replacement is increasingly the concern of those seeking to speed up the process of development throughout Brazil.

## Hoe Culture

The aborigines of America apparently had no hoe prior to the coming of Columbus, although the Incas of Peru had developed a highly perfected type of digging stick which enabled energy to be applied simultaneously by both the foot and the hand. Often this has been described rather uncritically as a "foot plow," although it would be more accurate to call it an approximation of a wooden spade. The hoe, the traditional implement of all Mediterranean peoples, was brought to the New World by the Spaniards and the Portuguese, and hoe culture as such remains today as the chief reliance of the great mass of the rural people who live between the Rio Grande and Cape Horn. In Brazil its chief competitor is the felling and burning just described. It is relied upon principally not only in the production of the beans, the manioc, the rice, the corn, and other food crops which sustain the masses of the Brazilian population, but also in the growing of many of the highly commercialized export crops such as coffee, cotton, and tobacco. In many sections even sugar cane is produced almost exclusively by a system of hoe culture.

## Rudimentary Plow Culture

The fourth of the systems of agriculture (whose core elements are the crude, wooden, rooting plow; the slow, lumbering ox; and the antiquated two-wheeled oxcart) remains as a major factor to be reckoned with in all endeavors to inventory or improve the ways in which Brazilians go about deriving a livelihood from the soil. Like hoe culture this was the mainstay of the Mediterranean world at the time of the discovery of America, and it was one of the chief contributions which the stock-raising conquerors made to the agricultural activities of their Indian vassals in all of Spanish America and some parts of Brazil. In 1500, however, neither the plow itself, nor the draft animals, the oxcart, and the harness and hitching equipment brought to America from the Iberian Peninsula were substantially improved over those which the Egyptians were using thousands of years previously. Nor have they undergone any noteworthy changes from 1500 to the present. As for the system itself, the depth to which it is rooted in custom and tradition constitutes a primary obstacle to the improvement of life and labor in some parts of Brazil and vast areas elsewhere in Latin America.

*Advanced Plow Culture*

The fifth, and in many ways the most significant of all the six basic ways of farming, began taking form in northwestern Europe during Roman times; and it reached its acme of perfection in the northern and western portions of the United States and the "Prairie Provinces" of Canada about 1915. Its key components are the improved plow, equipped with a moldboard, which glides through the soil cutting and turning as it goes, in sharp contrast to the rooting and tearing done by the old Egyptian plow and its Hispanic descendants; the fast, even-gaited draft horse, equipped with the all-important horse collar and hundreds of other highly adjusted pieces of harnessing and hitching equipment; and the four-wheeled farm wagon. The English colonies, and particularly the northern ones, received this sociocultural system in a fairly advanced form from the mother country, and it was brought to perfection in the Midwest of the United States and the adjacent parts of Canada. There, in such states as Michigan, Indiana, Illinois, Wisconsin, Iowa, and Minnesota (and in the Canadian provinces of Manitoba, Saskatchewan, and Alberta), immense numbers of immigrant farmers from northwestern Europe have had a large part in one of the most remarkable cultural transformations the world has ever seen. These immigrants from England, Germany, Denmark, Sweden, Norway, Ireland, and a few other countries, were ravenously "land hungry," they were driven by unbounded aspirations for a better life for themselves and especially their children, they were already habituated to the system in general, and they were subject to almost no restrictions that would inhibit the development of the highest type of society made up of the middle-class operators of substantial family-sized farms.

A mention of the development of this system in northwestern Europe, the United States, and Canada is pertinent in this article for two reasons: (1) it is probably the factor which did most to generate the immense differences between the levels of living in northern Europe and southern Europe, and between those in the United States and Canada and those in Brazil and the other Latin American countries; and (2) advanced plow culture neither has nor is likely to contribute very much to agricultural and socioeconomic development in most parts of Brazil (and in most of the Spanish-American countries as well). In connection with the second of these points it should be indicated that there are some exceptions to the rule. The European farmers who emigrated to south Brazil, southern Chile, and Argentina late in the nineteenth century carried with them the system of advanced plow culture in a moderate stage of development, and thereby contributed immensely to the efficiency of agricultural production in the areas which they settled. More recently, especially in southern Brazil (and in Uruguay and Argentina), later immigrants from Europe have had a major role in the superimposition of a fairly modern agricultural way of life upon the old pastoral culture which long had dominated large areas of what potentially are among the best farming areas of the entire world. Generally speaking, though, repeated attempts, from about 1800 on, to introduce the improved plow into Latin America have failed utterly. Apparently the difficulty is that only the improved metal plow has figured in the endeavors or the "experiments"; and this instrument by itself has not proved equal to the abuses to which it was subjected, not to mention the expectations of those who misguidedly sought to fit it into a total system of rudimentary plow culture. Be this as it may, however, the failure of advanced plow culture to become established throughout Brazil during the nineteenth century and the opening half of the twentieth, retarded the development of most parts of the country so greatly that it may be almost impossible for most of them to overcome the handicap.

## *Mechanized Farming*[3]

The extent to which agriculture in most parts of Brazil can be made to enter the twentieth century probably will be due almost exclusively to the replacement of a rudimentary pastoral economy and the four traditional and antiquated systems of agriculture by the highly perfected mechanized system of farming. Indeed this phenomenal change has already been accomplished in a few favored locations. The system itself is readily available for transplantation and, fortunately, no one seems inclined to attempt to fit a few of its central features into the traditional rudimentary plow culture system.

Moreover, tractors and motor trucks are now so widely used for nonagricultural purposes throughout Brazil that the lines of supply for parts are thoroughly established and skilled mechanics are widely distributed.

The way of farming which now is enabling the modernization of agriculture to take place in Brazil and other ''developing'' sections of the world was developed directly out of the advanced plow culture. In the parts of the United States and Canada mentioned above, the tractor, the motor truck, and the automobile quickly replaced the horse; the number of plow bottoms, cultivators, harrows, disks, and so on, per implement was increased, their balance improved, and all the machinery was made of lighter and stronger metals; the grain combine and the corn picker were perfected; and the equipment for handling hay and that used in the preparation of silage were greatly improved; electricity was brought to the barns to power milking machines and other labor-saving devices; and gasoline motors became the sources of energy used to pump water, grind feed, and perform hosts of other farm tasks. Perhaps the most revolutionary aspect of all these improvements, however, was the attainment of what was the major objective of all these world-shaking transformations, namely, to enable one man, usually the farm operator himself, to perform any one of the large and complicated processes. Simultaneously, improvements were made in the highways to the extent that even the farm-to-market roads became ''all-weather'' arteries of traffic; and hundreds of other highly useful features became integral parts of the most remarkable system of agriculture and animal husbandry that the world has ever known. By 1950 this superbly effective sociocultural entity was not only widely used in Europe and almost universally disseminated throughout the United States, but it was available for transplantation in other parts of the world.

Brazil should be among the chief beneficiaries of an ultramodern mechanized farming system. This is largely because the great bulk of its potentially most productive land has never felt the fructifying influence of the plow. Even the best land in many of its thickly populated districts has never grown anything but a native grass. Thus to the extent that the large landed proprietors can turn their thoughts from pastoral activities to agriculture, huge expanses of land are readily available for cultivation by highly mechanized methods. Moreover, at an increasing pace, the superimposition of such a type of farming upon the traditional pastoral culture actually is taking place. Furthermore, unlike the situation in the United States, where the mechanization of agriculture has been both a response to the flight of people from the land and a factor promoting the rural-to-urban exodus, in large portions of Brazil the introduction of the mechanized system of agriculture results in a need for many additional families to assist in the cultivation of the soil. The beneficial results of the change already are available for all to see in many areas. Among those that I have seen personally, some of the more impressive are: the highly productive cotton farms in the Triangulo of Minas Gerais; some of the rice farms in the states of Rio Grande do Sul and São Paulo; and some of the large sugar-cane plantations in São Paulo and the state of Rio de Janeiro. All of this, however, is of modest proportions in relation to the task that needs to be done. It will require the skillfully directed and untiring efforts of all those interested in the well-being of the massive rural population of Brazil in order to teach the great majority of those who live by agriculture and pastoral activities even the elements of modern ways of farming. Fortunately, the Brazilians have now developed a highly effective agricultural extension service, the Associação Brasileira de Crédito e Assistência Rural; and its thousands of dedicated workers aided by personnel of the Ministry of Agriculture, the experts of various international agencies, and technicians of firms engaged in the processing of farm products are doing much to modernize Brazilian ways of farming.

# 12

## Recent Social Changes

During the 1960s Brazil entered a new epoch in her history, in her relationships with the United States, and in her international role. By 1963 she also appeared to be on the verge of an upheaval that might range all the way from a seizure of power in some kind of coup d'etat (generally called "revolution" when Latin America is involved) to a destructive civil war. The unheaval that did take place was far less extreme than might have been the case, but even so the type of society prevailing in Brazil prior to the Second World War was gone forever; and in the 1970s those who would understand life and work in the Portuguese-speaking half of South America must reckon with an important set of new factors. This includes an extreme nationalism, which involves an aspiration to be the leader of a regional bloc of nations; the determination to become a highly industrialized country; increased importance of the masses in the political and other power struggles going on at the local, state, and national levels; and apparently less dependence upon improvisation while planning ahead more in order to meet the exigencies of social, economic, and political life. In the paragraphs that follow, an attempt has been made to describe a few of the momentous social changes which underlie the tremendous ferment and demand for change currently prevailing in Brazil. Only seven of these are treated here, namely, the phenomenal increase of population; the rush of people to the cities and the resulting urbanization and suburbanization; the changes in the prevailing type of social solidarity; the development of a middle class; the widening gap between the standards of living and the level of living; the

First published in *Social Science* 48, No. 1 (Winter 1973): 3-15, and republished by permission of the editors.

increasing scarcity of goods, capital, professional and technical skills, and other components of a modern and industrialized society; and the rapid homogenization of Brazilian society.

## The Growth of Population

For the simple reason that the growth of Brazil's population itself is the principal factor bringing about many of the other changes in Brazilian society, it will be considered first in our brief discussion of the recent developments in that country. Many striking superlatives are being used nowadays to describe the phenomenal increase of population that is taking place throughout the world; but their use is most appropriate in connection with the changes now going on in Brazil and Spanish America. Since at least 1925 the population of Brazil has been characterized by an exceptionally high rate of natural increase and consequently by rapidly mounting numbers of people. Furthermore, since 1950 the rate of growth has risen to an even higher level than prevailed prior to that, and there is every reason to suppose that during the 1970s the population of Brazil will maintain its record-breaking rate of increase.

That the population of Brazil was multiplying at a very rapid rate has, of course, been known for some time. Census counts made in 1940 and 1950 enabled us to calculate that the rate prevailing during the decade between these two enumerations was an exceptionally high 2.5 percent per annum. As a result of this, most of those dealing with Brazilian population matters (including the Instituto Brasileiro de Geografia e Estatística and the present writer) anticipated that Brazil's population in 1960 would be about 66 million. Much to the surprise of all of us, however, the 1960 census reported a total of almost 71 million. This means that the rate of increase had risen to about 3.3 percent per year, a truly astounding rate that also was equaled for the same period by the growth of population in the Spanish-American half of South America. Prior to this recent development in South America, never before in human history had the population of an entire continent increased at such a pace. As a matter of fact, it is probable that the United States between 1790 and 1860, when the rate of population growth ran about 3.2 percent per year, is the only other large nation that previously had experienced such a rapid increase of population.

Between 1960 and 1970 Brazil's population continued burgeoning with the actual increase reported being from 71 million to almost 95 million, or about 34 percent, so that the annual rate remained above 3 percent per annum. About 1965 she also passed the landmark at which the population became predominantly urban; and during the year 1972 she passed the 100 million mark in number of inhabitants.[1]

It is also important to note that between 1960 and 1970 the rates of population increase were substantial throughout all parts of the Brazilian half continent. In none of the states were they lower than that of the United States (13 percent). On the other hand, though, the new Federal District almost trebled in population during the decade under consideration, and the growth rates in most of the other populous sections of Brazil were very rapid. This was especially true in Goiás, in which the new Federal District containing Brasília forms a small enclave, and its big neighbor, the state of Mato Grosso. But the recent increase also was very great in Paraná, which also more than doubled in population between 1950 and 1960.

**Urbanization**

After centuries of existence as an overwhelmingly rural, agricultural, pastoral, and collecting society, Brazil presently is caught up in a mad rush to urbanize and industrialize. The small elite minority who belong to the traditional families and, to an even greater extent, the ''new rich''—those who command and direct—seem to have become convinced that industrialization is the only solution for the host of acute and chronic problems which confront Brazilian society. Millions of simple country folk are fleeing the huge estates and flocking into the cities or squatting in the huge circular belts of misery, or shanty towns, which surround most of the towns and cities. In a few locations, such as the areas in and about the cities of São Paulo and Rio de Janeiro, great industrial complexes are arising; but most Brazilian cities still have no substantial industrial bases, and industry and jobs in factories are almost nonexistent in many of the large and rapidly growing centers. Moreover, few of the uprooted country folk who have migrated to the cities have more than the most rudimentary ideas about their chances for remunerative work and improved levels of living. Nevertheless, during the 1960s and 1970s the drastic changes which are the order of the day from the Amazon Basin to the State of Rio Grande do Sul have urbanization, both as a cause and as an effect, at the core of the modifications that are under way.

The most publicized aspects of the phenomenal increase of urban population in gigantic Brazil are, of course, the almost fantastic expansion of the cities of Rio de Janeiro and São Paulo. As late as 1920 there were no more than 1,250,000 persons in the area now occupied by metropolitan Rio de Janeiro, an extremely limited portion of Brazilian territory which now contains a population of well over 7 million people. In 1900 the city of São Paulo had only 240,000 residents, and a remarkable increase brought this figure up to 579,000 by 1920. In 1970, however, as the capital of a state having almost 18 million inhabitants, of whom about three-fourths were urban, São Paulo had become the greatest industrial center in all of Latin America. Its built-up areas had spread out far beyond the boundaries of the município in which it is located, a political subdivision of the state which alone contained 5,902,000 residents in 1970, to make the central city into the core of a metropolitan area of more than 8 million human beings. Thus, São Paulo, and even Rio de Janeiro, has the right to dispute with Buenos Aires and Mexico City for the distinction of being the largest city in Latin America and the second largest in the Western Hemisphere.

One must stress, however, that the great speed with which these two huge conurbations are growing is merely indicative of the upsurge of urban development throughout the nation. In this connection it is important to note that in 1940 only 31.2 percent of Brazil's 41,236,000 inhabitants was placed in the urban (including suburban) category, whereas by 1950 36.2 percent of its 51,944,000 people was so classified; by 1960 45.1 percent of its 70,967,000 inhabitants qualified as urban, and by 1970 about 55 percent of the 95 million inhabitants lived in urban areas. Such changes were possible only because the bulk of extremely rapid additions to the country's population was accounted for by the growth of urban centers.

It also is important to note that by 1970, sixty of Brazil's cities had populations of 100,000 or more, whereas as late as 1940, the center occupying the thirty-first place in the rank order (Bauru, São Paulo) had only 32,796 inhabitants.

*Urbanization and Urbanização*

There is one feature of the rapid urbanization process presently going on throughout Brazil to which I attribute the utmost significance. It is what I style as the lag of *urbanização* in comparison with urbanization.

*Urbanización* throughout Spanish America and *urbanização* in Brazil, both of which I translate as "urbanization," are widely used in a technical sense to denote the work of planning and constructing the physical parts of a city. This is to say that in Brazil *an* "urbanization" is a subdivision or other areas in which aligned streets have been laid out, public squares and parks have been provided, streets and sidewalks have been paved, and central water systems and lighting systems have been installed; it also indicates that, except for a broader use of the term by a few sociologists and economists, urbanização almost always is employed in Portuguese in the limited sense indicated. As a rule throughout Brazil the public improvements that are called "urbanizations" are concentrated in the central portions of the cities, and the surrounding sections, many of them very densely populated, are practically devoid of facilities.

Perhaps the difference between "urbanized" and "nonurbanized" areas, in the Latin American sense, is best expressed in the following translation of the distinction as used in Brazil for census purposes. This states that "an urbanized area is considered as that part of the territory that is served, or due to be served, by public improvements, as well as that included in the planned zone of expansion, including that along the highways. Considered as a non-urbanized area is that constituted of groups of buildings or dwellings in which there is a predominance of huts or rude dwellings constructed without obedience to any plan, outside the area of aligned streets, without legal rights of occupation [i.e., huts erected by squatters], and not served by public facilities."[2] This translation is presented not merely for the primary purpose of clarifying the connotations of the terms urban, *urbanização,* and so. forth in Brazil, but also in order to suggest some of the bases for the generalization that "urbanization" is not keeping pace with urbanization throughout Brazil. The mere fact that "the problem of the suburbs" is now generally recognized as one of the chief social problems afflicting the populations of Brazil (and also all of the other countries from Mexico to Argentina and Chile) alone is eloquent testimony to the validity of this proposition.[3] Moreover, some years ago the publication of comprehensive data for Brazil relating to "The Process of *Urbanização* and the Deficiency of Public Service or Those of Collective Utility in the Seats of Municipios," makes possible for that country a fairly adequate analysis of the situation. Even though substantial changes have taken place since the study was made the materials are important:

> Even leaving out of consideration the small towns and villages, which in general are of less importance demographically, and taking into account only the seats of municipios [counties], there is to be observed an accentuated deficiency of public services and those of collective utility in the interior of the nation. According to data published by the Section of Urbanistic Activities of the former Ministry of Education and Culture, the following was the situation on December 31, 1954: of the 2,399 seats of municipios existing in Brazil, 1,080 had no pavement whatsoever, 1,354 had no systems for supplying drinking water, 1,939 lacked systems for disposing of sewage, and 349 were without the benefits of electrical illumination. . . .Furthermore, in some of the capitals the situation was no better: there were no mains for drinking water in Rio Branco, and no sewage system in this same city nor in Boa Vista, Teresina, Maceió, or Cuiabá.[4]

The call for improvement made in this report along with a more general recognition of some of the basic requirements of life in large urban aggregations are producing much greater efforts to provide the essential facilities and services under consideration. Thus, according to the 1960 issue of Brazil's *Anuário Estatístico*,[5] by the close of the year 1958, 47 percent of the seats of the municipios were served by water mains and 34 percent had sewer systems, proportions that are substantially higher than those of 1954.

Comparable data for subsequent years are lacking; and only three items relating to "urbanization" are carried in the most recent issues of the *Anuário Estatistico,* namely public water systems, sewer systems, and garbage collection. Between 1960 and 1967, based on materials in the 1969 issue of the *Anuário,* the number of households in Brazil served by water meters rose from 850,514 to 1,495,058, and the number of buildings with sewer connections from 1,370,152 to 1,912,306. Even more significant, however, as a

demonstration of the extent to which "urbanization" in Brazil lags
in comparison with urbanization, is a compilation in the same issue
of the great statistical compendium showing estimates of the number
of people served by public water systems and sewers classified
according to the sizes of the municipio seats. These are presented in
summary form in Table 8. These materials make it evident that
about a fourth of the households in Brazil's cities of 100,000 or
more inhabitants still lack connections with water mains, and that
only about two-fifths of them are served by sewer systems.
Moreover, recent painstaking surveys of conditions in parts of
Salvador, the huge capital of Bahia, and in burgeoning Campina
Grande in the heart of the great Northeast, show that in many large
urban districts adequate and safe water supplies and facilities for
disposing of human wastes are still a thing of the future.[6]

TABLE 8

Estimates of the Number of People Served by
Public Water Systems and Sewers, by Size of the Seats
of the Municipios in which They Reside, 1967

| Number of inhabitants in the seat of the municipio | Population | Percentage served by | |
|---|---|---|---|
| | | Public water system | Sewers |
| Total | 85,783,003 | 26.9 | 13.1 |
| 2,000 or less | 49,066,558 | 1.1 | 0.2 |
| 2,001-10,000 | 7,858,490 | 35.3 | 11.4 |
| 10,001-20,000 | 3,478,847 | 51.5 | 22.2 |
| 20,001-50,000 | 3,694,745 | 61.9 | 31.0 |
| 50,001-100,000 | 3,034,558 | 73.8 | 40.5 |
| 100,001-over | 18,649,805 | 72.2 | 38.0 |

Source: *Anuário Estatístico do Brasil,* 1969, pp. 476, 478.

Earlier a reliable sociological survey of Rio de Janeiro's favelas
provided a wealth of detail to substantiate the conclusions one must
reach from the type of statistical data just presented. Thus the
perceptive authors of this report[7] state that "from the sanitary point
of view the favelas appear to us as suburbs embodied in the heart of
the city; and some even resemble certain parts of the rural zone with
their extremes transplanted into the heart of the nation's capital."
As a result of their comprehensive studies of the families who live
in the hundreds of thousands of hovels that cover the hills within

Brazil's famed and picturesque metropolis, the sociologists who conducted the studies concluded that "with rare exceptions water is the number one sanitary problem of the favelas. Water not only for the bath, a general problem in many of Rio de Janeiro's middle-class and even upper-class residential districts; but water to drink, water for the minimum necessities of the human being. In the favela of Escondidinho, for example, near the Laranjeiras-Rio Comprido tunnel, if the persons who live on the hill-top want water to drink, they must descend flights of stairs having 352 steps and then cross a stretch of steep hillside in order to get it, a kilometer away, in the Rua Almirante Alexandrino."[8] In general the data this same team supplies with respect to the facilities, or lack of them, in this great city, fully justifies anyone in reaching the conclusion that the lack of hygienic ways for disposing of bodily wastes and garbage create a problem that is only slightly less than that arising from the difficulty of getting water for drinking, bathing, and culinary purposes.

## Increasing Social Differentiation and the Change in Social Solidarity

Accompanying the mushrooming of cities and towns throughout Brazil are substantial changes in the size and structure of the rural community and in the nature of social cohesion in social groupings as a whole. These matters are important sociologically for they seem to determine in a large measure the personality types produced in a given society. Societies in which social differentiation has not proceeded to any great extent, as was the case in most parts of Brazil prior to the twentieth century, are made up of many small, homogeneous, and highly cohesive social groupings. The "experience world" of a given person is limited almost entirely to the small community or neighborhood, that is, to the little cluster of families in a small locality, into which he was born. All members of that community are essentially alike with respect to most of the fundamental characteristics and the social bonds which unite individuals into groupings. Occupationally, religiously, educationally, politically, ethically, and morally they are almost as similar as peas in a pod. In addition, centuries of inbreeding frequently develops a physical type that is highly uniform. Age and sex are the major bases for the division of social labor, and social cohesion is very strong. The latter is of the type that comes almost exclusively from the recognition of basic similarities between the members of the small locality group, of the type that has given rise to the sayings that "birds of a feather flock together," and "blood is thicker than water." Until recently the comparatively slight development of social differentiation and social solidarity based upon similarities on the part of the people making up each little homogeneous community have been characteristic of the masses of the people in extremely rural Brazil. (The sharp differences between the masses and the members of the small upper class were, of course, indicative of the one major cleavage that did exist, but even this does not invalidate the generalization that social differentiation was not highly developed.)

As a community grows, as societal horizons expand, and especially as contacts develop between those living in different locality groups, the process of social differentiation goes on rapidly. Occupational division of labor and specialization are accompanied by similar diversification in religious activities, education, politics, government, and all other parts of the social organization or structure. The mores and other standardized uniformities of behavior cease to command complete acceptance and compliance on the part of those residing in a given locality. Heterogeneity becomes the rule, and the cohesion or solidarity of the particular group and of society as a whole comes to be based in large measure upon the lack of self-sufficiency of any given part and the resulting interdependence which this brings about. Emile Durkheim, whose thinking in this respect I follow, designated this type of solidarity as *organic* because he thought it analogous with the interdependence of parts of a living organism. That based upon similarities he styled as *mechanistic*.

The changes in social differentiation and social solidarity presently taking place in most parts of Brazil resemble those which were going on in the United States about fifty years ago. It is likely, however, that the changes in the Brazilian social body show a greater variation from one part of its extensive territory to another than was true in the United States. This is to say that despite the comparative isolation and lack of contact of those living in such sections of the United States as the Southern Appalachians, the Ozarks, or the swamps of south Louisiana, that country in 1910 was less a superimposition of various epochs than Brazil is in the 1970s. Thus today one may find areas in São Paulo in which social differentiation seems to be keeping pace with that in the United States; but at the same time it is possible for anyone to visit many sections of Brazil in which the social order is only beginning to emerge from the colonial epoch. Lourenço Filho's proposition that one leaves behind a century of time with each day's journey inland from the coast still has considerable validity.[9]

Nevertheless, with the mushrooming of cities and towns, the improvement of transportation facilities, the development and spread of new and revolutionary means of communication, and the increasing spatial mobility of the population, the masses of the people in Brazil no longer are living in almost hermetically sealed-off little neighborhoods and communities. The division of labor in all lines of activity is increasing rapidly. Within each small locality group social solidarity of the mechanistic type is giving way to that based upon division of labor, specialization, and the consequent lack of self-sufficiency of the various parts. But although each community is becoming more heterogeneous in its make-up, Brazilian society as a whole is becoming less segmented and more of an integrated entity. Its various segments in different parts of the nation are coming to resemble one another more closely, or, in brief, the process of the homogenization, as indicated below, of Brazilian society is making great strides. This is to say that the individual Brazilian is coming to be less completely submerged in and circumscribed by his own small kinship and neighborhood groupings and more a citizen of his countylike municipio, his state, and his republic. Although this has not affected greatly the way of life of the members of the upper classes, it is of far-reaching significance for the humble folk who make up the mass of the population.

## The Rise of a Middle Class

Slowly but surely a middle class is arising in many parts of Brazil to help fill the large void that long existed between a small upper class at the top of the social scale and the impoverished, servile or semiservile, uneducated, and underprivileged masses that made up its inordinately large base. It should be stressed, though, that the change is not rapid in most places, is hardly under way in many, and that if Brazil ever is dominated by persons of middle-class status and mentality, this probably will be many decades in the future. The most headway has been made in the small-farming districts of Rio Grande do Sul, Santa Catarina, and Paraná, and in all of the larger cities. The immigration during the last quarter of the nineteenth century of a sturdy peasantry who were settled on small farms in south Brazil played a major role in the rise of Brazil's middle class, both in the rural districts, and in the cities to which large numbers of their offspring have migrated. These immigrants were strongly influenced by middle-class standards, and, even though there has been some tendency for their descendants to ape upper-class ways, relatively few of them could attain firm positions in the limited space on the upper rungs of the social ladder. In the middle ranges, though, their rapidly increasing numbers contribute greatly to the growth and development of the intermediate social strata which probably are properly denoted as middle-class people.

The rise of "the new middle class" has been traced in a substantial section of his excellent book by Professor Charles Wagley.[10] He first points out that since early in the nineteenth century there have been in Brazil "a small group of people who might be classified as middle class. These were originally the families of men who were clerks in government offices or who had other white-collar occupations. . . . Since the mid-nineteenth century, the immigration of Europeans, especially to southern Brazil, has added to the small Brazilian middle class." But he stresses that "until very recently this middle segment has been relatively insignificant in numbers and might even be said to have been actually the lower and poorer fringes of the upper class." In line with this, perhaps I should stress that I personally have been amazed at the extent to which the Brazilians I know, who appear to live at a middle-class level, actually are the descendants of those who once occupied the very apex of Brazilian society.

Relative to the most recent developments Wagley has the following to say:

> Everyone who has known Brazil for the last two decades agrees that the middle class has increased many times over and is rapidly expanding. This is reflected in an enormous increase

in demand for consumer goods, in the expansion of middle-income housing, and in the heavier pressure on all public services. Perhaps the best index of middle class expansion is the increase in white-collar jobs, for the middle sectors still consider manual labor in any form as a lower-class occupation. The tremendous expansion of federal, state, and municipal civil service has opened up many white-collar positions, and government employment has been perhaps the most single important road to membership in the middle class. With the growth of industry and commerce, numerous jobs have become available in offices and stores. Furthermore, opportunities in the professions have increased with Brazil's population explosion and with the increased buying power of its people. There is an urgent need for chemists, nurses, engineers, and the like. The expanding economy calls for white-collar workers and specialists, as well as for labor. The new middle sector has new demands, and is becoming at least superficially similar to the middle classes of the United States and Europe.[11]

## The Widening of the "Zone of Exasperation"

Many of Brazil's major problems, including in a large measure those involving her relationships with the United States and the countries of Europe, arise out of the recent, rapid widening or spread of the gap between the level of living of her people and the standard of living to which they now feel they are entitled. In other words, the difference between the level of accomplishments and the magnitude of the aspirations of her population increased greatly during the last fifty years. Indeed, since the outbreak of the First World War a veritable revolution has taken place in the expectations of the masses of the population throughout the length and breadth of Brazil. This got under way in the southern portions of the country, and especially in the cities of Rio de Janeiro and São Paulo, and various parts of the state of which the latter is the capital. Gradually, however, it has spread to all parts of the huge Brazilian half continent. To a considerable extent this rise in expectations, or the amounts of goods and services to which the people consider themselves to be entitled, has been accompanied by substantial rises in the amounts of such things they actually have been privileged to consume. Nevertheless the rise in expectations (or the standard of living) has greatly exceeded that in the actual levels or planes of living. Thus, in spite of the sizable advances in actual accomplishments, in the 1970s the difference between the two is much greater than it was in 1914. Thus one may say that the area of frustration or the zone of exasperation has been increasing rapidly.

The point to this is that since 1914, and especially since 1935, the masses of the Brazilian population have come to believe that they and their children are entitled to far better real wages, housing, dress, educational opportunities, health services, and so forth, than they have enjoyed in the past. As a matter of fact, and this is in sharp contrast to the situation prevailing not long ago, Brazilians by the millions now aspire to the ownership of small farms, to the personal possession of automobiles, to voices in political affairs, and to a way of life they see being enjoyed by the more favored portions of Brazilian society, by large numbers of foreigners who live and work in their midst, and by people in some other parts of the world of which they have heard. But, and this qualification must be underscored, it always is easier for politicians to promise than for statesmen to satisfy, for those willing to promote change to draw up and present three hundred projects for agrarian reform than it is to put a few substantial reform measures into practice,[12] for agitators to arouse than for those having the responsibilities of administrative positions to satisfy, for individuals to aspire than for them to attain, or for the standard of living to advance than for the level of living to keep pace with its upward movement. As a result, and this is one of the most important recent social changes in Brazil, the difference between the actual plane on which Brazil's masses live and that on which they now feel entitled to live is much greater than it was fifty or even twenty-five years ago.

Moreover, one could contend with much reason that this spread between aspirations and attainments is a fairly good indicator of the degree of ferment and discontent among the masses with those who direct affairs in their local communities, in the states, and in the nation; and that it measures fairly well the hostility they feel and frequently express with the managers and white-collar employees of the foreign firms doing business in their midst, with the officials and representations of the countries in which these firms have their home offices, and even with the people in the countries with which, in the past, they have been united in trade, commerce, and even military alliances. Thus social and economic ferment is the order of the day, and there is little or no effort to distinguish between the elements of the old order which have worked to the advantage of the masses and those which are responsible for the bulk of their ills. When the area of frustration or the zone of exasperation is as broad as it is in contemporary Brazil, rational behavior in local, state, national, and international relationships becomes even more of a rarity than usually is the case.

## The Growing Plague of Scarcities

One of the consequences of the rapid transition from an overwhelmingly rural, agricultural, pastoral, and collecting society to one that is far along the path to urbanization and industrialization is a growing plague of scarcities that afflicts a large part of Brazil's inhabitants. Food shortages, inadequate transportation, the precarious condition and sporadic services of the public utilities, and a host of other scarcities must be reckoned with daily by millions of people, and especially by those of middle- and lower-class status who live in the major cities.

Brazilian leaders are, of course, well aware that they cannot achieve their goals as long as 30 to 40 percent of those ten years of age and over are illiterate, only two or three million people in a population of 100 million have completed high school, and the number of thtse with university degrees does not exceed 400,000 to 500,000. Yet these facts are made known by the recent censuses. They underscore what is well known to all, namely, a lack of teachers for schools at all levels, a scarcity of engineers and technicians to man the industrial plant, a shortage of all kinds of skilled workers, or, in brief, a paucity in the labor force of most of the skills needed to develop and maintain an industrial basis for urban life and an agricultural economy that is capable of producing the food, fiber, and other raw materials needed by a large population in the nuclear era.

But the lack of adequate training of the members of the labor force is only one aspect of the growing plague of scarcities with which Brazil and its people are confronted on all fronts. In monetary matters, for example, the problems faced by the married couple are matched at all levels of government, local, state, and national. As yet even the national government can raise by taxes only a fraction of the funds it so badly needs, and at the state and local levels there is in effect no adequate means for getting from all the equivalent of a significant amount of their annual income, so that schools, health services, protection of life and property, roads and bridges, and so on may be provided. Even the pittances that the local government may try to raise through the imposition of license fees and so on quickly lose their values because of the rapidity of the inflationary process. At the state and national levels the shortages of funds also are acute because adequate taxes are not imposed and those that are levied are paid in money that has lost much of its value between the time the assessments are made and the date on which the taxes are collected. At the same time the entire national economy suffers because the proceeds from the export of coffee, cotton, cocoa beans, sugar, iron ore, lumber, manganese, and other products of lesser importance are insufficient to purchase the things that Brazilians need to meet their present standard of living. Merely to secure the petroleum and oil products consumed each year requires a large share of the amount grossed from exports; and to obtain the other capital and consumer goods demanded by the economy, pay the interest on the loans, supply the funds which many of those who can do so deposit in foreign banks,[13] and so on, taxes all sources of international exchange to the utmost. In short the lack of purchasing power at home and abroad is acute.

And so it would be with almost any aspect of Brazilian society that we would elect to examine. School buildings, teachers, roads, railroads, foodstuffs, fibers, fertilizers, trained workers, or, in summary, nearly all of the essentials for the type of society Brazil is attempting to develop are in increasingly short supply. Recent changes have produced a type of social existence that is radically different from the quiet, uneventful, listless, and easy abundance that many associate with life in the tropical zone in which the larger part of Brazil is located.

## Homogenization of Society

As was mentioned incidentally above, during the 1970s the homogenization of Brazilian society is progressing at a rapid rate.[14]

This is to say that with the passage of time all of the various components (ethnic or racial, religious, demographic, cultural, economic, social, and so on) of which society is made up are becoming more uniform throughout the length and breadth of the settled portions of Brazil's immense territory. Indeed the migration of population from one region to another, the dissemination of cultural traits from one area to another, the spread of behavior patterns from the city to the country and from section to section, and so on, rival those presently going on within the United States and Argentina, and probably considerably outdistance the comparable tendencies in Colombia, Peru, Venezuela, and most of the other countries of Latin America. This is to say that societal features long limited to Rio Grande do Sul, to Bahia, to the Northeast, to the great cities such as Rio de Janeiro and São Paulo, presently may be observed as integral parts of the way of life of the people in various other parts of the immense ·nation. Dietary practices, dress, music, the dance, ideologies, machines and implements, agricultural practices, labor organizations, educational content and norms, and social values are only a few of the specific items involved in the momentous redistribution of societal components that is going on.

All this means, of course, that as one decade succeeds another, the composition of any given territorial segment of Brazilian society, any specific community or neighborhood, or of each one of the thousands of small parts of which the national fabric is made up is becoming much more diverse or heterogeneous. At the same time, however, because of the tendency for all of the components to become more equally distributed throughout the entire body of society, the culture, social organization, and social processes in each of the country's various subdivisions are coming to resemble more closely those which make up the way of life and labor in other sections. Thus the very fact of increasing diversity within the neighborhood or community is bringing about more homogeneity on the national scale. As a result, in comparison with the situation fifty or even twenty-five years ago, one who now comes to know any one area in Brazil is far more likely to be acquiring a knowledge of Brazilian society in general and not merely one of a highly distinctive segment of it.

# 13

## Urbanization in the 1970s:
## A Study of Sociocultural Change

When Brazil entered the Second World War in 1942 it was a huge, loosely integrated assortment of agricultural and pastoral areas plus a few large cities of which Rio de Janeiro, São Paulo, Recife, Porto Alegre, and Bahia (Salvador) were by far the most important. Even by counting as urban all of the villages and hamlets that figured as seats of municipios into which the states were divided and those of the *distritos de paz* of which the municipios were composed, the census of 1940 could include only 12,880,000 inhabitants, 31.2 percent of the total, in the urban category. During the next decade, that of the war itself, a net migration of more than 2,500,000 persons helped greatly to increase the urban total to 18,783,000 in 1950, but even so only 36.1 percent of the population fell in the liberally defined urban segment. As soon as the war was over, however, the floodgates of rural-urban migration were opened widely, and the process of urbanization quickly began to transform an entire half continent from an overwhelmingly rural, agricultural, pastoral, and collecting economy into one where manufacturing, trade and commerce, and other nonagricultural activities are dominant.

By 1960 the urban part of the population had been swelled to 32,000,000, or 45.1 percent of all Brazilians, at the close of a decade of unprecedentedly rapid sociocultural change. During the ten years a net of 6,500,000 of those who figured in the 1960 census had moved from rural to urban areas. It is doubtful if this mass exodus of people from the country to the city had ever been paralleled in the entire history of mankind, but even so in Brazil itself this tremendous movement from country to city was to be

208

exceeded, both on the absolute and relative bases, during the following decade.

With the results of the 1970 census now available, we are able to take stock of this momentous change. Between 1960 and 1970 the urban population came to exceed the rural; and by 1970 the urban part of Brazil's population had mushroomed to 41,600,000 persons, a number equal to the nation's entire population in 1940. In the 1970 census, 55.9 percent of all Brazilians were classified as urban; and our computations show that between 1960 and 1970 a net of 10,300,000 persons had transferred their resieences from rural to urban areas. To recapitulate, between 1940 and 1970, the net movement of persons who personally migrated from rural areas to urban districts rose from 2,560,000 for the period 1940-50, to 6,335,000 between 1950 and 1960, and to 10,300,000 during the ten years ending in 1970.[1] Perhaps the essential facts about the mass transfer of population from Brazil's vast rural districts to her now-teeming cities since the close of the Second World War are best epitomized by the three following sets of calculations: (1) on a net basis, the proportions of all Brazilians enumerated in a given census who had migrated from rural to urban areas during the decade before the next census was taken rose from one in twenty in 1950 to one in eleven in 1960 and to one in nine in 1970; (2) during the same thirty-year period, with the data given in chronological order, the net rural-urban migration rose from a figure equal to 24 percent of the total increase in Brazil's population during the decade 1940-50 to 33 percent for that ending in 1960 and finally to 44 percent for the years 1960-70; and (3) net rural-urban migration accounted for 43.4 percent of the increase in urban population between 1940 and 1950, 47.9 percent of that from 1950 to 1960, and 49.3 percent of that during the decade 1960 to 1970.

These demographic changes portend or betoken changes during the 1970s that will make the life and labor of the typical Brazilian vastly different from what it was in the 1950s or even the 1960s. In the years immediately ahead, urbanization as a cause and also as an effect should be by far the most engrossing matter confronting the Brazilian people who live in a country which in 1972 joined the 100-million club, along with China, India, Soviet Russia, and the United States, almost simultaneously with the entrance into that select group of Japan and Indonesia. The cities and towns inhabited by the majority of the 100-million plus Brazilians are all bursting at their seams; and the problems arising from the sudden concentration of tens of millions of persons in urban districts are overwhelming, to say the least. Those interested in sociocultural change, societal problems, and all the other dynamics of life late in the twentieth century can hardly find a richer field for observation and study than that offered by present-day Brazil. Indeed the almost overnight transformation of the Brazilian half continent from an immense area in which a rural way of life, based upon an agricultural, pastoral, and collecting economy had completely dominated the scene for over four centuries, into one in which nonagricultural industries, occupations, and activities greatly predominate presents opportunity for case studies of tremendous significance.

## The Rural Threshold

Efforts to appraise the metamorphosis of Brazilian society represented by the kind of "wildfire" urbanization currently under way should start with an understanding of the extreme degree of rurality prevailing in Brazil as late as 1940. My own personal observations began in 1939 when a grant of $800 from the Julius Rosenwald Fund helped pay the cost of visits to Cuba, Panama, and all of the South American countries except Venezuela. Four months were spent on that journey, including about three weeks in Brazil. Then I came to know that on the eve of the Second World War the entire area was highly rural and that a substantial urbanization was under way only at a few places of which Buenos Aires, Montevideo, Rio de Janeiro, and São Paulo were the most outstanding examples. In fact when I compare the cities in Spanish America and Brazil that I saw in 1939 then and now I have difficulty in convincing myself that they are the same places. In reality perhaps they are not, unless one assigns every importance to the point of intersection of specific degrees of longitude and latitude and ignores all of the culture traits, social patterns, and sociocultural systems and subsystems of which a city is composed. In other words, the only things that have not changed are the central portions of the locations and the names.

While I was returning from Brazil to New Orleans, war in Europe erupted; and shortly thereafter I undertook an assignment that enabled me to get first-hand experience with the growth, development, and feeding of Brazilian cities. Specially commissioned by Cordell Hull, then Secretary of State, I was one of three sociologists dispatched to the embassies in Buenos Aires, Rio de Janeiro, and Mexico City to study and report upon society in Argentina, Brazil, and Mexico, with special relation to the war effort. I drew the assignment to Brazil. Carl C. Taylor went to Argentina, and Nathan L. Whetten to Mexico. Out of this work came, among many other things, the three volumes that have come to be known as "the country studies."[2] An entire year was spent in Brazil on that assignment, and during that time a series of trips took me into all parts of the country. Visits were made to all of the state capitals and other major cities, and some of them, including São Paulo and Belo Horizonte, were visited repeatedly.[3] Those who think that the metamorphoses observed in the animal world, such as that from tadpole to frog or from caterpillar to butterfly, are dramatic should attempt to compare and contrast such Brazilian cities as Santos, Niterói, Juiz da Fora, Campinas, Vitoria, Natal, Aracaju, Maceió, Campina Grande, Fortaleza, São Luiz, Manaus, and Belém, or even Curitiba, Belo Horizonte, and Salvador, as they were in 1942 with the same cities today. My observations during a full year convinced me that Brazil was overwhelmingly rural, that the degree of rurality of its society was extreme, and that the process of urbanization hardly had got under way in most parts of the immense country. My conclusions were as follows:

> Quantitatively and qualitatively, Brazil's population is one of the most rural in the entire world. Undoubtedly, the percentage of the nation's population who are living in communities that must be classed as strictly rural is hardly to be equaled elsewhere. On the other hand, the immense extent of the thinly populated country, the great dispersion of its nodules of settlement, the use of scattered farmsteads in arranging the population on the land, the very high proportion of the population who engage directly in agricultural, stock raising, or hunting and fishing activities, and the undeveloped state of the means of communication and transportation are evidences that the degree of rurality is also a very high one. As yet urban influences reach large expanses of the Brazilian countryside only rarely and then in a weakened condition.[4]

The manuscript of the first edition of *Brazil: People and Institutions* went to press in December 1944, when the data from the 1940 Brazilian census were still unavailable. When at long last they were published they showed that even with the criteria used (which placed in the urban category the inhabitants of every hamlet, village, town, or city that served as a seat of a municipio, and also the people living in the aggregation of dwellings in every little seat of a *distrito de paz,* including large numbers with populations of less than 100) only 31 percent of the population was classified as urban. Subsequently the reports of the 1950 census gave a more extensive listing of population centers than those of the 1940 census. For 1950 it was possible to subtract from the urban category the inhabitants of "cities," i.e., seats of municipios, and seats of distritos de paz having populations of less than 2,000 inhabitants. At that time 44.3 percent of the 1,887 seats of municipios and 95.8 percent of the 3,482 seats of distritos de paz had less than 2,000 inhabitants. When the residents of these small places were subtracted from the urban total, even in 1950 only 31.2 percent of Brazil's population remained in the urban category,[5] and the generalizations quoted above remained almost fully as valid as they were in 1942 and 1943 when all those who ventured into Brazil's backcountry personally experienced the effects of a hyperrural society.

## The Growth of Cities and Towns

As is evident from the data given above, the great metamorphosis of Brazil from an extremely rural society to a predominantly urban one took place during the 1950s and 1960s and continues unabated in the 1970s. New villages, towns, and cities are springing up in the interior, and especially along the highways that are being pushed into the nation's great heartland that for centuries has remained almost devoid of inhabitants. During the 1950s the changes were most pronounced in central Goiás, where Brasília was being built and dozens of new places were coming into existence and dozens of older ones (such as Anapolis and Goiania) were bursting at their seams; in the 1960s the most spectacular developments were the hundreds of new population centers that sprang up along the new Belém-Brasília highway resembling beads on a string; and in the

1970s attention is focused upon the dramatic growth of population in Altamira and all the other *agravillas* (larger, more complete trade and service centers) that are either taking on new life or being brought into existence as a result of the construction of the Transamazonian highway and related roads that are being pushed through the Brazilian part of the great Amazon Basin.[6]

In order to supply some of the essential facts about the recent spectacular developments in the urbanization of Brazil, Tables 9 and 10 and Figures 10 and 11 have been prepared. In Table 9 the materials presented show the growth of the thirty-five largest cities in Brazil during the period 1950 to 1970. This is the twenty-year period in which Brazil's population almost doubled in size, in which it came to be predominantly urban, in which it mounted to almost 100 million, and in which the urban population alone came to be as large as the entire population of the nation only thirty years earlier. In interpreting these data one should keep in mind that the huge figures for São Paulo and Rio de Janeiro actually greatly underemphasize the size and importance of these two immense conurbations which have eight or nine million inhabitants apiece. Fully as significant as the huge concentrations of people in these two great metropolitan areas, however, are the burgeoning of other great metropolitan centers such as Belo Horizonte, Recife, and Salvador, which had passed the one-million mark prior to the 1970 census, and Porto Alegre and Fortaleza, which probably passed that mark early in the 1970s. Nova Iguaçú, though, is just one of many integral parts of the city of Rio de Janeiro, indistinguishable by the visitor from other highly congested portions of the city, which is separated administratively from the metropolis by the boundary which divides the state of Guanabara (in which the municipio of Rio de Janeiro is located) and the state of Rio de Janeiro in which many of the suburbs and most of the satellites of Brazil's former capital are situated.

In Table 10 are some of the hard facts about the sudden rise of hundreds of new population centers and the rapid growth of the older ones. State-to-state comparisons of rural/urban population distribution in 1950, the magnitudes of population changes between 1950 and 1970, and the extent to which these changes took place in rural and urban areas are shown in Figure 10. And in Figure 11, the location and growth between 1950 and 1970 of all Brazil's principal cities are shown.

**TABLE 9**

**Growth of Brazil's Major Cities, 1950-70**

| Municipio and State | Population (000's) 1950 | 1970 | Increase 1950-70 Number | Percent |
|---|---|---|---|---|
| São Paulo, São Paulo | 2,198 | 5,980 | 3,782 | 172 |
| Rio de Janeiro, Guanabara | 2,337 | 4,316 | 1,939 | 82 |
| Belo Horizonte, Minas Gerais | 358 | 1,255 | 897 | 251 |
| Recife, Pernambuco | 525 | 1,084 | 559 | 107 |
| Salvador, Bahia | 417 | 1,027 | 610 | 146 |
| Porto Alegre, Rio Grande do Sul | 394 | 903 | 509 | 129 |
| Fortaleza, Ceará del | 270 | 873 | 603 | 223 |
| Nova Iguaçú,[1] Rio de Janeiro | 146 | 732 | 586 | 401 |
| Curitiba, Paraná | 181 | 642 | 461 | 255 |
| Belém, Pará | 255 | 624 | 369 | 145 |
| Brasília, Distrito Federal | 000 | 546 | 546 | — |
| Duque de Caxias, Rio de Janeiro[1] | 92 | 435 | 343 | 373 |
| São Gonçalo, Rio de Janeiro[1] | 127 | 434 | 307 | 242 |
| Santo Andre, São Paulo[2] | 127 | 421 | 294 | 232 |
| Goiania, Goiás | 53 | 390 | 337 | 636 |
| Campinas, São Paulo | 153 | 382 | 229 | 150 |
| Santos, São Paulo | 204 | 350 | 146 | 72 |
| Niterói, Rio de Janeiro[1] | 186 | 330 | 144 | 77 |
| Campos, Rio de Janeiro | 238 | 321 | 83 | 35 |
| Manaus, Amazonas | 140 | 314 | 174 | 124 |
| São João de Meriti, Rio de Janeiro[1] | 76 | 305 | 229 | 301 |
| São Luis, Maranhão | 120 | 271 | 151 | 126 |
| Natal, Rio Grande do Norte | 103 | 270 | 167 | 162 |
| Maceió, Alagoas | 121 | 269 | 148 | 122 |
| Juiz da Fora, Minas Gerais | 127 | 244 | 117 | 92 |
| Londrina, Paraná | 71 | 232 | 161 | 227 |
| Teresina, Piauí | 91 | 230 | 139 | 153 |
| João Pessoa, Paraíba | 119 | 228 | 109 | 92 |
| Ribeirão Preto, São Paulo | 92 | 219 | 127 | 138 |
| Pelotas, Rio Grande do Sul | 128 | 213 | 85 | 66 |
| Campina Grande, Paraíba | 173 | 197 | 24 | 14 |
| Petropolis, Rio de Janeiro[1] | 108 | 193 | 85 | 79 |
| Aracaju, Sergipe | 78 | 187 | 109 | 140 |
| Sorocaba, São Paulo | 94 | 178 | 84 | 89 |
| Ponta Grossa, Paraná | 54 | 129 | 75 | 139 |

[1]Part of metropolitan Rio de Janeiro
[2]Part of metropolitan São Paulo

Compiled and computed from data in Conselho Nacional de Estatística, VI, *Recenseamento Geral do Brasil–1950,* Vol. 1, Rio de Janeiro, 1956, pp. 179-201; *VII Recenseamento Geral do Brasil–1960,* "Sinopse Preliminar do Censo Demográfico," Rio de Janeiro, 1962, pp. 22-23; and *VIII Recenseamento Geral–1970,* "Sinopse Preliminar do Censo Demográfico," Rio de Janeiro, 1971, pp. 102-5.

**TABLE 10**

**Numbers of Towns and Cities in Brazil According to
Populations, 1950, 1960, and 1970**

| Number of | Number of places | | |
|---|---|---|---|
| inhabitants | *1950* | *1960* | *1970* |
| 2,500,000-over | 0 | 2 | 2 |
| 1,000,000- | 2 | 0 | 3 |
| 500,000- | 1 | 4 | 6 |
| 250,000- | 3 | 4 | 13 |
| 100,000- | 8 | 21 | 14 |
| 50,000- | 20 | 42 | 55 |
| 20,000- | 76 | 117 | 214 |
| 10,000- | 115 | 265 | 349 |
| 5,000- | 258 | 378 | 546 |
| 2,000- | 692 | 1,016 | 1,241 |
| Total | 1,175 | 1,849 | 2,439 |

Compiled from data in Conselho Nacional de Estatística, *Anuário Estatístico do Brasil*, Ano XII, 1951, Rio de Janeiro: Institute Brasileiro de Geografia e Estatística, 1952, pp. 45-49; *VII Recenseamento Geral do Brasil–1960,* "Sinopse Preliminar do Censo Demográfico," Rio de Janeiro: Instituto Brasileiro de Geografia e Estatística, 1962, pp. 16-19; and *VIII pecenseamento Geral–1970,* "Sinopse Preliminar do Censo Demografico," Rio de Janeiro: Fundação IBGE, 1971, pp. 82-95.

## Factors Responsible for the Growth of Cities

To understand urban growth in Brazil or elsewhere, it is necessary to consider first the primary factors that are responsible for the recent burgeoning of cities and towns. The more basic causes, or exactly why a great world region that for centuries had remained overwhelmingly rural, pastoral, and agricultural suddenly was caught up in a mad rush of people from the rural districts to urban areas, are matters requiring much more detailed study and analysis. Among the immediate factors, though, two call for specific mention. These are the tremendous rise in the rate of natural increase of population, and the huge rural-urban migration.

### The Rise in the Rate of Natural Increase of the Population

The sudden rise in the rate of natural increase in Brazil in recent decades was due almost exclusively to a dramatic reduction in the death rate. This, combined with a birth rate that remained at its traditionally high level, produced an annual rate of natural increase of about 3 percent per year, during the 1960s. In other words, since about 1940 the death rate has been reduced from around 30 or 35 per 1000 population to about 10 or 15, and this brought about a doubling of the rate of natural increase, or an increase in it from about 1.5 to approximately 3.0 percent per year. An almost unprecendentedly rapid population increase resulted. Had it not been

FIGURE 10.  Population, Rural and Urban, of Each State in 1950, and Population Increase between 1950 and 1970

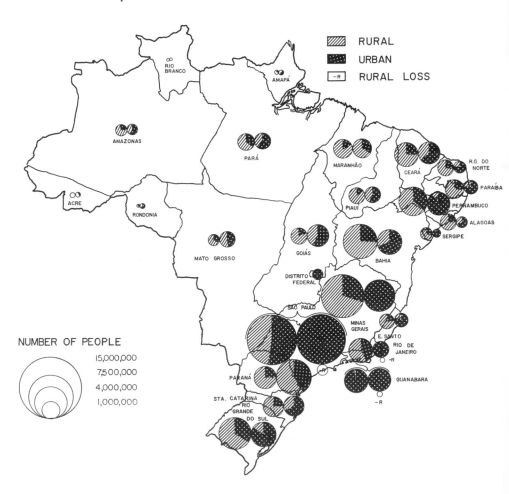

for this burgeoning of the population, the growth of cities and towns since 1950 would have been far less spectacular than has actually been the case.

Although there can be little question about the large sustained upsurge of population in Brazil, and in other parts of Latin America as well, one may very well be perplexed about its timing. Why is it that the growth of population in Latin America, which had been far from spectacular for four centuries following the days of Columbus,

FIGURE 11. Population in 1950 and Population Increases between 1950 and 1970 in Major Cities

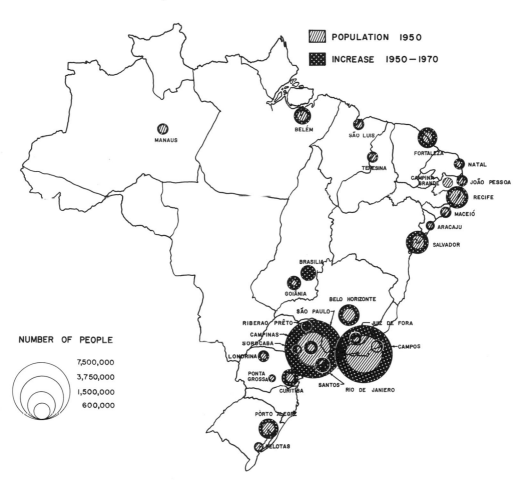

should become so rapid during the opening years of the second half of the twentieth century? An adequate rationale for the quick pace of urbanization in Brazil and the other Latin American countries must also include the answer to this question. Fortunately, we are able to give a fairly definite answer to it.

As indicated above, the recent rapid upsurge in the rate of natural increase of population is due to a recent sharp and dramatic drop in the death rate with no comparable change in the birth rate. The abrupt fall in the death rate that has taken place throughout Brazil and Spanish America since 1950, in turn, undoubtedly is due to the applications on a large scale of modern medicine and sanitation. Infectious and germ-transmitted diseases, which once accounted for large proportions of all deaths, were largely brought under control in many parts of the Western world during the first quarter of the twentieth century; and during the second and third quarters remarkable strides have been made in bringing them under control throughout Latin America. However, as is the case with social and cultural change generally, innovations begin in the cities and spread only gradually to rural areas.[7] Whenever society is in a rapid state of flux, as presently is true with respect to mortality throughout Brazil and Spanish America, the new patterns prevail in the city, the old ones in the country. As more effective measures against malaria have been taken, as ways and means of safeguarding water and milk supplies were adopted generally, as vaccinations and injections became as much a part of disease prevention in rural areas as had been the case in the towns and cities, the health and mortality of the rural population came to compare more favorably with those of the urban population. All of this has contributed immensely to the rise in the rate of natural increase of population and the growth of urban centers.

### The Mass Migration from Country to City

Immigration is of minor importance in the growth of Brazil's cities and towns. Therefore, even with the high rates of natural increase that now prevail throughout her large territory, her cities and towns would continue to be (as they were for centuries) merely urban islands in a sea of rural humanity had it not been for a tremendous movement of people from rural districts to population centers. Most of the immigrants do, of course, establish themselves in the urban centers. But this stream of immigrants is a mere trickle and its influence is slight in comparison with the huge migration of millions of persons from the farms and ranches to the central cities and to the miserable slums, favelas, or bands of misery that encircle these urban centers. In countries such as Brazil (or Colombia, Venezuela, and Peru) if the programs of colonization and settlement, agrarian reform, and agricultural development actually were commensurate with the opportunities and needs of the people, whereby the majority of the rural migrants would be directed to new agricultural districts, the cities and towns would grow far less rapidly and many of them probably would actually decline in relative importance.

This, of course, is not happening. In spite of the large-scale programs of colonization and settlement recently initiated, millions of migrants from the rural districts are flocking into the urban centers; and there they are contributing immeasurably to the host of acute and chronic social and economic problems with which those centers are afflicted. For this reason, it is pertinent to examine briefly the nature of the principal forces that are expelling millions of agricultural laborers and small subsistence farmers from their rural habitats and attracting them to the cities and to the miserable, mushrooming suburbs.

Comprehensive data pertaining to the rural-to-urban migration are, of course, largely lacking, just as is the case for almost all other parts of the world. It has been possible to show that almost one-half of the persons living in the central part of the city of Rio de Janeiro (i.e., the state of Guanabara) were born in other parts of the country. Until 1950 the administrative area involved was somewhat coterminous with the national capital, so that this is indicative that millions of migrants from elsewhere in Brazil had contributed to the growth of Rio de Janeiro.[8]

In addition, by means of more elaborate arithmetical computations it was estimated that between 1940 and 1950 about 60 to 65 percent of the growth of Rio de Janeiro and São Paulo was due to migration from elsewhere in Brazil;[9] and that between 1950 and 1960, as mentioned above, about one out of every ten persons enumerated in the 1960 census (a total of between six and seven million people) had moved from rural to urban areas during the decade.[10] And after the preliminary results of the 1970 census became available, comparable procedures indicated that between 1960 and 1970, this rural-urban migration had swelled to a total of around 10,300,000. Of course merely by comparing the rates of growth of rural and urban populations it is possible to infer, soundly, that a tremendous movement of people from rural to urban areas is taking place; and one who visits any Brazilian city and mingles with people in all walks of life soon knows that the recent influx of migrants from the surrounding rural areas has been very large. Neither of these procedures gives an exact quantitative basis for judging the relative importance of rural-urban migration in urban growth; but there is no valid reason for supposing that generalizations attributing the urban growth taking place in Brazil largely to rural-urban migration are seriously in error. In fact, what one political scientist stated about the mushrooming of Belo Horizonte, capital of Minas Gerais and, after Brasília, the most rapidly growing of all big cities in Brazil, can be safely said about the growth of almost every city in Brazil. From a city of 200,000 in 1940 Belo Horizonte increased to 1,255,000 inhabitants, according to the 1970 census. (See Table I.) And "this amazing rate of growth is due almost entirely to the massive migration from rural areas, and predominantly from the state of Minas Gerais itself."[11]

*Factors, Forces, and Media in Rural-Urban Migration*

It is useful to divide the factors, forces, and media responsible for the mass movement of Brazilians from the country to the city into two large groups. The first of these consists of the great socioeconomic changes that set the stage for the rural exodus, and the second is made up of the immediate influences or media which impinge upon specific persons and induce them to move from rural to urban areas. Each of these is discussed briefly.

Many pages might be filled with an analysis and description of the broad social and economic changes which Brazil has experienced since 1900 and especially since 1950. These are, in the last analysis, the factors or forces responsible for the tremendous movement of population from country to city. The development and extension of modern means of communication and transportation help to link one state with another, and also to unite the various sections of a given state. During the nineteenth century in most parts of Brazil the application of steam to move ships and railroads did little to revolutionize the system of transportation. Even today adequate rail facilities are few and far between in Brazil. Similarly, prior to 1920, the telephone and the telegraph did relatively little to modernize communications in Brazil. Since 1930, however, and especially since 1950, the automobile and the motor truck, airplanes, telephone systems utilizing the satellites, and radio and television have, with startling swiftness, brought rapid and relatively inexpensive means of transportation and communication to practically all settled parts of the huge country. For example, roads and trails in the interior of Brazil on which as late as the 1940s I spent days and weeks in which I encountered very few vehicles, today are jammed with trucks, buses, and automobiles moving thousands of persons and many tons of produce and merchandise from place to place. And for one who personally experienced the exasperation of trying to arrange a conversation between the cities of Rio de Janeiro and São Paulo in the 1940s, the present ease of communication by telephone on the part of people in Belém or Fortaleza with those in Porto Alegre or Curitiba is a thing of wonder. These improvements have done much to set the stage and provide the means for the rural exodus.

The recent rapid development of educational facilities throughout Brazil is another of the broad social changes that is playing a large role in internal migration. In sharp contrast with the situation that prevailed only a few decades ago, illiteracy of two-thirds or even three-fourths of the people, and still higher proportions of the rural population, no longer is considered to be natural and inevitable. It no longer is thought of as tolerable. In the Charter of Punta del Este, signed in August 1961, Brazil solemnly pledged: "To eliminate adult illiteracy and by 1970 to assure, as a minimum, access to six years of primary education for each school-age child in Latin America." And probably this is the goal of the Alliance for Progress that came nearest to attainment. However, the school and the books, newspapers, and magazines it teaches people to read are among the most powerful forces making for urbanization.

The increased contacts between Brazilians and foreigners is one of the features of the period since 1940 that most distinguishes it from all previous epochs. Especially since 1950 great numbers of Brazilians have visited distant parts of the world. Likewise, there has been a heavy influx of visitors from other continents into Brazil.

Especially numerous and important have been the contacts between Brazilians and people in those countries where a middle-class social heritage and industrialization have combined to produce the highest average standards of living that the world has ever known. Almost inevitably the Brazilian who has visited Europe, Canada, or the United States helps promote the process of urbanization upon his return. The foreign companies which, during their operations in Brazil, carry on training programs often play a much larger role than they may think in transplanting people from the country to cities and towns.

Intense social ferment among the rural masses during the second half of the twentieth century is another powerful force in promoting this movement of people. Once docile and tractable under the paternalistic direction of the proprietors of the large estates, millions of these humble people have become increasingly discontented with their own lot in life and with their children's prospects. This, of course, is fomented by demagogues of every stripe. It results also from conscientious endeavors of devoted people to bring about programs of agrarian reform, community development, and other changes that would promote the welfare of the rural masses. Whatever its cause, this social ferment is a powerful factor in the flow of people from the country to the city.

The enactment of extensive social legislation, especially during the regime of Getúlio Vargas, must also be included in even a short list of broad changes which are contributing heavily to the flight of people from the land. Ever since the organization of the old League of Nations, Brazil has been among the first to enact into law the numerous models of social legislation that have been designed and recommended by the various international agencies. Measures dealing with hours of work, minimum wages, security of tenure, severance pay, paid vacations, sick leave, and the like are on the list. Many of these measures have been largely ineffectual, but the fact remains that they have been much more effective in urban than in rural areas. This has helped to broaden the already wide differentials of working conditions in the two areas. Indeed, in many cities these social enactments have done much to better the lot of the workers, and word of this has spread quickly to the rural districts. This factor, too, has played an important role in causing Brazil's rural people to flock into its urban centers.

This type of analysis might be continued indefinitely. Many

Brazilian leaders have come to feel that only through industrialization could they hope to cope with their rapidly mounting list of chronic and acute social problems. However, the enumeration given above should suffice for present purposes, and it is best to turn to the specific media that have caused individual Brazilians to migrate from the country to the city.

In Brazil, as elsewhere, word-of-mouth reports of persons who, for one reason or another, have made the move from country to city to their friends and relatives back home are one of the more potent forces in determining exactly which ones of Brazil's tens of millions rural people will make the move to her cities. Traditionally, rural Brazilians have been an extremely migratory lot, with a great deal of interregional movement (from the Northeast to the Amazon region, from Minas Gerais, Bahia, and the Northeast to the state of São Paulo and the city of Rio de Janeiro), and this has been followed by much visiting back home of those who pioneered the shift from rural to urban areas.[12] Thus, just as letters and other personal reports of those who first immigrated were the effective factors in causing persons in the "old countries" to swell the tide of European immigration to the United States,[13] so throughout Brazil at the present time word-of-mouth reports and letters are among the decisive factors helping João and Maria to decide to leave the rural neighborhood and join their relatives and friends who have preceded them in going to the city.

Practically no secondary schools are located in the rural sections of Brazil, and they are also lacking in many towns of considerable size. In much of the area from Rio Grande do Sul to Roraima they are present only in national and state capitals and other fairly good-sized population centers. Therefore, even the affluent landowner who lives on his fazenda or estancia must choose either (1) to allow his children to arrive at adulthood with no more schooling than the three or four years provided in the primary schools of the municipio in which he lives; (2) to send his children to the state capital or some other city to live with friends or relatives while they pursue their studies; or (3) to move with his entire family to one of the cities in which a secondary school is located. Very frequently, the third option is the one chosen. In recent decades, many persons of middle-class status and even some who originated in the lower strata are going to the city in order to obtain the education that will enable them to rise in the socioeconomic scale.

The standard of living of upper-class Brazilians makes it necessary for them to have a host of servants (maids, cooks, gardeners, chauffeurs, laundresses, and so on) at their beck and call in and about the palatial city homes in which they reside. Furthermore even those of middle-class status must have a servant or two if they are to maintain the appearance commensurate with their social positions. The practice of recruiting country people for service as servants in city homes probably is less prevalent in Brazil than it is in some Spanish-American countries, where since 1940 it has not been unusual for high-born city women literally to scour the surrounding rural districts in search of servants when they had difficulty in finding domestic help in the city. Nevertheless it is a significant factor in rural-urban migration.

Other inducements or attractions that may bring workers from the rural to the urban community include: the employment of rural youths on construction projects involved in the expansion of urban areas and the water, power, and other systems needed to supply them; the effectiveness with which the young men who drive the cars and trucks throughout the countryside are able to persuade some of the girls they meet in the cafes, restaurants, hotels, public squares, and so on, to accompany them to the cities; the values and inspirations which the urban-reared or trained teacher is able to transmit to the students in her classes; and even, in some places, such as northeastern Brazil, the drumming up of business in the rural communities by those who secure their means of livelihood by trucking human beings over the long, hot, dusty roads that lead to the great cities in the south.

Finally, especially in the 1970s, rural-urban migration is being fostered by the development in small cities and large towns of hosts of basic industries connected with the modernization of agriculture. These include plants for producing fertilizers, modern establishments for the production and distribution of seeds and feeds, factories for the manufacture of farm implements and machines, chemical industries devoted to the production of herbicides and pesticides, and so on. They also include establishments for processing farm products, such as plants for pasteurizing milk and producing dried milk, mills turning out a host of cereal products, factories for converting sugar, milk, and chocolate into a rich variety of delicacies, and establishments for the processing of meat and other animal products. In Brazil during the 1970s, as was the case earlier in the United States, a huge transfer of all of these aspects of agricultural production and processing from the farms and plantations to towns and small cities is taking place. Much movement of people from rural to urban residential areas is resulting from it.

## *Value Systems and Rural-Urban Migration*

It would be a mistake to attribute the recent phenomenal growth of cities and towns in Brazil to a sudden change or "explosion" in values that has made the Brazilian outlook more favorable to urban life. As a matter of fact, an image favorable to urban life goes back at least to the national crisis which accompanied the abolition of slavery (1888) and the establishment of the Republic (1889). The fundamental change is that in recent decades the rural masses gradually have been liberated from economic, social, cultural, and legal bonds which long bound them to a creaturelike existence on the large landed estates in the rural sections of their country. In their desire to become urban residents, which seems to be the most widespread current societal driving force in Brazil, the humble rural people are merely imitating the upper classes.

Ever since 1888 when slavery in Brazil was abolished, followed quickly by the consolidation of the old family plantations and other rural principalities into large modern corporations, there has been a tendency on the part of upper-class Brazilian families to reside in the urban centers. As a result, throughout the nation, an attitude has developed in which everything rural is disparaged, whereas the urban mode of existence is extolled.

Consider for example the following extract, in rather literal translation, from one of the most incisive and objective studies ever made of the great favelas in the city of Rio de Janeiro. "From the sanitary point of view the favelas appear to us as suburbs in the hearts of the cities; and some even resemble certain parts of the rural zone with their extremes transplanted into the heart of the nation's capital."[14]

## Some Effects and Concomitants of Urbanization

The effects or at least the concomitants of urbanization in Brazil conform closely to those of urbanization in general. The concentration of the population in the cities undoubtedly brings about a rapid rise in the standard of living, including improvements in educational status, increased use of health and medical services, and many other features of higher levels of living. It is likely, also, that the standards of living (i.e., the levels of aspirations) rise more rapidly than the actual levels of living, thus greatly increasing the gap between the two (the "zone of exasperation"). I have chosen to conclude this chapter with a brief discussion of a few of the major social problems caused by urbanization.

Undoubtedly, with the metamorphosis of Brazilian society since 1950, some of the most pressing of society's problems have ceased to be those dealing with agriculture and rural life, and become those of the cities and towns. In the 1970s it is even difficult to maintain public interest in the issue of agrarian reform. Many of the new problems are the direct result of the migration which almost overnight transferred a very large segment of the total population from a great rural proletariat into an urban one. Even the attempts by extremists to use violent revolutionary tactics to effect what they claim will be reforms in society seem largely to have been transformed from guerrilla activities in the countryside into attempts to organize guerrilla warfare in the cities. This chapter will conclude with brief treatments of what I consider to be the three most serious contemporary urban problems in Brazil: (1) the problem of rural-urban migration itself; (2) the problem growing out of the lag in what the Brazilians call *urbanização* in relation to what we call *urbanization* in English; and (3) the problem of the "suburbs." Attention is focused upon each of these in turn.

## The Influx of Migrants from the Rural Areas

It would be unwise to omit from any list of urban problems in Brazil the great cause of burgeoning urban populations, namely the tremendous influx of poorly prepared people coming from the rural areas. In this connection one should keep in mind the fact that relatively few of the migrants were sought out in their rural homes and recruited for jobs in trade and commerce, industry, transportation and communication, and most other urban, nonagricultural activities in the urban centers. Rather most of those who migrate do so because of the hard, difficult, miserable, almost hopeless situations which have been their lot on huge landed estates and poor little subsistence farms from whence they come. As stressed above, word-of-mouth reports from relatives and friends who preceded them, from people they really could trust, have convinced them by the millions that the city offers opportunities for life and labor vastly superior to the servile or semiservile positions they occupy and the creaturelike existence they lead in the rural districts. Irrespective of the motivations for migration, however, the real problem is that of trying to integrate people of limited skills, little or no education, practically no experience in self-directed political activities, rudimentary knowledge of health and sanitary measures, low standards and levels of living, and unsophisticated beliefs of what to expect in urban situations into a highly differentiated urban society. Moreover, in many cases, the problem of integrating them into urban life has barely begun, although unrealistic talk of solving the problem by returning the migrants to the rural districts is less pronounced in the 1970s than it was in the 1950s.

## The Lag of "Urbanização" in Comparison with Urbanization

The most embracing of all urban problems in Brazil during the second half of the twentieth century is the lag between *urbanização* and what generally is meant by the word urbanization in the English language. I translate the former as "urbanization," and in Brazil it is used in a technical sense to denote the work of planning and building the physical parts of a city. Thus, as indicated in Chapter 12, *an* "urbanization" is a subdivision or other area in which aligned streets have been platted, public squares and parks have been laid out, streets and sidewalks have been paved, storm sewers and sewer systems have been constructed, central water systems and lighting systems have been installed.

In addition to the data given in Chapter 12, Professor José Arthur Rios of Rio de Janeiro, able lawyer-sociologist who carried the main responsibility for the excellent study of the favelas of Rio de Janeiro cited above, more recently did the sociological parts of a comprehensive survey of a huge, fairly new slum in Salvador, Bahia. This area, Alagados, had a population of about 75,000 or 8 percent of those in the city. These people lived in "an agglomeration of (15,000) sub-habitations" and suffered from "the most degrading housing and hygenic conditions." The survey showed that only 11 percent of the dwellings were connected with the municipal water mains, and that the families living in the others carried water from the homes of their neighbors or from twenty-two spigots scattered about in the area. Nearly all the houses were equipped with old oil drums for catching and storing rain water from the roofs. Electricity was available, at least intermittently, in 5,012 of the dwellings, but the only sewer system was that provided by the ebb and flow of the tide over the mud flat along the bay on which the people had erected their rude habitations.[15]

Another of Rios's surveys was of Campina Grande, a mushrooming trade and transportation center in the immense, problem-ridden Northeast. In 1960 this city had a population of about 126,000. In 1963, though, when the survey was done, in the entire city "the percentage of the people who drank uncontaminated water was less than 30 percent," the "sewer system served less than 20 percent of the inhabitants," and the infant mortality rate of from 200 to 500 per 1,000 live births could be explained "by the general nutritional and hygenic deficiencies."[16]

Before leaving the subject of the slowness with which essential facilities are provided for the millions of people, largely of lower-class status, who recently have flocked into Brazilian cities, it seems necessary to consider briefly the basic reasons for the lag over and above those due purely to the magnitude of the task. In view of the chaos that has developed in the cities of the United States since 1960, one should be able to avoid feelings of superiority in this respect; but it is probably fair to say that most of the woes that are causing the mayors of our great cities to run to the federal government about are compounded several times over in Brazil.

All local government in Brazil, rural and urban alike, is very debile. There is no substantial system of local taxation, such as the general property tax; and taxes upon gasoline, cigarettes, and so on are used very sparingly in efforts to secure from the residents of a community of any size substantial contributions to be used for public purposes. Nor have I ever been able to learn of a single instance anywhere in Brazil of anything comparable to a local election in which the people of a village, town, or city would vote on a bond issue in order to secure the sums needed to finance the construction of some facility such as a municipal water or sewer system, or to pay for an expansion of school facilities. Brazilian cities still lack effective means of pooling resources to meet the costs of essential services.

In general the cities and towns are dependent upon subventions from national and state governments in order to construct and maintain streets, storm sewers, lighting systems, water mains, sewer systems, and so forth. In the national and state capitals, and at considerable cost to other parts of the country, this may result in fairly adequate and even luxurious facilities in favored sections of the cities. But it leaves most urban centers sadly deficient in essential public utilities and services. And the inhabitants of the huge slums that develop on the hills near the hearts of some cities, on the mud flats washed by tidal waters on others, and on the outskirts must struggle to survive in settings that are practically devoid of any of these necessities of urban life.

## The Problem of the "Suburbios"

The problem of the suburbs is, of course, merely the extreme form of the failure to expand the physical features of the city rapidly enough to keep pace with the rate at which people are congregating in and about cities and towns. Not all the great slum districts of the cities are located on the peripheries, and not all the outskirts of the cities are slums. The notorious favelas on the hills of Rio de Janeiro are prominent examples of huge slums near the central business districts. And the exclusive residential areas extending along the coast in the southwestern part of Rio de Janeiro are striking specimens of ecological patterns in which the finest residential districts are not in the hearts of the cities. Moreover, as transportation facilities improve, many more departures from the general rule will come into existence. But the fact remains that in general the Brazilian city is encircled by a broad belt of poverty and misery.

This general situation became apparent about 1960; and it has been described by many sociologists and other professional people. An excellent example, and one which brings out the problems of the suburbs, is the following paragraph by one of Brazil's able social scientists:

In all urban centers there generally are sections which are distinguished from the others by the almost complete lack of public improvements and by the uncomfortable conditions in their dwellings. As a rule these districts, in which the poorest layers of the population live, form the periphery of the cities, and they constantly spread to greater distances from the centers of greatest activity, carrying along their human agglomerations, with greater or less mobility, to the degree that the urban expansion becomes more intense. The social groups of high economic levels generally are located in the central districts, or in proximity to them, whereas those lacking resources live on the outskirts.[21]

These extracts are merely illustrative. My own files alone contain documentation that these huge bands of misery surround almost every city of any importance in Brazil, and that in Brazil (as also is true throughout Spanish America), the problem of the suburbs truly is one of the greatest urban difficulties with which its society must deal.

# Some Comparisons of the Process of Urbanization in Brazil and in the United States

Since 1950 a quickening of the process of the homogenization of society throughout the world has greatly reduced the differences in the urban ways of life in Brazil and the United States. This process, which is the societal equivalent to that of homogenizing milk, brings about the equal distribution throughout the societal body of all the various components of which it is formed; it produces a much greater heterogeneity within any given segment of society at the same time that it brings about a greater similarity between the various segments. Much like Spencer's concept of evolution it results in far greater uniformity between ever increasing heterogeneities.[1] Even so, however, there have been and still are many significant differences between urbanization in Brazil and the United States; and a few of the more important of these are analyzed briefly in this chapter. The ones selected for treatment here are as follows: (1) differences in the timing of the outbursts of city building; (2) striking contrasts between the sources of the inhabitants for the burgeoning cities; and (3) differences in the basic sociocultural ecological forms, i.e., the ground plans of cities in Brazil and the United States. Each of these is treated in turn.

## The Timing of the Outbursts of City Building

It is important to note that the great outbursts in city building in Brazil and the United States took place in quite different periods of time. This fact alone has had much to do with the ways in which

231

the process of urbanization in the one have differed from those in the other. In this opening section, therefore, attention is focused upon a few of the more significant features of the timing of the rush to the cities in the two largest and most populous countries in the Americas.

Evidence readily available makes it apparent that the recent, sudden concentration in urban centers of the bulk of the Brazilian population came about some fifty years later than the comparable, but much more gradual, aggregation of people in the cities of the United States. This is indexed fairly well by the difference in the dates in which the populations of the two countries became predominantly urban. In the United States the year in which the urban population came to exceed the rural in number was around 1918, whereas in Brazil the corresponding landmark was not reached until about 1965. Moreover the total number of inhabitants involved when the residents of urban centers became more numerous than those in rural districts was somewhat smaller in Brazil (about 90 million) that it was in the United States (just over 100 million). Even more important than this, however, is the fact that the majority of the population of the United States did not crowd into cities and towns until after the frontier had been pushed from the eastern limits of the country to the western (i.e., until the supply of virgin territory that could be transformed into farms and ranches had been exhausted), whereas in Brazil, even after it had become a predominantly urban country, fully one-half of the national territory remained to be occupied and settled. Indeed only after Brazil had become more urban than rural did its leaders set in motion a gigantic effort to open up and settle the immense wilderness of the Amazon Basin.[2]

The great lag in urbanization in Brazil, in comparison with that in England, France, the United States, and other of the more developed countries, means that many of the essentials of the contemporary urban way of life originated elsewhere through the slow and difficult process of trial and error before they were transplanted to the Brazilian scene. Probably the most critically important of these are the systems through which industrial energy is produced and applied. It may be affirmed categorically, without fear of rational contradiction, that the present stage of urbanization throughout the world could never have been attained without the perfection of the internal combustion engine and its application to propel automobiles, motor trucks, and aircraft. Some people have amused themselves by calculating the number of inches of horse manure that would blanket the earth's surface had the present degree of urbanization been attained with the energy coming from horses and mules and the hay and grain needed to feed them. It is, of course, utterly preposterous to think that horses and mules could ever have provided the energy required for the world's modern cities. But it also is entirely possible that eventually the course of the development of civilization would have been determined by industrially produced electric energy, nuclear power, or some other means of moving vehicles and burdens even though the internal combustion engine had never been invented. But this is mere speculation. As events transpired it actually was the perfection of the internal combustion engine that enabled mankind to move from the "horse-and-buggy" stage of civilization to the nuclear age; and in the last analysis the widely heralded pollution of the air by the emissions from internal combustion engines is not only one of the chief threats to urban existence in Brazil, the United States, and elsewhere, but these engines, themselves, are the instruments that made possible the present immense concentration of populations in cities large and small.

What we have witnessed in the last sixty years has been two stages in the development of cities and towns. First, in countries such as Canada, England, France, Germany, and the United States, the technology was developed that produced a complete reversal in the flow of energy between farm and city; and second, later on the technology involved in that reversal was applied in Brazil and many other countries in which farm-produced energy never provided the base for any considerable degree of urbanization.

My own studies of the specifics of the reversal of the flow of energy between farm and city have been confined largely to the developments in the United States and in Brazil and other Latin American countries, so the discussion in these paragraphs is confined to the changes in the Western Hemisphere. In the United States as late as 1910 practically all of the energy that was used to move people and things within the already teeming cities came directly from the farms. It was supplied by means of about three million horses and mules, and the hay and grain to feed them, that were used to pull the drays and wagons, the cabs and carriages, the buggies and carts, which were the mainstays of the intraurban systems of transportation. A few streetcars, moved by electricity, were the chief exceptions to this rule; but even they had replaced the old "horse cars" on the city's streets only a decade or so earlier. Between 1910 and 1920 in the cities of the United States the automobile and the motor truck began taking the places of horses and mules to a considerable extent, and by 1940 this process was almost complete. It also should be mentioned that at first the "clean" automobiles, which did not litter the city's streets with dung nor slicken them with urine, was viewed as the answer to the problem of keeping the cities in a habitable condition. It also should be stated explicitly that from about 1950 on, practically all the energy used for work on the farm and in the transportation of people and things between farm and city in the United States was and is produced in urban industrial plants.

As indicated above, Brazil did not enter the stage of rapid urbanization until after the internal combustion engine and electric motors were readily available for use in vehicles for moving people and commodities about within the cities. As late as 1939-42, when I personally visited all of Brazil's major cities, from Manaus in the north to Porto Alegre in the south, Brazil was still overwhelmingly in the rural, agricultural, and pastoral stage of its existence. In 1940 about 80 percent of her people lived in extremely rural environments, and her cities were only on the threshold of the phenomenal growth that was to get under way soon after the close of the Second World War. Moreover at that time even the inhabitants of Rio de Janeiro and São Paulo did not have to contend with the millions of motor vehicles that now jam the streets of these great metropolises with bumper-to-bumper traffic. Nor in 1939 were the streets choked with horse-drawn carts, wagons, carriages, cabs, and other vehicles, such as was true about 1920 when I first came to know life in some of the major cities in the United States. As a matter of fact, the notes in the journals I kept in 1942-43 as I traveled in all parts of Brazil are replete with entries about the reliance upon porters for the transportation of heavy burdens from place to place in the cities; and these notes are more than a little reminiscent of the descriptions left by visitors who recorded their observations in Brazil's cities during the nineteenth century.[3]

It is not necessary, however, to rely on personal observations to document that the extensive use of wheeled vehicles in Brazilian cities, both those drawn by draft animals and those propelled by internal combustion engines, has been confined largely to the period since 1950. There are abundant statistical data to support the same generalization, and it may be indicated that since these data are taken from records of the collections of fees they are far more reliable than most of the estimates that fill the pages of the statistical yearbooks. In 1940 the built-up areas of the city of Rio de Janeiro still were confined largely to the old Distrito Federal which at that time had a population of 1,764,000. In 1937, however, there were in this huge national capital only 22,261 automobiles, 854 auto busses, 89 ambulances, and 585 motorcycles, along with 8,368 motor trucks and other motor vehicles used in trucking. At that time the vehicles drawn by animals were registered in the following numbers: for passengers, 44 carts and 15 carriages; and for transporting goods, 852 ordinary carts, 213 common wagons, and 809 enclosed wagons. In addition there were in use 4,496 handcarts propelled by human energy.

The census of 1940 showed the city of São Paulo to have a population of 1,326,000, somewhat smaller than that of Rio de Janeiro. In 1937, however, the number of private automobiles circulating in its streets came to 23,847, but it is credited in the official statistical compilations with only 568 buses, 515 motorcycles, and no motor-driven ambulances. The number of motor trucks totaled only 7,842. And the vehicles drawn by animals were as follows: carts for passengers, 951; carts for cargoes, 6,749; and wagons for carrying goods, 652. No data on pushcarts are included in the tables.

There is little need to continue the elaboration, since in 1937 the cities of Rio de Janeiro and São Paulo alone accounted for 74 percent of all the automobiles (62,207) and 72 percent of all the motor trucks (22,318) in use in Brazil.[4] It was to be decades before the transformations portended by the use, on the eve of the Second World War, of a few thousand motor vehicles in Brazil's two great metropolitan centers were to spread to large cities in other parts of the country.[5] These statistics emphasize the fact that Brazil never knew the ''horse-and-buggy days'' or even the horse-and-wagon stage of transportation. By about 1965 when urban life became the rule for the majority of its population, modern motor vehicles suddenly became integral parts of the rapidly expanding intra- and interurban transportation systems. These alone made possible the degree of urbanization now prevailing in Brazil, and also, of course, the much higher degree prevailing in the United States and many European countries. Moreover, the production by industrial processes of energy for use on farms and plantations is one of the major factors in the process of industrialization presently contributing heavily to the metamorphosis of Brazilian society. The net effect of all this is to reduce greatly the differences once prevailing between the urban ways of life in Brazil and the United States.[6]

## Sources of the Cities' Burgeoning Populations

The differences in timing of the great surges of city building in Brazil and the United States is related to some extent to the sources of the people who swelled the urban populations of the two countries. In both cases, of course, the dramatic achievements in the control of mortality, so that the city ceased to be a kind of colony that had to be repopulated every year through rural-urban migration, was an important factor. As is well known, the dramatic breakthrough in this respect came about fifty years earlier in the United States than in Brazil; and indeed in the latter, further substantial reductions in the death rate are sure to be accomplished during the 1970s, whereas in the former the principle of limits means that little or no more prolongation of the average duration of life is likely to be forthcoming. In Brazil the death rate can still be lowered considerably merely by measures to insure that larger proportions of the children who arc born live out the established life span. In the United States and Western Europe, on the other hand, any additional substantial reduction in the death rate can be achieved only by lengthening the span of life itself. However, with the process of urbanization in Brazil also lagging about fifty years in comparison with that in the United States, the tremendous reductions in the death rates in the two countries have affected both of them in about the same stages of their urban development. On the other hand, in the United States a tremendous fall in the birth rate took place between 1870 and 1933, and, following a substantial recovery between 1935 and 1955, again from 1956 on. There has been, however, no corresponding change in Brazil. Therefore the role of natural increase in the growth of Brazilian cities doubtless has been considerably greater than it was in the comparable stage of urban development in the United States. Nevertheless in both countries migration has been the big factor in urban growth, and differences in the migrations, both of immigration and rural-urban migration, are chiefly responsible for the ways in which the process of urbanization in the one country has differed from that in the other.

During the eventful years in which the United States was transformed from a nation that was predominantly rural, agricultural, and pastoral, into one in which urban and industrial activities were dominant, the migrants who participated in the work of city building were of two distinctive kinds. Highly motivated European immigrants by the millions settled in the nation's cities, mostly those located in the eastern and northern portions of the country, where they played great roles in the metamorphosis of society that took place. And their work of city building was shared by about equally large contingents of migrants from the parts of the country in which middle-class operators of family-sized farms were busy perfecting the most highly developed system of agricultural production the world has ever known. The immigrants and the sons and daughters of middle-class farmers resembled one another in that they were highly motivated to seek better stations in life for themselves and their children, and were habituated from childhood to make decisions of their own and to enjoy the benefits or suffer the consequences of the same. Few of them had had their entire personalities formed in the highly regimented ranks of plantation laborers, the order-and-obey systems of personal relationships, and the servile or semiservile way of life generated and perpetuated by any plantation system be it in Brazil, the southern part of the United States, the West Indies, or any other part of the world. As a result, and despite the fact that until very recently over half of the rural population of the United States lived in the southern states, where the plantation system was dominant, only about 1917 did any considerable number of the human products of that system begin to migrate to cities and towns. They had practically nothing to do with urban life in the United States before 1920.

Since 1932, however, all of this has changed. That year marks the point when the public relief and welfare rolls began to replace farm labor and mere subsistence farming as "the employer of last resort"; and since then tens of millions of ill-prepared migrants from the plantation system have made festering slums out of the central districts that once were the pride of the cities of the United

States. In fact the plantation sections of the southern part of the United States and some of the West Indies, along with the economically marginal sections in all parts of the country, have proved to be the great rural taproots of contemporary poverty in the cities of the nation. In this respect, moreover, even though public assistance of various kinds has not yet become the "employer of last resort" in Brazil, the sources of the people who have flocked into her cities since 1950, with the migrants coming as they have from the plantations and the areas of the most marginal kinds of subsistence farming, are far more similar to those of the people who settled in the cities of the United States after 1930 than they are to the ones who migrated from rural to urban areas and those who came from overseas prior to that date. In the final explanation of why the processes of urbanization and industrialization in the United States took place as they did it would be difficult to overemphasize the importance of the immigrants who swelled the populations of the cities between 1870 and 1914 and of the hosts of migrants from the family-sized farming districts who joined them there. Together they participated in the work of developing the industries, building the systems of communication and transportation, developing the trade and commerce, perfecting the health and sanitary systems, and initiating most of the other measures and services on which the modern urban life depends.

So important in the urbanization of Brazil and the United States are the roles of immigration, on the one hand, and those of the radically different types of migrants from the rural areas, on the other, that it seems essential to supply a few more of the details about each.[7] The rural-urban classification of the United States population used before 1920 leaves a great deal to be desired, and it is not possible to determine with as much precision as is desirable the extent to which immigrants were concentrated in cities and towns prior to 1900. It is easily demonstrated, however, that the great influx of Europeans took place between 1900 and 1914, with the number arriving rising above the 1,000,000 mark in 1910 and 1913, and reaching its all-time peak of 1,218,500 in 1914.[8] Therefore, for present purposes, it seems sufficient to indicate that the census data show that in 1910, the foreign-born white (European) part of the urban population was about 9,600,000 or 22.5 percent of the total. Thereafter it rose to around 10,380,000 in 1920 and to approximately 10,730,000 in 1930, and then began to fall off. However, because of the shutting off of the supply of immigrants, the proportion of the foreign-born in the nation's urban population fell from the 22.6 percent recorded for 1910, to 15.6, 8.8, amd 5.8 percent for the years 1930, 1950, and 1970, respectively. The numerical importance of immigrants and their children in the cities of the United States reached its apex in 1920, when they made up almost one-half (48.0 percent) of the entire urban population, a figure that was cut to 19.3 percent in 1970. Moreover, in 1880 when the surge of urban development was bursting forth, data for specific cities show that immigrants alone made up the following proportions of the populations of some of the larger ones: San Francisco, 45 percent; Chicago, 41 percent, New York, 40 percent; Milwaukee, 40 percent; Detroit, 39 percent; Cleveland, 37 percent; and St. Paul, 36 percent.

Some of my own as yet unpublished studies demonstrate that in the United States before 1915 the overwhelming proportion of those who left farms for cities was from the middle-class, family-sized farming districts of the northeastern and midwestern parts of the country. In the heavily populated rural districts of the South (a section long dominated by the plantation system and the two-class social system that it generated and perpetuated, and in the hilly and less fertile parts of the area by the concentration of large numbers of small general and subsistence type farmers), on the other hand, rural-urban migration was limited. The fact that before 1920 there were very few cities of any size and importance in the entire South also contributed heavily to this lag.

During the course of the great conflict in Europe, however, all of this began to change drastically. The shutting off of immigration as a source of supply for the labor needed in overtaxed war plants produced an intensive campaign of recruitment throughout the South. This produced a flow of unskilled workers, persons who by no stretch of the imagination could be classified other than of lower-class status, from the southern part of the United States to the great industrial cities like Boston, Chicago, St. Louis, and Minneapolis-St. Paul. The features of these migrants were most visible in the form of the hundreds of thousands of Negroes who flocked into northern cities at the time, but undoubtedly the movement of white people of lower- and lower-middle-class status from the rural districts of the South to the cities of the North was equally important or even greater numerically than that of Negroes.[9]

The onslaught of severe economic depression in the rural parts of the United States immediately after the close of the First World War speeded up the flow of the sons and daughters of the operators of family-sized farms to the cities during the 1920s; but this was brought to virtual cessation, and a tremendous rise in the volume of the reverse movement was generated by the severe urban and industrial depression that began in 1929. Very quickly, however, the measures designed to combat the Depression were initiated, including the institution by the federal government in 1932 of public assistance as the "employer of last resort," or the replacement of economically marginal subsistence farming by programs designed to reduce and control the production of crops and livestock. These soon produced the conditions that resulted in the movement of some 55 million people from the farms to cities, towns, and villages of the United States between 1932 and 1970.[10] Even the net movement during these eventful years was about 30 million persons. Furthermore, of those who left the farms, fully 80 percent were of strictly lower- or lower-middle-class status, and they were drawn in highly disproportionate numbers from the rural parts of the South. It is very important to note that they included about 1 million families, or well over 5 million persons, who once made up the semiservile agricultural labor category called "sharecroppers," which replaced that of slavery itself, following the freeing of the slaves, in the production of cotton which long was the nation's most valuable crop. These 1 million families were almost equally divided between blacks and whites. Their mass movement into the cities along with that of other millions of families of small subsistence farmers from various parts of the United States are what helped change completely, after 1930, the sources of the people who swelled the nation's urban population.

As suggested above, the sources of the people who participated in the burgeoning of Brazilian cities, between 1950 and 1970, differed substantially from those that supplied the newcomers who were largely responsible for the comparable stage of urbanization in the United States, between about 1870 and 1920. The new inhabitants of Brazil's teeming cities were, however, much more similar in origin to those who pushed the process of urbanization to its critical stage, possibly even to the breaking point, between 1930 and 1970. This is to say that with a few exceptions, of which the city of São Paulo is the most striking example, immigrants and their children are conspicuous by their scarcity in Brazil's modern cities; and relatively few migrants from family-sized farms operated by middle-class farmers have figured in the mass movement from rural to urban areas since 1950. As in the United States since 1930, the bulk of those who now make up Brazil's urban population are either persons themselves born in cities and towns or migrants of lower- or lower-middle-class status from areas where the huge landed estates or small subsistence farms dominate the rural scene.

To demonstrate these propositions is fairly simple. Consider first the minor role played by the immigrants. As shown by Brazil's 1950 census, there were in the entire country in that year, on the eve of the great rural exodus that has metamorphized Brazilian society, only 1,244,184 persons (2.3 percent of the 52,000,000 population) who had been born outside Brazil. And of these, 626,943, or 50.4 percent of all the foreign-born in the country, lived in the municipio of São Paulo and the part of the city of Rio de Janeiro that was located within the boundaries of the old Distrito Federal. In these two ultraurbanized areas the 416,589 persons enumerated in São Paulo and the 210,354 foreign-born in a part of metropolitan Rio de Janeiro comprised 19.0 percent of the inhabitants of the former and 8.9 percent of those living in the latter. Between 1950 and 1970, immigration to Brazil totaled only about 750,000, so that it is evident that in the immense burgeoning of cities and towns during that period immigrants played a very small part.[11]

No extensive documentation of the fact that relatively few of the Brazilians who flocked into cities and towns between 1950 and 1970 had migrated from substantial family-sized farms is called for. Such farms simply do not exist in any large numbers.[12]

There remains merely the task of indicating some of the salient features of the staggering mass movement of people from Brazil's rural areas to her cities since 1950. Elsewhere I have tried to take stock of the nature and magnitude of this migration,[13] and here, now that the preliminary data from the 1970 census are available, additional and as yet unpublished facts on that momentous development may be included in the summary. In brief my own studies show that the net movement of population from rural to urban areas in Brazil during the period 1940 to 1970 was as follows: 1940-50, 2,560,000; 1950-60, 6,335,000; and 1960-70, 10,300,000. These data may be interpreted to mean that between 1940 and 1950, a net of 1 out of every 20 Brazilians enumerated in the 1950 census had moved from rural to urban areas during the decade; and that subsequently, those ratios rose to 1 out of 11 for the years 1950 to 1960, and to 1 out of 9 for the decade ending in 1970. These amounts of net rural-urban migration were sufficient to account for 43.4 percent of the increase in urban population between 1940 and 1950, 47.9 percent of that from 1950 to 1960, and to 49.5 percent of the immense (almost 21 million) increase between 1960 and 1970.

## Ground Plans of Cities

Among the more significant determinants of the organization and flow of life in modern cities is the street plan or the ground plan of the city itself. This aspect of social ecology is responsible for many of the striking differences between cities in all that is related to the physical spacing of dwellings and their location with respect to places of work, the sites of commercial and recreational facilities, the journey to work and other aspects of the flow of pedestrians and vehicles, and all the rest. These differences exist between cities that occupy terrains that are similar, and they are multiplied by great differences in topography such as those that are found in the locations of Rio de Janeiro, San Francisco, and Caracas, at the one extreme, and Belo Horizonte, Chicago, and Lima, at the other. In this connection one would do well to reflect briefly upon the differences in the flow of traffic in cities such as Paris, London, Milan, and Seville, on the one hand, and in Belo Horizonte, Chicago, and Indianapolis, on the other, although all are located on practically level ground. Likewise, on sites where the terrain is rugged, there are equally great differences in the basic ecological patterns and the flow of social and economic activities. To take stock of some of these one needs only to compare such cities as Rome, Salvador (Bahia), São Paulo, and Pittsburgh, in one group, with Denver, San Francisco, and Salt Lake City, in another. Merely within the United States itself a difference in ground plans about as sharp as that between day and night is to be observed if one compares the cities that are located in areas in which the land was alienated prior to 1787, i.e., in areas occupied before the system of land surveys designed by Thomas Jefferson went into effect, with those situated in districts that were settled subsequent to that historic event. Brazil, however, has lacked the institutionalized forces required to produce a similar dichotomy in the ground plans of its cities.

In order to gain an understanding of the principal differences between the ground plans of various cities in the United States and Brazil, or elsewhere for that matter, one must take into account three general considerations. One of these is the nature of the plats used in establishing settlements on the original sites. This, however, is of significance only in connection with the layout of streets in the very oldest part of a city, and in general at present this is a very small part of the area occupied by a large city. In exceptional cases, such as that of the city of Rio de Janeiro, where the leveling of hills, the filling of parts of the bay, and the cutting of broad new avenues through the old part of the city have figured heavily in the modern arrangement, the original plat is of even less significance than is usually the case. There is no comparable case, however, in the United States.

A second and more important determinant of the ground plans of modern cities is the nature of the land surveys used in establishing the boundaries of rural properties in the areas surrounding the cities' original sites. These zones, the ones into which the cities have expanded, now include the bulk of the territory within the urban perimeters of cities in both Brazil and the United States, thus making the nature of the old rural surveys into the influence of primordial importance in determining the ground plans of their modern cities.

The size of the rural properties in the area surrounding the original plats of cities is a third ingredient that has had much to do with the ground plans of modern cities, in general, and those of Brazil and the United States, in particular. Where the tracts in the once agricultural-pastoral outskirts of cities were small, or about 160 acres in the cases of Chicago, Indianapolis, and dozens of other places in the United States that are now cities of many hundreds of thousands or millions of inhabitants, the urban "developers" had to work with small additions of land, and in these cases the nature of the original surveys have been all-important. But where the tracts near cities were large landed estates, as was the case near Rio de Janeiro, Recife, and many other of Brazil's major cities, the roles of the property lines of the original surveys were considerably less important. These three factors, i.e., the original plats, the system of rural land surveys, and the size of the farms and estates in the areas adjacent to the original settlements, are the ones whose influences in combination have largely determined the ground plans of modern cities. (It is recognized, of course, that considerable importance is to be attached to recent large-scale and costly projects to cut broad avenues, often on the diagonal, through thickly built-up urban areas, to construct expressways and interchanges. These have radically changed the ground plans in the central portions of some of the larger cities; but they do not change the importance of the three factors indicated above.) The role of each of the three factors is discussed briefly below.

## Original Town Plats

Essentially the original ground plans of cities fall into two basic types. These are: (1) *grids,* on which the city's streets intersect at right angles; and (2) *radial* patterns, in which the major thoroughfares radiate from the center of the city like the spokes of a wheel. Ancient Roman cities, of which Pompeii is an excellent fossil specimen, are among those that originally were laid out on the grid plan; and those of medieval Europe, many of which were built about castles on the hilltops, are splended illustrations of the radial type. In many cases (including Milan, Italy, and Cordova, Spain, to mention only two outstanding specimens) the central portion of the modern city represents a radial pattern that was superimposed on a site where the Romans had used the grid plan. Merely because a grid was used in laying out the plan of the settlement that eventually grew into a large modern city, however, does not mean that such a regular pattern will prevail in its contemporary street plan. This is because most of the space presently within the urban perimeters of Rio de Janeiro, São Paulo, Recife, New York, Chicago, Detroit, and all the other large cities in Brazil and the United States, consists of areas in which the original lines were etched through the institution of property rights to land by means of the surveys used in recording the original deeds through which the land passed from the ownership by the state to that by individuals. Today these are reflected in shapes of the various subdivisions that have been added as the cities grew, the courses of major thoroughfares, and many other physical expressions of the vagaries that distinguish one city from another.

## Original Land Surveys Used in the Areas over which the City has Expanded

Elsewhere I have classified rural land surveys into three principal varieties, namely (1) those featured by the use of metes and bounds, which result in highly irregular, often almost chaotic or "crazy-quilt" patterns of boundaries between the holdings of various proprietors; (2) riverfront types of surveys in which the use of a waterfront (river, lake, oceanfront) or a road as the base of departure, and the employment of straight lines to delineate the sides of the properties, brings a considerable degree of regularity into the system of surveys; and (3) rectangular surveys based upon the lines of latitude and longitude of which the principal embodiments are the official system designed by Thomas Jefferson. As indicated above this type was used in the description of all of the public domain of the United States that was alienated after 1787; and it also was that used in the western provinces of Canada.[14] As stressed below, whether a given city was located in an area in which metes and bounds, riverfront patterns, or rectangular types of land surveys were used has proved to be a major determinant of the present layout of its streets.

## The Size of the Rural Estates in the Areas Now within City Limits

Only a word is needed about the third factor mentioned above, or the size of the rural tracts over which the cities have expanded. As mentioned above, and as anyone who uses the helicopter to get between Midway and O'Hare airports in Chicago may readily observe, the basic layout of that great city has been vitally affected by the relatively small tracts into which the farm lands in Illinois originally were subdivided. The ground plan of modern New Orleans, on the other hand, in which the riverfront pattern of land surveys was used inside one of the huge meanders of the Mississippi River, would have been vastly different from what it is had the tracts of land on either side of the original site consisted of small holdings. As it was, when the first new subdivisions were laid out across the canal (present Canal Street) at the one extremity of the original site, there was plenty of room *within* a small part of the huge tract having a front of over half a mile on the Mississippi River, which belonged to John Gravier, and which itself was only a part of the old plantation that once belonged to the Jesuits. Hence Poydras, Girard, Julia, and St. Joseph streets were laid out quite differently than would have been the case had the developers been faced with the necessity of dealing with a number of previously existing boundaries between small tracts of ground.[15]

If only the three factors considered here are taken into account (namely the grid and the radial types of original plats, the three sharply different kinds of rural land surveys, and the dichotomy of relatively small or large rural land holdings) the possible combinations might give rise to twelve distinct types of street patterns. Neither in Brazil nor the United States, however, have most of these possibilities gained physical expression. Actually in the vast majority of the settlements in both countries a grid plan was used in laying out the original town plat; and in both countries, with a few notable exceptions (such as Belo Horizonte, Gioania, and Brasília, in the former, and Washington, D.C., Philadelphia, and Salt Lake City, in the latter) the plans used in making the original plats have been of relatively little importance in determining the layout of the cities' streets as they are found in the 1970s. This is because the areas occupied by the original villages and towns are now only very small segments of the cities that have developed out of those nuclei; and in practically all cases the expansion of the limits of the cities has taken place piecemeal and on relatively small tracts in the additions that were made year after year. Essentially the net result of all this has been to produce only the two basic types of ground plans in the modern cities of Brazil and the United States. Irrespective of the nature of the original town plats, wherever metes and bounds were used in the surveying and patenting of the original grants of land, the cities in those areas now tend towards the radial ground plan, and wherever the rectangular patterns of survey were employed the grid now prevails as the major feature in the layouts of cities and towns. In both countries, however, in a few cities the peculiar configurations of the waterfronts in such cities as Rio de Janeiro, New York, and Seattle have played decisive roles in determining the existing ecological features of the cities we now see.

Strange as it may seem, because of the piecemeal fashion in which the cities have grown, to an overwhelming degree the ground plans of today's metropolitan areas in both Brazil and the United States have been determined by the old rural surveys that early blanketed the districts that now make up the bulk of the territory within the cities' perimeters. Moreover, despite the existence of a few notable exceptions (among which New Orleans and Detroit are the best examples) the riverfront patterns of land division have affected the present ground plans of relatively few large urban places.[16] The use of metes and bounds in surveying rural lands throughout Brazil and in the parts of the United States settled before 1787, however, has done much to make the ground plans of Brazilian cities and those in the eastern part of the United States take on a form that corresponds to the radial type. One needs only to look at the layouts of Boston, Baltimore, Richmond, Atlanta, Nashville, St. Louis, Louisville, and Dallas, as these are conveniently found in the modern highway atlases, to mention a few cities in the one country, or those of almost any large city in the other, to determine the validity of this generalization. Thus there is a great deal of similarity between the ground plans of Brazilian cities, in general, and those located in the oldest parts of the United States, simply because the areas now within the limits of the cities in both cases originally were surveyed and patented according to a system of metes and bounds.

Throughout most of the area of the United States, however, the original surveys and patents were made in accordance with the provisions of the rectangular surveys prescribed in the Ordinance of 1787. Therefore as places such as Chicago, Indianapolis, Milwaukee, Minneapolis-St. Paul, Kansas City, Oklahoma City, Denver, and Miami expanded into the areas surrounding their original nuclei, the additions were made by adding piecemeal relatively small blocks in which the old property lines ran east-west and north-south. This almost prohibited anything except the grid pattern for even the newest and best-planned subdivision, and the departures from it are mostly the large and expensive expressways that have been cut through densely inhabited sections of the grids. Herein lies one of the most striking differences between the sociocultural ecological patterns of cities and towns throughout most of the territory occupied by the United States, those in the oldest portions of the same country, and those throughout the length and breadth of Brazil.

Finally, because as a rule the rural estates in the areas now occupied by cities were much larger in Brazil than in the United States, in the building of the new subdivisions in the former, the developers were much less restrained by the sizes and shapes of the original grants of land than was true of those responsible for the additions in the latter.

# Notes

## Chapter 1

1. Baton Rouge: Louisiana State University Press, 1946, 1954, 1963, and 1972.

2. The Brazilian materials, as well as the remainder of the reference library we have assembled, have been acquired by the Zimmerman Library of the University of New Mexico where, in their permanent home, they are to be known as the Smith Collection.

## Chapter 2

1. Cf. Don Martindale, *The Nature and Types of Sociological Theory* (Boston: Houghton, Mifflin Company, 1960), pp. 16-17.

2. Fernando de Azevedo, *Brazilian Culture,* translated by William Rex Crawford (New York: The Macmillan Company, 1950), p. 160.

3. Even this had some unfavorable consequences, however, as exemplified by the case of Harvard University. In that noted institution of higher learning, which I myself was privileged to attend during the academic year 1930-31, the "bastard" (combination of Greek and Latin roots) neologism was eschewed until 1930, when prestigious Pitirim A. Sorokin was employed to establish a department. Later, after campus politics had made the situation so distasteful to him that he relinquished the headship, the name of the department was changed from "Sociology" to "Social Relations."

4. Cf. L.L. Bernard, "Henry Hughes, First American Sociologist," *Social Forces* 15, No. 2 (Dec., 1936): 154-74.

5. Cf. L.L. Bernard, "The Historic Pattern of Sociology in the South," *Social Forces* 16, No. 1 (Oct., 1937): 1-12; and the essay entitled "George Fitzhugh, Sui Generis," published as a Preface to C. Van Woodward, editor, *Cannibals All! or Slaves without Masters by George Fitzhugh* (Cambridge, Mass.: The Belknap Press of Harvard University Press, 1960), pp. vii-xxxix. For a more complete account of the life and work of Fitzhugh see Harvey Wish, *George Fitzhugh, Propagandist of the Old South* (Baton Rouge: Louisiana State University Press, 1943).

6. Cf. L.L. Bernard and Jessie Bernard, *Origins of American Sociology: The Social Science Movement in the United States* (New York: Thomas Y. Crowell, 1943), pp. 205-19 and passim.

7. Azevedo, *Brazilian Culture,* p. 361.

8. Baton Rouge: Louisiana State University Press, 4th edition, 1972, p. 513.

9. Cf. T. Lynn Smith, *Agrarian Reform in Latin America* (New York: Alfred A. Knopf, Inc., 1965), pp. 20-21, and 65-79; idem, "Some Notes on the Life and Work of A.P. Figueiredo," *West Georgia College Studies in the Social Sciences* 6, No. 1 (June, 1967): 119-26.

10. T. Lynn Smith, "Studies of Colonization and Settlement," *Latin American Research Review* 4, No. 1 (Winter, 1969): 100-101; idem, *Agrarian Reform,* pp. 21-22.

11. On this point see T. Lynn Smith, "Rural Sociology: A Trend Report," *Current Sociology* 4, No. 1 (Paris: UNESCO, 1957): 10, 28-29.

12. For studies on the development of sociology in Brazil see Donald Pierson, *Survey of the Literature on Brazil of Sociological Significance Published up to 1940* (Cambridge, Mass.: Harvard University Press); and Roger Bastide, "Sociology in Latin America," in Georges Gurvitch and Wilbert E. Moore, editors, *Twentieth Century Sociology* (New York: The Philosophical Library, 1945), pp. 615-37.

13. This information I had from Dr. Park personally after he retired from Chicago. At that time he established his headquarters at Fisk University in Nashville, Tennessee, and each year he came to Baton Rouge, Louisiana, where I was living, and spent many hours conversing with me in my office and in my home. At this time, he also indicated to me that he got his idea for his ecological work from Dr. Charles J. Galpin and the latter's study of Walworth County, Wisconsin, the classic *Social Anatomy of an Agricultural Community* (Madison: Wisconsin Agricultural Experiment Station, 1915).

14. Among the most important of his publications is the monograph, *Cruz das Almas: A Brazilian Village* (Washington, D.C.: The Smithsonian Institution, 1951). A second edition of *Negroes in Brazil* was published by the Southern Illinois University Press in 1967.

15. It remains for a future generation to give Zimmerman the recognition due him. Here, I would merely mention that in addition to working with Sorokin on the now-classic *Principles of Rural Urban Sociology* (New York: Henry Holt & Company, 1929), and the monumental three-volume *A Systematic Source Book in Rural Sociology* (Minneapolis: University of Minnesota Press, 1930-1932), three great works of enduring value in three fundamental fields of sociology all were produced by Zimmerman alone. These are *Consumption and Standards of Living* (New York: D. Van Nostrand, 1936); *The Changing Community* (New York: Harper & Brothers, 1938); and *Family and Civilization* (New York: Harper & Brothers, 1947). But these are only three in a long list of books and monographs he wrote. Few scholars in the field of sociology or out of it can point to a record of achievement even remotely rivaling that of Zimmerman.

16. Also Richard Pattee had translated and published in 1939 a translation of one of Ramos's books under the title *The Negro in Brazil* (Washington, D.C.: Association Press).

17. Baton Rouge: Louisiana State University Press, 1946, 1954, 1963, and 1972.

## Chapter 3

1. Unless otherwise indicated, the statistical data used in this chapter are taken from T. Lynn Smith, *Brazil: People and Institutions,* 4th edition (Baton Rouge: Louisiana State University Press, 1972), and from Brazil's Departamento de Divulgação Estatística, *Anuário Estatístico do Brasil–1973* 34 (Rio de Janeiro: Instituto Brasileiro de Geografia e Estatística, 1973).

2. *Anuário Estatístico do Brasil, 1970* (Rio de Janeiro: Instituto Brasileiro de Geografia e Estatística, 1970), p. 83.

3. "O Povo Brazileiro e sua Evolução," *Recenseamento do Brazil, 1920,* Vol. 1 (Rio de Janeiro: Imprensa Nacional, 1922), p. 281.

4. *Anuário Èstatístico do Brasil, 1973,* p. 51.

5. Cf. T. Lynn Smith, "A Demographic Study of Widows," *International Population Conference, New York, 1961* (London: International Union for the Scientific Study of Population, 1963), p. 312.

6. T. Lynn Smith, *Brazil: People and Institutions* (Baton Rouge: Louisiana State University Press, 1946), pp. 232-35; cf. idem and Paul E. Zopf, Jr., *Demography: Principles and Methods* (Philadelphia: F.A. Davis Company, 1970), Chapter 12.

**Chapter 4**

1. As late as 1821 James Henderson wrote about São Paulo: "It is a great misfortune to the Brazil, that extensive tracts of land have been granted to donatories, who do not possess the means of cultivating one-hundreth part of it, but hold on under the expectation that the gradual improvement of the country will render it daily more valuable, and the residence of the court here induces them to adhere more strongly to this impression: if they dispose of any part of it, they generally subject it to a fine, and the consequences attending such a contract will present a decided obstacle to the agricultural improvement of this country, not at all proportioned to its extent or superabundant powers. Individuals who would devote their exertions and property to the culture of the soil, where this mode prevails, must be effectually deterred. The province of St. Paulo, which may be estimated to contain one hundred and twenty thousand square miles, has no land devoluto, or ungranted, although one-thirtieth part of it is not in a state of cultivation." *A History of the Brazil; Comprising Its Geography, Commerce, Colonization, Aboriginal Inhabitants, &c.* (London: Longman, Hurst, Rees, Orme, and Brown, 1821), pp. 86-87.

In other places the concentration of land ownership was probably even greater. In Bahia a large share of the land early came into the hands of two families, that of the Senhor da Torre and of Antonio Guedes de Britto. The first possessed "260 leagues of land on the right hand side of the upper São Francisco River and running to the south," and "running on the said river towards the north . . . 80 leagues." The second had "160 leagues . . . from the Morro dos Chapéos to the headwaters of the Rio das Velhas." Gilberto Freyre, *Casa Grande & Senzala,* 3rd edition (Rio de Janeiro: Schmidt, 1938), p. 37.

2. The exceptions are relatively rare instances under the Jesuits.

3. Oliveira Vianna, "O Povo Brazileiro e sua Evolução," *Recenseamento do Brazil, 1920,* Vol. 1 (Rio de Janeiro: Typographia de Estatística, 1922), p. 282.

4. Ibid., p. 289.

5. Ibid., p. 290.

6. Cf. Alfred Ellis, Jr., *O Bandeirismo Paulista y o Recúo do Meridiano,* 3rd edition (São Paulo: Companhia Editora Nacional, 1938). This, along with the works of other Brazilian scholars, such as those of Afonso de E. Taunay, indicates how these "raids" of the bandeirantes secured for Brazil the vast areas of its territory which lie west of the line which the pope established to divide the American possessions of Portugal and Spain.

7. For this phase of their activities consult Thomas J. Page, *La Plata, the Argentine Confederation, and Paraguay* (New York: Harper & Brothers, 1859), pp. 473-83. Page sets at 60,000 the number of Indian slaves sold in the public square in Rio de Janeiro in the years 1628 to 1630, the time of these depredations. See also Vianna, "O Povo Brazileiro," pp. 289-90.

Details of the reduction of these Jesuit missions are given in the following extract from the writings of one of the Jesuit fathers. Even if allowance is made for a large margin of error in the figures, one may be certain that the number of Indians captured and carried to the slave marts for sale was very large. "These rapid progresses in the Christian cause have been miserably retarded by the Mamalukes from Brazil, a bordering country, and principally from St. Paulo. The Mamalukes are a set of people born of Portuguese, Dutch, French, Italians, and Germans, and Brazilian women, celebrated for skill in shooting and robbing, ready for any daring enterprize, and thence distinguished by the foreign name of Mamalukes: for it was their constant custom to carry off the Indians, led by the Fathers into the freedom of the children of God, into the hardest slavery. By their incursions, repeated for a number of years, they overthrew the towns of Asumpcion in Yeyuy, of Todos Santos in Caarõ, of the holy Apostles in Caazapaguazú, of St. Christopher on the opposite side of the Ygay, of St. Joachim in the same place, of Santa Barbara, on the western bank of the Paraguay, and of St. Carlos in Caapi. The Guarany inhabitants of these colonies, with the exception of a few who escaped by flight, were led away to Brazil, chained and corded, in herds, like cattle, and there condemned to perpetual labour in the working of sugar, mandioc, cotton, mines, and tobacco. The sucking babes were torn from the bosoms of their mothers, and cruelly dashed upon the ground by the way. All whom disease or age had rendered imbecile were either cut down or shot, as being unequal to the daily march. Others, in sound health, were often thrown by night into trenches prepared for them, lest they should take advantage of the darkness, and flee. Many perished by the way, either from hunger or the hardships of a journey protracted for many leagues. In this hunting of the Indians, they sometimes employed open violence, sometimes craft, equally inhuman in both. They generally rushed into the town in a long file, when the people were assembled in the church at divine service, and, blocking up every street and corner, left the wretched inhabitants no way of escape. They frequently disguised themselves as Jesuits, wearing rosaries, crosses, and a black gown, and collected companies of Indians in the woods. Many towns that were liable to the treacherous hostilities of the Mamalukes, such as Loretto, St. Ignatius, &c. were removed to safer places, by a journey of many months, and with incredible labor, both of the Fathers and the Indians. Nor did the Mamalukes spare our colonies of the Chiquitos and Moxos, nor others in the hands of the Spaniards, which were administered both by the secular and regular clergy. The Indian towns settled on the banks of the Yeyuy, in Curuquatí, and many others, were entirely destroyed by the Mamalukes. The same fate attended Xerez, Guayra, (Ciudad real), Villarica, &c. cities of the Spaniards. Who can describe all the devastation committed in Paraguay? Hear what is said on this subject in the collection of *Lettres Curieuses et Edifantes:*–'It is asserted,' they say, 'that in the space of one hundred and thirty years, two millions of Indians were slain, or carried into captivity by the Mamalukes of Brazil; and that more than one hundred thousand leagues of country, as far as the river Amazon, was stripped of inhabitants.' It appears from authentic letters, (sent by the Catholic King ------ in the year 1639, 16th Sept.) that in five years three hundred thousand Paraguayrian Indians were carried away into Brazil. . . . Pedro de Avila, Governour of Buenos-Ayres, declared that Indians were sold openly, in his sight, by the inhabitants of the town of St. Paulo, at Rio Janeiro; and that six hundred thousand Indians were sold, in this town alone, from the year 1628 to the year 1630.'' Martin Dobrizhoffer, *An Account of the Abipones, An Equestrian People of Paraguay,* trans., Vol. 1 (London: John Murray, 1822), p. 159. Robert Southey, *History of Brazil,* Vol. 2 (London: Longman, Hurst, Rees, Ormes, and Brown, 1817), pp. 309 ff., gives an account that is more charitazle to the Paulistas.

8. The Indian's role of fighter was an important one. "During the 16th and 17th centuries each sugar engenho had to maintain on a war footing its hundreds or at least its tens of men ready to defend the house and the stores accumulated in the warehouses against savages and pirates: these men were almost exclusively Indians or caboclos armed with bows and arrows." Freyre, *Casa Grande & Senzala,* p. 62.

9. But there was some. Sir Harry H. Johnston, *The Negro in the New World* (London: Methuen & Co., 1910), p. 98, states that 4,000 to 6,000 Negroes from Brazil returned to Africa between 1850 and 1878. See also Donald Peirson, *Negroes in Brazil* (Chicago: University of Chicago Press, 1943), p. 39, who calls attention to the fact that certain towns on the west coast of Africa may have been named by Negroes who had once lived in Brazil. See also Gilberto Freyre, *Nordeste* (Rio de Janeiro: José Olympio, 1937), pp. 130 ff.

10. Despite the fact that slaves were probably well fed and housed and very well treated in Brazil, there seems to have been considerable effort to prevent their reproduction. Note the observations of H.M. Brackenridge, who served as secretary to the commission which the United States sent to South America in 1817 to report the situation in the provinces that were revolting from Spain. He stated that the annual importation of slaves into Brazil was about 30,000, of whom the larger share were males. He also added that it was considered cheaper to import slaves at the prevailing prices of $200 or $300 per head than to rear them. *Voyage to South America,* Vol. 1 (Baltimore: J.D. Toy, Printer, 1819), p. 167.

In São Paulo: "The black slaves have very few children, which is not entirely explained by the proportion of the female to the male slaves (16:22). One cause may be, that the male slaves, being almost always employed in the labors of agriculture, and tending the cattle, pass the greater part of the year alone in the remote *chacaras* and *fazendas de criar gado,* whereas the female slaves are employed in household services." J.B. Von Spix and C.F.P. von Martius, *Travels in Brazil,* Vol. 2 (London: Longman, Hurst, Rees, Orme, and Brown, 1824), p. 11.

A few years later Commander Charles Wilkes of the U.S. Navy stated more positively: "The slaves do not increase, as procreation is prevented as much as possible. The two sexes are generally locked up at night in separate apartments. The number of slaves imported into Rio and Bahia previous to the prohibition of the slave trade in 1830, was about forty thousand a year for the former, and ten thousand for the latter, as follows:

|  | Rio | Bahia |
|---|---|---|
| 1828 | 41,913 | 8,860 |
| 1829 | 40,015 | 12,808 |
| 1830 half year | 29,777 | 8,588 |

"About one-third of these were lost by death, leaving two-thirds as an accession to the labour of the country.

"The number annually imported since 1830, contrary to law, is estimated at seven to ten thousand." *Narrative of the United States Exploring Expedition During the Years 1838, 1839, 1840, 1841, 1842,* Vol. 1 (New York: G.P. Putnam & Co., 1856), p. 86.

A British writer, Alexander Majorbanks, in the middle of the nineteenth century, also indicated that the Africans in Brazil did not reproduce sufficiently to maintain their numbers: ". . .but who can tell how many slaves it will take to glut the market of Brazil? The half of the population of the continent of Africa would scarcely be sufficient to supply the demand that would spring up under such circumstances. Treated as her slaves are, and as the Brazilians think it their interest to treat them, the time will never come when they will dispense with the necessity of fresh importations from the coast of Africa. But let her be forced to adopt a different policy in relation to the treatment of her slaves, and be made to rely upon the natural increase of those already in the country, and the time is not far distant when we may reasonably expect the Brazilians themselves to be utterly opposed to any further accessions to her slaves from the coast of Africa." *Travels in South and North America,* 5th ed. (London: Simpkin, Marshall, and Company, 1854), p. 60. Herbert H. Smith in the 1870s referred to the practice of locking up Negro men and women in separate quarters at night. *Brazil, the Amazons and the Coast* (New York: Charles Scribner's Sons, 1874), p. 526.

More recently Calmon generalized: "The Negro, as a rule, did not survive the third generation. Until 1850 the pure blood Negroes were Africans or children of Africans. The number of mulattoes increased as a function of the slave's sociability: that of the Negroes oscillated with the traffic." Pedro Calmon, *Espirito da Sociedade Colonial* (São Paulo: Companhia Editora Nacional, 1935), p. 157.

11. Renato Mendonça, *A Influência Africana no Portugues do Brasil* (São Paulo: Companhia Editora Nacional, 1935), p. 53.

12. The last discussion of this subject by Arthur Ramos, Brazil's most noted authority on the Negro, is found in Chapter 6 of T. Lynn Smith and Alexander Marchant, editors, *Brazil: Portrait of Half a Continent* (New York: The Dryden Press, 1951). See also Arthur Ramos, *O Negro Brasileiro,* 2nd edition (São Paulo: Companhia Editora Nacional, 1940), pp. 22-25, and especially the posthumously published work of Nina Rodrigues, *Os Africanos no Brasil* (São Paulo: Companhia Editora Nacional, 1932); cf. Oliveira Vianna, "O Povo Brazileiro e sua Evolução," p. 319.

13. Of the Minas Negroes in Rio de Janeiro, Wilkes wrote in 1838: "The negroes of Brazil who have been brought from North and South Africa, are divided into two distinct and very dissimilar classes. The natives of that portion of the continent known under the general name of Upper Guinea, include the countries in the interior as far as Timbuctoo and Bornou, being the whole of that region lately explored by the English expeditions. The slaves from this quarter, though of various nations and languages, have yet a general likeness, which stamps them as one race. In Brazil they are known under the name of Minas.

"The Minas slaves are said to be distinguished from others by their bodily and mental qualities. They are generally above middle height, and well formed. The forehead is high, and the cheek-bones prominent; the nose sometimes straight and sometimes depressed; the lips not very thick; teeth small and perpendicularly set; the hair is wooly, and the colour an umber or reddish brown, approaching to black.

"The look and bearing of the Minas blacks are expressive of intelligence and dignity, and they betray little of the levity usually ascribed to the negro race.

"In Brazil they occupy the highest positions that slaves are allowed to attain, being employed as confidential servants, artisans, and small traders. They look down upon, and refuse to have any connexion with, or participation in the employment of other negroes. Many of them write and read Arabic, and all can repeat some sentences of it. The greatest number of slaves who purchase their freedom belong to this race.

● ● ● ● ● ●

"The Minas are held in much fear in Brazil. They are extremely numerous at Bahia, and it is understood, that during a late insurrection, they had fully organized themselves, and were determined to institute a regular system of government. They had gone so far as to circulate writings in Arabic, exhorting their fellows in bondage to make the attempt to recover their liberty." *Narrative of the United States Exploring Expedition,* pp. 54-56.

Wilkes also described the southern, or Bantu, types: "The nations to the South of the equator, have the usual form of the negro, agreeably to our ideas. Those of the slaves at Rio de Janiero, are, in general, short, badly formed, or clumsy, with narrow foreheads, flat noses, protruding jaws and teeth, and prominent cheek-bones, with the chin sloping backwards. They are indolent, thoughtless and licentious. They may be seen in the streets at all hours, employed as carriers, earning the stipulated sum for their masters. And when this is gained, they are to be found stretched out on the sidewalk, under the porticoes, or on the steps of churches, enjoying themselves as mere animals, basking in the sun or sleeping in the shade. They are not deficient in intelligence: the defect is less in their intellectual powers than in their character, which appears to want energy." Ibid., p. 57.

14. Cf. Freyre, *Casa Grande & Senzala,* pp. 6, 164. See also his *Sobrados e Mucambos* (São Paulo: Companhia Editora Nacional, 1936), pp. 40 ff.

15. See Gilberto Freyre, "Some Aspects of the Social Development of Portuguese America," in Charles C. Griffin, editor, *Concerning Latin American Culture* (New York: Columbia University Press, 1940), p. 86. Cf. Rodolfo Garcia, "Os Judeus no Brasil Colonial," in Afranio Peixoto et al., *Os Judeus na Historia do Brasil* (Rio de Janeiro: Uri Zwerling, 1936), pp. 42, 43, who shows that numerically, financially, and professionally the Jews also played a considerate part in the peopling of Brazil's sugar-growing coastal fringe. In spite of the fact that Brazil was by no means too distant for the long arm of the Inquisition, the new Portuguese colonies were for many years a refuge for Jews and "new Christians." Although late in the sixteenth and early in the seventeenth century representatives of the Bishop and Inquisitor General of Portugal set up tables of the Holy Office in Bahia, Recife, and other population centers, the local ecclesiastics frequently were accused of assisting persons suspected of adhering to the practices of Judaism to evade detection and judgment. A century later, and especially in 1713, the work of the inquisitors sent from Portugal was much

more effective. This year saw thirty-two men and forty women condemned in Rio de Janeiro alone. Those sent to Lisbon for judgment included a large number of *senhores de engenho,* and in part the persecutions may have been motivated by jealousy and covetousness. The definitive work on Jews in colonial Brazil and inquisitorial activities in this part of the New World is Arnold Wiznitzer, *Jews in Colonial Brazil* (New York: Columbia University Press, 1960). See also *Narrativa da Perseguição de Hippolyto Joseph da Costa Pereira Furtado de Mendonça* (London, 1811).

16. Cf. Freyre, *Casa Grande & Senzala,* pp. 138-39.

17. This factor is very important. In the first place, relatively few Portuguese women were among the settlers. In the second place, of the white children born in Brazil, a very high percentage took religious orders. Said the captain general of Minas in 1731, ''I suppose every woman in Brazil will be a nun,'' and eight years later the Count of Gaveas complained that in Bahia, ''the heads of families refuse to give their daughters in marriage, placing them in convents,'' with the result that in 1738 there were only two marriages in the entire city. Calmon, *Espirito da Sociedade Colonial,* pp. 90-95.

18. Later, after Africans became an important element in the population, many priests left numerous mulatto offspring. This is especially important because the rich inheritances left by their ecclesiastical fathers were the means by which men of the mulatto class came into the possession of wide expanses of lands. Says one of the *Cartas Soteropolitanas* (letters from Bahia) quoted by Calmon: ''There are ecclesiastics, and not a few, who in that ancient and bad manner without remembering their estate and character, live thusly in disorder with mulatresses and negresses, by whom they leave at death children as heirs to their property; and by this and similar means there have come into the hands of presumptuous, arrogant, and vagabond mulattoes many of the most valuable properties in Brazil, such as the sugar plantations of this area, which in a short time are destroyed.'' *Espirito da Sociedade Colonial,* p. 160. By 1774 mulattoes in Brazil came into the enjoyment of full privileges before the law. Ibid., p. 162. See also Freyre, *Casa Grande & Senzala,* p. 323.

19. Cf. introductory chapter in Pierre Denis, *Brazil,* trans. by Bernard Miall (London: T. Fisher Unwin, 1911), pp. 32-35.

20. Some of the evidence indicates that upper-class men frequently preferred their dark mistresses to their white wives. Said La Barbinnais, the French traveler of the early eighteenth century, as quoted by Calmon: ''To the most beautiful women they prefer the negresses and mulatresses. I know one, a very charming woman from Lisbon, who is married to a Bahiano; however, disorder prevails in their home, because her husband disdains her for the love of a negress who does not merit the attentions of the ugliest negro in all of Guinea.'' There is also a little rhyme in the folklore of the state of Rio de Janeiro that runs, in a literal translation, as follows:

> If white women were for sale,
> Either for gold or for silver,
> I should buy one of them
> For a servant for my mulata.

Cf. Calmon, *Espirito da Sociedade Colonial,* p. 161. See also Freyre, *Casa Grande & Senzala,* p. 9, who quotes the old Brazilian saying about ''a white woman for marriage, a mulatress for a mistress, and a negress for work.'' Cf. Freyre, ''Some Aspects of the Social Development of Portuguese America,'' pp. 83-84.

21. Says Oliveira Vianna: ''In reality during the Colonial epoch the latifundium was the breeding field par excellence. In it the whites—the owners, their relatives, their agregados—exercised a dominating role. They were the sires, the great impregnators of the Indian women, the fiery stallions of the Negro females. Some of them, even among the most noble, left only *'filhos naturaes e pardos'* [illegitimate children and mulattoes] according to the testimony of the Conde da Cunha.'' *Populações Meridionaes do Brasil* (São Paulo: Companhia Editora Nacional, 1938), pp. 78-79. And again: ''The half bloods, are, then, a

historical product of the latifundia. To serve as a field for race crossing, a center for integrating the three distinct races, is the second social function of the rural dominion. This function is one of the most important in our history—because in it is the genesis and formation of our nationality." Ibid., pp. 79-80.

Similar is the analysis of Dr. João Pandiá Calogeras: "And the conditions of life on the old fazendas, in which the master possessed unrestricted control of the lives and goods of his slaves and retainers, like the past feudalism, facilitated greatly the production of half bloods, quadroons, and even of children with higher proportions of Aryan blood.

"Among the slaves, appeared a scale of all shades which varied from almost-white, with an almost imperceptible African tint, to the most characteristic Congo." *A Politica Exterior do Imperio,* Vol. 1 (Rio de Janeiro: Imprensa Nacional, 1927), pp. 293-94.

To this facility with which a few thousand Portuguese males *(machos)* produced offspring by women of color, Freyre attributes much of tiny Portugal's success as a colonizing nation. Cf. *Casa Grande & Senzala,* p. 7. Certainly this small country seized and maintained control of huge expanses of the earth's surface at a time when competition with larger countries was keen. Furthermore, the biological and cultural factors involved preserved the colonies for the Portuguese crown, even though it was long subordinated to Spain.

22. Oliveira Vianna, *Populações Meridionaes,* p. 79. Only rarely does one find in the literature descriptions of the cafuso groups. Thus, while von Spix and von Martius, Mawe, Prince Maximilian, Koster, St. Hilaire, Burton, and other early travelers make frequent reference to communities of domesticated Indians and caboclos and of communities composed wholly of Negroes and mulattoes, rarely did they observe settlements of cafusos. When von Spix and von Martius did encounter a group of these people in Taruma in the province of São Paulo, it was the occasion for a detailed description of their features and characteristics. *Travels in Brazil,* Vol. 1, pp. 323-24.

23. This interpretation was stressed by Brazil's outstanding historian, Dr. Arthur Cezar Ferreira Reis, in conversations with the author at Belém during December 1942. However, when von Spix and von Martius visited the Coroados of the River Doce in Minas Gerais in 1818 they reported: "The Indian women, we were told, showed more attachment to the negroes than to their own Indian husbands. Runaway negroes, therefore, frequently appear in the woods as the *cicisbei* of the Indian women, and are passionately sought by them. The contrary is the case with the Indian men who consider the negresses as below their dignity and despise them." Ibid., Vol. 2, p. 229.

24. Even this modern attitude has deep roots in the past. Thus long before slavery was abolished in Brazil, visitors were struck by the freedom with which persons of all colors mingled with lack of racial discrimination. For example, Wilkes wrote in 1838: "Every one, on his first landing at Rio, will be struck with the indiscriminate mingling of all classes, in every place, all appearing on terms of the utmost equality;—officers, soldiers, and priests, both black and white, mixing and performing their respective duties, without regard to colour or appearance. The only distinction seems to be that of freedom and slavery. There are many wealthy free blacks, highly respectable, who amalgamate with the white families, and are apparently received on a footing of perfect equality." *Narrative of the United States Exploring Expedition,* Vol. 2, p. 45.

25. Says Manoel de Oliveira Lima, *The Evolution of Brazil Compared with that of Spanish and Anglo-Saxon America* (Palo Alto: Stanford University Press, 1914), p. 20: "Indeed, not only has the genealogical tree of many families of distinction been jealously guarded from contact with all strains of inferior blood, but the whites of the colonies maintained and defended their titles and rights to certain posts and functions which had been reserved to them by the laws of their respective mother countries." See also Calmon, *Espirito da Sociedade Colonial,* pp. 158-59. Girls were sent from Portugal, sometimes by the queen herself, for the explicit purpose of preserving the "social rank and the aristocratic status of the planters." Freyre, "Some Aspects of the Social Development of Portuguese America," p. 83.

Testimony of others is similar. John Codman, who sometimes was inclined to be severely critical, wrote: "Some years ago, when a census was to be taken, it was proposed to divide the classes of the community, and to enumerate separately the white, black, and mixed. The Brazilians themselves laughed at the imbecile who wasted his ink in the suggestion. 'Mixed!' There is black blood everywhere stirred in; compounded over and over again, like an apothecary's preparation. African blood runs freely through marble halls, as well as in the lowest gutters, and Indian blood swells the general current. There is no distinction between white and black, or any of the intermediate colors, which can act as a bar to social intercourse or political advancement.

"The whole population of Brazil, according to the latest census, was 9,083,755, of whom 1,357,416 were slaves; of the remaining 7,726,339, called 'free,' it was wisely determined to make no further classification." *Ten Months in Brazil,* 2nd edition (New York: James Miller, 1872), pp. 153-54.

As an explanation of the reason for the Portuguese lack of discrimination against peoples of darker color one should keep in mind that Portugal was the last part of the Iberian Peninsula to be occupied by the Moors. For centuries in Portuguese society the darker ethnic elements occupied the higher social positions. Under the circumstances marriage with a person of darker hue generally meant moving up the social scale. This economic factor undoubtedly had much to do with disassociating the combination of dark or black with bad or undesirable, which has generally prevailed in the Western world. Probably a great deal of the Brazilian's racial tolerance has stemmed from this factor. Cf. Roy Nash, *The Conquest of Brazil* (New York: Harcourt, Brace and Co., 1926), p. 37; and Freyre, *Casa Grande & Senzala,* p. 7. The popularity in Portugal of the legends about the "enchanted Mooress" *(moura-encantada),* and especially their settings (ibid., pp. 7-8), also indicates that Portuguese men were by no means immune to the mystical appeals of dark eyes and raven tresses. See also Freyre's contribution in Griffin, editor, *Concerning Latin American Culture,* p. 83.

26. There are certain studies such as Alfred Ellis, Jr., *Populações Paulistas* (São Paulo: Companhia Editora Nacional, 1934), pp. 178-96, which purport to show that the Japanese are assimilating rapidly; the numbers and proportions of mixed Japanese-Brazilian marriages are given as evidence. However, since any child born in Brazil is counted as a Brazilian, all the data really show is that children born in Brazil of Japanese parents have reached a marriageable age. Since Japanese were first imported in 1908, this is not surprising. A much more significant and penetrating study is that by R. Paula Souza, "Contribuição á Etnologia Paulista," *Revista do Arquivo Municipal de São Paulo* 31 (1936): 95-105, which takes into account the racial characteristics of the parties contracting marriages. This piece of research revealed that even among Japanese families with children in the university, i.e., those least isolated socially from the Brazilians, no race mixture whatever had taken place. See also Oscar Egidio de Araujo, "Enquistamentos Étnicos," *Revista do Arquivo Municipal de São Paulo* 65 (1940): 227-46.

27. Cf. Sud Mennucci, "A Subdivisão do Municipio de Blumenau," *Geografia* 2, No. 4 (1936): 20.

28. Even an upper-class Brazilian will make reference to his remote Indian ancestry or feel complimented if another calls him a "caboclo." Similar reference to possible African ancestors is taboo. Says Freyre: "To call someone a 'caboclo' in Brazil almost always is a eulogy of his character or of his capacity for physical and moral resistance. This is in contrast to 'mulatto,' 'negro,' *'muleque,'* 'creole,' 'pardo,' *'paravasco'* [brownish], *'sarará,'* which in general have a depreciative connotation with respect to the moral, social, or cultural situation of an individual. Many a Brazilian mulatto of high social or political position makes a practice of calling himself 'caboclo': 'we caboclos,' 'if I were not a caboclo.' And Julio Bello informs us that old Sebastião do Rosario, a well-known senhor de engenho in Pernambuco during the 19th Century, a pure Wanderley of means, of the Wanderleys of Serinhaem—a people almost all of ruddy European skin, of blue eyes, of flaxen hair—when in a expansive

mood, highly contented, at one of his elaborate dinners, used to speak of himself, falsely, as being a 'caboclo.' Mulatto or touched with negro blood is what no one cares to be when he is in the *alturas* [higher social levels]. Extremely rare are the exceptions." *Casa Grande & Senzala*, p. 48. E. Franlin Frazier, after studying fifty families in Bahia, cautiously wrote: "There is reason to believe some of those claiming caboclo ancestors preferred the term to mulatto which implied Negro ancestry." "The Negro Family in Bahia, Brazil," *American Sociological Review* 7 (August, 1942): 470.

29. See Freyre, *Casa Grande & Senzala*, pp. 47-49.

30. The darker and lower-class elements live in the suburbs of the city. Rather generally throughout northern Brazil, and even on the outskirts of large cities such as São Luís, the owner of the land permits "squatters" to build a house providing they use thatch for the roof. A more permanent construction with a tile roof, however, may not be built by the squatter.

A young mulatto from southern Piauí, whom I encountered in Teresina, the capital of that state, complained bitterly that the landowners in that section did not comply with this time-honored custom but "kicked out" anyone who tried to build a house on the outskirts of that city. He personally longed for the day when he could go back to his own *terra* where the donos were more understanding. His statement, however, was probably not a complete description of the prevailing situation, because in the outskirts of Teresina, as in other northern cities, the wattle-and-daub walls, the thatched roofs, and the dirt floors of the huts and especially the confused patternless arrangements of the streets and houses seem to indicate an almost complete freedom to build whatever was wanted in the nature of a shelter wherever it was desired to locate a habitation.

In Teresina I made the following entry in my notes: "Cities and towns here (north Brazil) are all of a type and all exactly contrary to the Chicago ecological theories. The center of town is an area of paved streets, electric lights, water, and houses of masonry with tiled roofs. Farther out the facilities give out, but some plastered houses and aligned streets continue. On the edges of town there are no facilities, streets are winding and unaligned, houses are all of thatch or wattle and daub, with thatched roofs. Undoubtedly the center of town is much freer of mosquitoes and, consequently, much less dangerous from the standpoints of malaria and yellow fever."

31. For materials on these trends and relationships in the United States, see T. Lynn Smith and Paul E. Zopf, Jr., *Demography: Principles and Methods* (Philadelphia: F.A. Davis Company, 1970), Chapters 5 and 13.

32. For data on the age distribution of the population of Brazil in 1950, the ratio of children to women in 1960, and other features of the population profile for the period 1950 to 1960 see T. Lynn Smith, "The People of Brazil and Their Characteristics," in John V.D. Saunders, editor, *Modern Brazil: New Patterns of Development* (Gainesville: University of Florida Press, 1971), Chapter 3.

## Chapter 5

1. Cf. T. Lynn Smith, *Brazil: People and Institutions* (Baton Rouge: Louisiana State University Press, 1946), pp. 160-64, and the corresponding sections in the second, third, and fourth (1972) editions of the same.

2. For somè of the detailed data on this aspect of Brazil's population policy, see ibid., 4th edition, Chapter 8; and for a classic account of the British blockade, see Edward Wilberforce, *Brazil Viewed Through a Naval Glass with Notes on Slavery and the Slave Trade* (London: Longman, Green, Brown, and Longmans, 1856).

3. Cf. T. Lynn Smith and Paul E. Zopf, Jr., *Demography: Principles and Methods* (Philadelphia: F.A. Davis Company, 1970), pp. 534-44.

4. The data given here were secured from the 1969 issue of the *Anuário Estatístico do Brasil* (Rio de Janeiro: Instituto Brasileiro de Geografia e Estatística, 1960), pp. 144, 162.

5. For some information on these movements see T. Lynn Smith, "The Role of Internal Migration in Population Redistribution in Brazil," *Revista International de Sociologia* 29 (January-April, 1971): 109-14.

6. For descriptions of life in the small towns and villages in this part of Brazil as it was in the nineteenth century, see George Gardner, *Travels in the Interior of Brazil* (London: Reeve, Benham, and Reeve, 1849), Chapters 9 and 10; and James W. Wells, *Three Thousands Miles Through Brazil* Vol. 2 (London: Sampson, Low, Marston, Searle & Rivington, 1886), Chapters 12-15.

7. Alfred K. Homma, "O Marahão Está Chegando," *Correio Agopecuario* 9, São Paulo (August, 1969): 6.

8. Materials on the early stages of this great project are given in Smith, *Brazil* (1972), pp. 647-50.

9. Curiously enough, the way in which this highly commercialized form of monoculture, with its rigid regimentation of a large servile labor force, the very antithesis of the old European feudal system, was generated and spread seems never to have been described in specific terms, but that is a subject for another essay.

10. *The Mechanization of Agriculture in Brazil: A Sociological Study of Minas Gerais* (Gainesville: University of Florida Press, 1969), p. 49. See also pp. 62, 74, and 80 for supplementary statements of the same induction.

11. My first systematic presentation of this schema is in *The Sociology of Rural Life,* 3rd edition (New York: Harper & Brothers, 1953), Chapter 14; and subsequent applications of it are found in *Brazil,* 3rd edition, Chapter 15; idem, *Colombia: Social Structure and the Process of Development* (Gainesville: University of Florida Press, 1967), Chapter 5; and idem, *The Sociology of Agricultural Development* (Leiden: E.J. Brill, 1972), Chapter 4.

12. Cf. ibid., *Brazil,* 4th edition, pp. 357-58.

13. Washington, D.C.: The Brazilian Embassy, 1959, p. 1.

14. Cf. T. Lynn Smith, "Agricultural-Pastoral Conflict: A Major Obstacle in the Process of Rural Development," *Journal of Inter-American Studies* 11, No. 1 (January, 1969): 16, passim; idem, "Problems of Agriculture in Latin America," in Committee on Foreign Relations, *Survey of the Alliance for Progress,* Senate Document No. 91-17, 91st Congress, 1st Session (Washington, D.C.: U.S. Government Printing Office, 1969), pp. 256-56, passim; and idem, "Some Sociocultural Systems Obstructing the Modernization of Agriculture in Spanish America," *Revue Internationale de Sociologie* 7, Series 2, No. 1 (1971): 1-10.

## Chapter 7

1. Richard F. Burton, *The Highlands of the Brazil,* Vol. 1 (London: Tinsley Brothers, 1868), p. 47.

2. T. Lynn Smith, *Brazil: People and Institutions* (Baton Rouge: Louisiana State University Press, 1946), p. 483.

3. F.J. Oliveira Vianna, "O Povo Brazileiro e Sua Evolução," *Recenseamento do Brazil, 1920,* Vol. 1 (Rio de Janeiro: Imprenta Nacional, 1922), p. 282.

3. Edward A. Ross, *South of Panama* (New York: The Century Company, 1915), p. 144. The italics are in the original.

4. Translated from Gilberto Freyre, "La lucha no es de clases," *Life en Español,* May 11, 1964, pp. 25-26.

## Chapter 8

1. Cf. Charles J. Galpin, *The Social Anatomy of an Agricultural Community,* Wisconsin Agricultural Experiment Station Bulletin No. 34, Madison, 1915; Carle C. Zimmerman and

Carl C. Taylor, *Rural Organization: A Study of Primary Groups in Wake County,* North Carolina Agricultural Experiment Station Bulletin No. 245, Raleigh, 1922; Edmund deS. Brunner, *Village Communities* (New York: Doubleday, Doran & Company, 1928); Dwight Sanderson, *The Rural Community: The Natural History of a Sociological Group* (Boston: Ginn & Company, 1932); Carle C. Zimmerman, *The Changing Community* (New York: Harper & Brothers, 1938); Olen E. Leonard and Charles P. Loomis, *Culture of a Contemporary Community: El Cerrito, New Mexico,* U.S. Department of Agriculture Rural Life Studies No. 1, Washington, D.C., 1941; Lowry Nelson, *The Mormon Village* (Salt Lake City: University of Utah Press, 1952); Irwin T. Sanders, "Community Development Programs In Community Perspective," in James H. Copp, editor, *Our Changing Rural Society* (Ames: Iowa State University Press, 1964), pp. 307-40; George A. Hillery, Jr., *Communal Organizations: A Study of Local Societies* (Chicago: University of Chicago Press, 1968); T. Lynn Smith, *Colombia: Social Structure and the Process of Development* (Gainesville; University of Florida Press, 1967), Chapter 8; and idem and Paul E. Zopf, Jr., *Principles of Inductive Rural Sociology* (Philadelphia: F.A. Davis Company, 1970), Chapter 10.

2. *Society: A Textbook of Sociology* (New York: R. Long and E.R. Smith, Inc., 1937), pp. 9-10.

3. Robert E. Park and Ernest W. Burgess, *Introduction to the Science of Sociology* (Chicago: University of Chicago Press, 1933), p. 163.

4. See Charles H. Cooley, *Social Organization* (New York: Charles H. Scribner's Sons, 1925), p. 23.

5. Zimmerman, *The Changing Community,* pp. 73-84.

6. Cf. T. Lynn Smith, *La Sociologia y el Proceso de Desarrollo de la Comunidad,* Documentos Técnicos UP/Ser. H/VII. 20.2, Washington, D.C.: Pan American Union, 1964, pp. 17-19; and idem, *Colombia,* pp. 295-99.

7. Cf. Emilio Willems, *Cunha: Tradição e Transição em uma Cultura Rural do Brasil* (São Paulo: No publisher given, 1948); and Charles Wagley, *Amazon Town: A Study of Man in the Tropics* (New York: The Macmillan Company, 1953).

8. This actually seems to be taking place in the colonization of the zones through which the new Transamazonian Highway is being pushed.

9. This trend should be analagous to one that has already run much of its course in the United States since the automobile became a factor about 1910. See, for the results of careful work about this aspect of community development, Dwight Sanderson, *Rural Social and Economic Areas in Central New York,* Cornell University Agricultural Experiment Station Bulletin 614, Ithaca, N.Y., 1934, p. 95; and T. Lynn Smith, *Farm Trade Centers in Louisiana, 1901 to 1931,* Louisiana Agricultural Experiment Station Bulletin No. 234, Baton Rouge, 1933, pp. 54-55.

## Chapter 9

1. Translated from Arthur Ramos, *O Negro Brasileiro,* 2nd edition (São Paulo: Companhia Editora Nacional, 1940), pp. 30, 35.

2. Ibid., pp. 406-7. For more details see T. Lynn Smith, *Brazil: People and Institutions,* 4th edition, pp. 528-31.

3. Daniel P. Kidder, *Sketches of Residence and Travels in Brazil* (Philadelphia: Sorin & Ball, and London: Wiley & Putnam, 1845), p. 398.

4. Ibid., pp. 399-401.

5. Ibid., p. 401.

6. Roger Bastide, "Religion and the Church in Brazil," in T. Lynn Smith and Alexander Marchant, editors, *Brazil: Portrait of Half a Continent* (New York: The Dryden Press, 1951), pp. 546-47.

7. Ibid., p. 348.

8. For additional details and sources of the materials taken from publications in Portuguese given above, see Smith, *Brazil: People and Institutions,* 4th edition, pp. 718-22.

9. Cf. Emilio Willems, *Followers of the New Faith* (Nashville: Vanderbilt University Press, 1967).

10. See the rich variety of materials on syncretism in James Hastings, *Encyclopedia of Religion and Ethics* (New York: Charles Scribner's Sons, 1924).

11. Ramos fell victim to a heart attack in Paris, where he had gone to head UNESCO'S Social Science Division, just as he was completing arrangements to undertake research in Angola and Mozambique.

12. See Smith and Marchant, *Brazil: Portrait of Half a Continent,* pp. 125-46. Among Ramos's earlier works are *As Culturas Negras no Nova Mundo* (Rio de Janeiro: Civilização Brasileira, 1937); *O Negro Brasileiro,* cited above; *Introdução á Antropologia Brasileira,* 2 vols. (Rio de Janeiro: Casa do Estudante do Brazil, 1943 and 1947); and *Aculturação Negra no Brasil* (São Paulo: Companhia Editora Nacional, 1942).

13. Nossa Senhora is the Portuguese equivalent of Our Lady.

14. Originally this word was used in Brazil to designate the Indian who had been brought under the influence of the Roman Catholic priests, as distinguished from the wild Indians of the forests and plains; soon it came to designate the half-breed of white-Indian ancestry; and presently it is in general use to signify the ordinary rural Brazilian of low socioeconomic status.

15. Charles Wagley, *An Introduction to Brazil,* 2nd edition (New York: Columbia University Press, 1971), pp. 222-23. In this connection too, some of the information supplied in a UPI story filed from Rio de Janeiro during Carnival in 1972 is pertinent. This was carried in the *Florida Times-Union* of Jacksonville, Florida, on February 21, 1972. It features the role of Exú, Afro-Brazilian incarnation of evil, during Lent, when all the other orishas "go into retreat," and, according to the story, when "millions of Brazilian voodoo practicioners live an anxious 40 days." Their fears cause them to frequent the macumba ceremonial centers, or terreiros, where Edson Biito, a *sacerdote* trom Bahia, and other practicioners of the cults offer them "consultations" at the rate of about $4.00 for a 15-minute period. The journalist filing this dispatch cited unofficial estimates placing the number of believers in macumba at about 500,000, stated that 20,000 of the terreiros were registered with the police in Rio de Janeiro alone, and indicated that on "New Year's Eve this year, more than a million persons flocked to the city's beaches to honor Yemanjá," the water goddess of the Afro-Brazilian religious cults. Indicative of the role these cults are planing in religious differentiation is the statement in the story that "formerly almost an exclusively Negro religion, macumba is gaining new adherents among middle-class white Brazilians."

16. J. Parke Renshaw, "A Sociological Analysis of Spiritism in Brazil" (Ph. D. diss., Gainesville: University of Florida, 1969), p. 6.

17. Ibid., p. 14.


**Chapter 10**

1. Shigeichi Sakai, *Brazil nikki* [Diary in Brazil] (Tokyo: Kawade Shobo, 1957), pp. 167-71; Tausan Kyoku, *Imin chosa hokoku* [Reports of the Survey of the Immigrants] (Tokyo: Gaimu Sho, 1910), passim; and Ijyu Kyoku, *Jinko no kokusai ido* (The International Movement of Population) (Tokyo: Gaimu Sho, 1957), p. 119.

2. T. Lynn Smith, *Brazil: People and Institutions,* pp. 218-19.

3. Seiichi Izumi, "Brazil niokeru Nikkei colonia" [The Japanese Brazilian Colonies in Brazil] in Seiichi Izumi, editor, *Imin* [Immigrants] (Tokyo: Kokin Shoin, 1957), pp. 17-19.

4. Ibid.

5. Frederic Normano and Antonello Geri, *The Japanese in South America* (New York: Institute of Pacific Relations, 1943), pp. 19-31.

6. Seiichi Izumi and Horoshi Saito, *Amazon* [Amazon] (Tokyo: Kokin Shoin, 1954), pp. 89-107.

7. Normano and Geri, *The Japanese in South America,* pp. 89-107.

8. Emilio Willems and Herbert Baldus, "Cultural Change Among Japanese Immigrants in Brazil," *Sociology and Social Research* 26, No. 6 (July-August, 1942): 527.

9. Izumi, "The Japanese Brazilian Colonies," pp. 88-89.

10. Hiroshi Saito, "Sengo imin no teichaku to doka" [The Fixation and Assimilation of Post-War Immigrants] in *Imin,* p. 609.

11. Izumi, "The Japanese Brazilian Colonies," pp. 83-91.

12. Willems and Baldus, "Cultural Change," p. 582.

13. Izumi, "The Japanese Brazilian Colonies," p. 93.

14. *Kaigai iju no koka* [The Effects of the Immigration] (Tokyo: Kaifai Iju Kyokai, 1957), pp. 19-26.

15. Saito, "Fixation and Assimilation," p. 607.

16. Willems and Baldus, "Cultural Change," p. 527.

17. Izumi, "The Japanese Brazilian Colonies," p. 529.

18. Saito, "Fixation and Assimilation," p. 606. Cf. John Embree, "Acculturation among the Japanese of Kona, Hawaii," *Memoirs of the American Anthropological Association,* No. 59 (1941): 31.

19. Saito, "Fixation and Assimilation," p. 645.

20. Masao Gamo, "Amazonia niokeru Nikkei colonia no koka katei" [The Process of the Acculturation of the Japanese Brazilian Colonies in the Amazon] in *Imin,* p. 525.

21. Tsutomu Ouchi, [*The Problems of Agriculture*], 7th edition (Tokyo: Iwanami Shoten, 1954), p.44.

22. Carlos Borges Schmidt, "Systems of Land Tenure in São Paulo," *Rural Sociology,* No. 3 (September, 1943): 243-47.

23. Akira Kinoshita, "Nomin" [Farmers], *Nihon Shakai Minzoku Jiten* 3 [Journal of Japanese Folk Society] (1957): 1145.

24. Kisaemon Ariga, "Sonraku" [A Village Community], *Nihon Shakai Minzoku Jiten* 3 [Journal of Japanese Folk Society] (1957): 855-56.

25. T. Lynn Smith, *The Sociology of Rural Life,* 3rd edition (New York: Harper & Brothers, 1953), p. 214.

26. Saito, "Fixation and Assimilation," pp. 614-15.

27. Vicente Unzer de Almeida, "Aspectos da Organização Social dos Japoneses em Registro," *Sociologia* 15, No. 4 (October, 1953): 357.

28. For a description of this system, see Smith, *Brazil,* Chapter 3.

29. Hiroshi Saito, "O Cooperativismo na Região de Cotia: Estudo de Transplantaçã Cultural," *Sociologia* 18, No. 4 (October, 1955): 350.

30. Ibid.

31. Eitaro Suzuki, *Nihon noson shakaigaku genri* [The Principles of Japanese Rural Sociology] (Tokyo: Jicho Sha, 1952), pp. 54-56.

32. Ariga, "Sonraku," pp. 853-61.

33. Tadashi Fukutake, *Nihon noson no shakaitaki seikaku* [The Social Characteristic of the Japanese Village Community], 8th edition (Tokyo: Tokyo University Press, 1954), pp. 51-52.

34. Ibid.

35. Ryozo Takeda, *Shakaigaku no kozo* [The Structure of Sociology], revised edition (Tokyo: Maeno Shoten, 1953), pp. 165-77.

36. John Embree, *Suye Mura* (Chicago: The University of Chicago Press, 1939), pp. 33-35.

37. Izumi, "The Japanese Brazilian Colonies," p. 69.

38. Ibid., pp. 70-72.

39. Tetsujin Tsukamoto, "Nikkei colonia no shudanchi no keita" [The Types of Clustered Japanese Brazilian Colonies] in *Imin*, pp. 254-58.

40. Morio Ono and Nobue Miyazaki, "Daitoshi shuhen noka no seiritsu" [The Establishment of Farmers around Large Cities] in *Imin*, pp. 320-26.

41. Saito, "Fixation and Assimilation," pp. 649-50.

42. Hiroshi Saito, "Amazon henkyo no izusha" [The Immigrants in the Amazon Valley] in Fumio Tada, editor, *Amazon no shigen to shakai* [Origins and Society of the Amazon] (Tokyo: Tokyo University Press, 1957), pp. 161-62.

43. Ibid., pp. 197-204.

44. Kisaemon Ariga, "The Family in Japan," *Marriage and Family Living* 16, No. 14 (November, 1954): 362-64.

45. Ibid.

46. Izumi, "The Japanese Brazilian Colonies," p. 59.

47. Ibid., p. 61.

48. Gamo, "The Process of Acculturation," p. 352.

49. Tsukamoto, "The Types of Clustered Japanese Brazilian Colonies," p. 260.

50. Izumi, "The Japanese Brazilian Colonies," p. 100.

51. Gamo, "The Process of Acculturation," pp. 513-14.

52. Izumi, "The Japanese Brazilian Colonies," p. 66; Sumi Shima, "Chiho shotoshi no nikkei Colonia" [The Japanese Brazilian Colonies in Small Local Cities] in *Imin*, pp. 444-45.

53. Izumi, p. 66.

54. Ibid., p. 67.

55. Saito, "Fixation and Assimilation," p. 602.

56. Emilio Willems, "Some Aspects of Cultural Conflicts and Acculturation in South Brazil," *Rural Sociology* 8, No. 4 (December, 1942): 384.

57. Unzer de Almeida, "Aspectos da Organização Social," p. 354. This writer seems to have mistaken *tokonoma* for *kamidana*.

58. Izumi, "The Japanese Brazilian Colonies," p. 99.

59. Marion T. Loftin, *The Japanese in Brazil: A Study in Immigration and Acculturation* (Ph.D. diss., Vanderbilt University, 1952), p. 238.

60. Ono and Miyazaki, "The Establishment of Farmers," pp. 322-23.

61. Gamo, "The Process of Acculturation," p. 518.

62. Gen Kondo, "Nogyo dantai" [Agricultural Bodies], *Nihon Shakai Minzoku Jiten* 3 [Journal of Japanese Folk Society] (1957): p. 1129.

63. Saito, "O Cooperativismo na Região de Cotia," p. 359.

64. Tetujin Tsukamoto, "Kaitaku gensen no Nikkei colonia" [The Colonies of the Japanese Brazilians in the Frontier Area], in *Imin*, pp. 383-85.

65. Izumi, "The Japanese Brazilian Colonies," p. 113.

66. Tsukamoto, "The Colonies of the Japanese Brazilians," pp. 257-58.

67. William F. Ogburn and Meyer F. Nimkoff, *Sociology* (Boston: Houghton, Mifflin Co., 1946), pp. 48-49.

68. Shigeichi Sakai, *Diary in Brazil*, pp. 118-19.

69. Ibid., pp. 129-30.

70. Izumi, "The Japanese Brazilian Colonies," pp. 120-25.

71. Ibid.

**Chapter 11**

1. For a fuller discussion of this sociocultural system, see T. Lynn Smith, *The Sociology of Rural Life*, 3rd edition (New York: Harper & Brothers, 1953), Chapter 14; and idem and Paul

E. Zopf, Jr., *Principles of Inductive Rural Sociology* (Philadelphia: F.A. Davis Co., 1970), Chapter 9.

2. For more extensive discussion of this and the other ways of farming in Brazil, see T. Lynn Smith, *Brazil: People and Institutions,* 4th edition (Baton Rouge: Louisiana State University Press, 1972), Chapter 15.

3. For a comprehensive and systematic study of the development of mechanized farming in one great Brazilian state (Minas Gerais), see Harold M. Clements, Sr., *The Mechanization of Agriculture in Brazil* (Gainesville: University of Florida Press, 1969).

**Chapter 12**

1. The data given here have been taken from T. Lynn Smith, *Brazil: People and Institutions,* 4th edition (1972), Chapter 24.

2. Alberto Passos Guimaraẽs, "As Favelas do Distrito Federal," *Revista Brasileira de Estatística* 14, No. 55 (1953): 259; cf. Louis J. Debret, José Arthur Rios, Carlos Alberto de Medina, and Helio Modesto, "Aspectos Humanos da Favela Carioca," *O Estado de S. Paulo, Suplemento Especial,* April 13, 1960, p. 7.

3. On the problems of the Latin American suburbs, see T. Lynn Smith, "Los Problemas Sociales de la Actualidad en la America Latina," in Asociación Venezolana de Sociología, *VI Congreso Latinoamericano de Sociologia, Memoria,* Vol. 2 (Caracas: Imprenta Nacional, 1961), pp. 315-17. The English version has been published in T. Lynn Smith, *Studies of Latin American Societies* (New York: Doubleday & Company, Anchor Book Series, 1970), pp. 209-26.

4. Alceu Vicente W. de Carvalho, *A População Brasileira* (Rio de Janeiro: Conselho National de Estatística, 1960), pp. 108-10. The cities enumerated are the capitals of the territories of Acre and Rio Branco and of the states of Piauí, Alagoas, and Mato Grosso, respectively.

5. Rio de Janeiro: Conselho Nacional de Estatística, 1960.

6. Cf. José Arthur Rios, Wit-Olaf Prochnik, Joel Ghivelder et.al., *Plano de Recuperação do Alagados: Estudo Preliminar,* Vol. 1 (Salvador; Instituto de Urbanismo e Administração Municipal, 1969), pp. 44, 57-62, and passim; and José Arthur Rios, *Campina Grande: Um Centro Comercial do Nordeste* (Rio de Janeiro: Serviço Social de Comercia, 1964), pp. 10, 45.

7. Debret, Rio, Medina, and Modesto, "Aspectos Humanos da Favela Carioca," p. 7.

8. Ibid., p. 25.

9. M.B. Lourenço Filho, *Joaseiro do Padre Cicero,* 2nd edition (São Paulo: Companhia Melhoramentos de São Paulo, 1929[?]), pp. 14-15.

10. *An Introduction to Brazil,* 2nd edition (New York: Columbia University Press, 1971).

11. Ibid., p. 112.

12. On this point see J.V. Freitas Marcondes, "Reforma Agrária a Luz das Ciencias Socias," *Sociologia* 24, No. 4 (1962): 273-85. A portion of these articles was translated and published under the title, "Salient Features of Agrarian Reform Proposals in Brazil," in T. Lynn Smith, editor, *Agrarian Reform in Latin America* (New York: Alfred A. Knopf, 1965), pp. 106-15.

13. This is far less important in the early 1970s than it was in the early 1960s.

14. For a development of the concept of the homogenization of society and an analysis of the manner and degree in which this is taking place in the United States, see T. Lynn Smith, "The Homogenization of Society in the United States," in the *Memoire du XIX Congrés International de Sociologie,* Vol. 2 (Mexico: Institut International de Sociologie, 1960), pp. 245-75.

## Chapter 13

1. No lengthy arithmetical computations have been made to deduct from these estimates of net migration the few thousands of persons who were living in small places that were in the rural category at the time of one census and in the urban category when the next enumeration was made. Such refinements would have no appreciable influence upon the figures given.

2. In order of their appearance these are T. Lynn Smith, *Brazil: People and Institutions,* (1946); Carl C. Taylor, *Rural Life in Argentina* (Baton Rouge: Louisiana State University Press, 1948); and Nathan L. Whetten, *Rural Mexico* (Chicago: University of Chicago Press, 1948). Somewhat later, Lowry Nelson, working on a similar assignment, produced *Rural Cuba* (Minneapolis: University of Minnesota Press, 1950).

3. Chapter 3, "Leaves from my Diary," in the first and second editions of *Brazil: People and Institutions* consists of extracts from notes taken on these trips.

4. Ibid., 1st edition, p. 189.

5. Cf. ibid., 4th edition, 1972, pp. 164-66.

6. For a striking specimen of the euphoria in Brazil which has followed the "kickoff" in 1970 of these gigantic efforts to open up and colonize the Amazon, see Jarbas G. Passarinho, *Amazonia: The Challenge of the Tropics* (Rio de Janeiro: Primor, 1971).

7. Cf. Pitirim A. Sorokin and Carle C. Zimmerman, *Principles of Rural-Urban Sociology* (New York: Henry Holt and Company, 1929), pp. 405, passim.

8. Cf. T. Lynn Smith, *Latin American Population Studies* (Gainesville: University of Florida Press, 1967), pp. 55-57.

9. Ibid., pp. 56-57.

10. See T. Lynn Smith, "Rural-Urban Migration in Brazil," in International Manpower Institute, *Symposium on the Role of Woroker Relocation in an Active Manpower Policy,* Washington, D.C.: Department of Labor, 1969, pp. 63-67.

11. Janice E. Perlman, "Dimensões de Modernidade numa Cidade em Franco Desenvolvimento," *Revista Brasileira de Estudos Políticos* 30 (Rio de Janeiro, 1971): 137.

12. Cf. Smith, *Brazil: People and Institutions,* Chapter 9.

13. See W.I. Thomas and Florian Znaniecki, *The Polish Peasant in Europe and America,* 5 vols. (Boston: Richard C. Badger, 1918-22).

14. Debret, Rios, Medina, and Modesto, "Aspectos Humanos da Favela Carioca." *Suplemento Especial,* p. 24.

15. José Arthur Rios, Wit-Olaf Prochnik, Joel Ghivelder et.al., *Plano de Recuperação dos Alagados: Estudo Preliminar,* Vol. 1 (Salvador: Instituto de Urbanismo e Administração Municipal, 1969), pp. 1, 57-62.

16. José Arthur Rios, *Campina Grande: Um Centro Comércial do Nordeste* (Rio de Janeiro: Serviço Social do Comércio, 1964), pp. 10 and 45.

17. Guimarães, "As Favelas do Distrito Federal," p. 250.

## Chapter 14

1. For the concept of the homogenization of society see T. Lynn Smith, "The Homogenization of Society in the United States," pp. 245-75.

2. For some of the basic information about this development see T. Lynn Smith, *Brazil: People and Institutions,* 4th edition, pp. 646-47.

3. For a few representative cases of the reliance upon human brawn as the mainstay in the intraurban transportation systems prior to 1900, see Wilkes, *Narrative of the United States Exploring Expedition,* p. 49, which states that in the city of Rio de Janeiro, "Few articles are transported in any other way than by slaves, and it is extremely rare to see a cart drawn by a

'beast of burden.' " See also the illustration on p. 53. Cf. Daniel P. Kidder and J.C. Fletcher, *Brazil and the Brazilians* (Philadelphia: Childs & Peterson, 1857), pp. 23-29.

4. The data used in these paragraphs have been drawn from the *Anuário Estatístico do Brasil, Ano IV–1938* (Rio de Janeiro: Instituto Brasileiro de Geografia e Estatística, 1940), pp. 250-51.

5. For information on the ownership of automobiles as "status symbols" rather than as means of locomotion in one large and burgeoning Brazilian city as late as the 1960s, see José Arthur Rios, *Campina Grande: Um Centro Comercial do Nordeste* (Rio de Janeiro: Servico Social do Comercio, 1964), p. 40, or the translation of the same in Smith, *Brazil: People and Institutions,* p. 699.

6. Perhaps the most significant evidence of the slight use of animal-drawn vehicles in nineteenth-century Brazil is that which indicates the virtual lack of hay in Rio de Janeiro and other cities. Hay making, it should be stressed, is not a part of the Mediterranean culture heritage; and in addition the inhabitants of countries where forage of some kind during all seasons of the year is not precluded by the presence of ice and snow, and this includes the southern part of the United States, never were compelled to master the techniques and to engage in the ardous efforts required in the production of hay. Therefore in Brazilian annals the materials pertaining to cities are not filled with incidents involving "haymarket square" as are those of Great Britain and the northern parts of the United States. In fact one cannot conceive of the setting being laid in Brazil for a story such as Anna Sewell's *Black Beauty.* Or consider the prosaic report of a U.S. consular official who for three years handled the papers connected with his country's commerce with Brazil's national capital. Near the close of the nineteenth century he was impelled to write: "The poetry of hay-making under the Southern Cross will have to wait till some future age, perhaps till Nature in her throes has elevated the Amazon plains. In a country where there is grazing the year round, hay can not be expected to figure largely as a crop. Still, there is a demand for it in the cities, and the supply called *alfalfa* comes from the River Plate. American sailing-vessels sometimes bring cargoes of it in bales from that region to Rio, where it is worth thirty dollars and upward a ton; but its fiber is coarse and it is inferior to good timothy. Some forty thousand bales of hay are annually imported at Rio from the River Plate, and occasionally a few bales come from Lisbon." C.C. Andrews, *Brazil: Its Condition and Prospects* (New York: D. Appleton & Company, 1887), p. 251.

7. For many of the essential data on immigration to the United States, and the high degree to which the immigrants' contributions were made in the nation's cities, see T. Lynn Smith, *Population Analysis* (New York: McGraw-Hill Book Company, 1948), Chapter 17 and passim; and for somewhat comparable materials for Brazil, see Smith, *Brazil: People and Institutions,* Chapter 8 and passim.

8. Smith, *Population Analysis,* pp. 314-15.

9. For details of the mass migration of Negroes from the plantations and farms of the area below the Ohio River to the one above it, see T. Lynn Smith, "The Redistribution of the Negro Population of the United States, 1910-1960," *Journal of Negro History,* 51, No. 3 (July, 1966), pp. 155-73.

10. Many of the data related to this are contained in some of my unpublished studies, although some of them are given in T. Lynn Smith, *Studies of the Great Rural Tap Roots of Urban Poverty in the United States* (New York: Carlton Press, 1974).

11. Data on the foreign-born population of Brazil in 1950 are from the *VI Recenseamento Geral do Brasil–1950,* Vol. 1 (Rio de Janeiro: Instituto Brasileiro de Geografia e Estatística, 1956), p. 1; vol. 24, Tomo 1 (1955), p. 1; and vol. 25, 1954, p. 89. Those on immigration are drawn from the compilations summarized in Smith, *Brazil: People and Institutions,* p. 634.

12. For data related to this point see ibid., Chapters 13, 14, and 15.

13. Ibid., pp. 682-84.

14. Cf. T. Lynn Smith, *The Sociology of Rural Life,* 3rd edition (New York: Harper & Brothers, 1953), Chapter 11.

15. In this connection one should consult the "Plan of the City of New Orleans and the Adjacent Plantations Compiled in Accordance with an Ordinance of the Illustrious Ministry and Royal Chapter, 24 December, 1798," which appears in Francois-Xavier Martin, *The History of Louisiana* (New Orleans: James A. Gresham, 1882).

16. For the best specimens of the role of this specific type of rural land survey one should observe such Canadian cities as Winnipeg and Montreal, and especially the former.

# Author Index

# Subject Index